JUSTICE FRAGMENTED

Suppose you have a dispute with your neighbour, and wish to secure redress for losses incurred. How might the issue be resolved? Is it worth the cost and time delay to take the matter to court? Or is there some other approach? Over the past few decades, a range of alternative resolution programmes has emerged to settle conflicts informally, outside the courtroom.

George Pavlich offers an innovative presentation of popular justice, relating it to an extensive account of key western ideas of justice. Existing debates between advocates and critics revolve around whether or not community mediation reduces or expands state controls. *Justice Fragmented* explores informal justice as an event rendered possible by the fragmentation of justice under postmodern conditions. It does not view community mediation as necessarily empowering, or an inevitable expansion of state control. Instead, using Foucault's ideas of governmentality, it describes community mediation as one of the many ways in which state regulation is 'governmentalised' by deferring to community-based controls. By identifying how one might engage with community justice this book shows how to avoid the political apathy that devalues many critical formulations.

George C. Pavlich is lecturer in Sociology at the University of Auckland.

JUSTICE FRAGMENTED

Mediating community disputes under
postmodern conditions

George C. Pavlich

London and New York

First published 1996
by Routledge
11 New Fetter Lane, London EC4P 4EE

Simultaneously published in the USA and Canada
by Routledge
29 West 35th Street, New York, NY 10001

Routledge is an International Thomson Publishing company

© 1996 George C. Pavlich

Phototypeset in Garamond by Intype London Ltd
Printed and bound in Great Britain by Mackays of Chatham PLC,
Chatham, Kent

British Library Cataloguing in Publication Data
A catalogue record for this book is available from the British Library

Library of Congress Cataloguing in Publication Data
A catalogue record for this book has been requested

ISBN 0–415–11312–1

For Carla, Seth, Tally and my siblings

CONTENTS

Acknowledgements   ix

1 IN SEARCH OF A BEGINNING . . .   1
   Approaching criticism or critical approach?   5
   Concepts, concepts, concepts   8
   Signposting the narrative   14

2 THE FRAGMENTED AUSPICES OF COMMUNITY JUSTICE   16
   Enunciating justice: two horizons of meaning   17
   Approaching justice in a modern ethos   19
   Justice talk in the interregnum   29
   Justice in search of idioms: the rise of mediation   39

3 CALCULATING COMMUNITY JUSTICE: MEDIATION IN
   BRITISH COLUMBIA   42
   The context: a social field emerges   43
   Community mediation in action   46
   Calculating community justice in British Columbia   51
   The 'neutral' mediator?   61
   Community mediation: a postmodern idiom?   64

4 THE CRITICS RESPOND: DARK SHADOWS OF
   COURTROOM JUSTICE   66
   Calculations as ideology: control through consensus   67
   The structural logic of community mediation   71
   Aporias in the early critics' discourse   78

5 REDRAWING CRITICAL LINES OF ENQUIRY:
   FOUCAULT, POWER AND COMMUNITY MEDIATION   82
   Fitzpatrick: taking community justice seriously   83
   Interpreting Foucault: methodological precautions   88
   A redrawn map: Foucault, criticism and community mediation   98
   Can Foucault take community mediation seriously?   101

CONTENTS

6 GOVERNING DISPUTES: MEDIATING BETWEEN
INDIVIDUALS, SELVES AND COMMUNITIES   106
  Community mediation and pastoral power   111
  Visions of community   113
  Individual, disputing selves   116
  Integrating community, individuals and selves   129

7 GOVERNMENTALISING THE STATE: INTERSECTING
POLITICAL RATIONALITIES   132
  The sovereign-law model   133
  Law and the identity of community mediation   136
  Community mediation and the law   139
  The symbioses of mutual constitution: 'remote control'   140
  *Community mediation and the future: dangers, resistance and
    strategic engagement*   145
  The promise: an alternative politics of dispute resolution   149
  In lieu of a conclusion   155

  Notes   159
  Bibliography   176
  Index   200

ACKNOWLEDGEMENTS

The text that follows has been with me for some years now and many people have contributed, often inadvertently, to its eventual form. I offer my appreciation to all those friends and colleagues who responded to my muses, helping me to develop my thoughts. Thanks to the participants of the case study in Vancouver for so generously helping with the study. I owe a special debt of gratitude to Bob Ratner, who offered detailed comments on the entire manuscript; his continued encouragement, friendship and critical fervour have left imprints well beyond the pages that follow. Barry Smart has unselfishly encouraged my endeavours and offered helpful advice; our numerous discussions about, and outside of, this project have contributed markedly to its form. My sincere thanks to Peter Fitzpatrick, Alan Hunt and David Schweitzer for their helpful comments on earlier versions/sections of this manuscript. Thanks also to the University of Auckland for providing a generous research grant to help complete the project. Finally, I offer my deepest gratitude to Carla Spinola, a venerable critic and unwavering friend, without whom what follows would never have emerged.

1

IN SEARCH OF A
BEGINNING . . .

Buying ecclesial indulgences for absolution is no longer common practice, but purchasing justice is. In secular worlds under postmodern conditions, the aim of such purchase is not to find salvation in the hereafter, but to rectify circumstances in the here and now. Many critical scholars engaged in legal thought, in *juris disciplina*, have suspended metanarratives pertaining to an eternal, singular justice, or a *lex eterna*, which promises equal treatment to all those who come before it (Lyotard and Thebaud 1985, Derrida 1992, White 1987/8). For, in the everyday, temporal processes of law, the *lex temporalis*, a steady stream of bewildered litigants must endure the costly, time-consuming and inhospitable processes of the courthouse. The liberal promise of equality before the law today rings as little more than a formal, hollow abstraction, largely favouring those with the means to play the legal game. Typically, the mechanisms of litigation usurp conflict from a given situation and transform it, often unrecognisably to those involved, into a professionalised legal dispute. In the process, the immediacy of dissension is transposed into conceptually distant legal categories that render conflict accessible to the courtroom's adversarial rules of procedure. As the trial proceeds, many litigants become further alienated from the process as they bear passive witness to an emerging 'case', interpretatively constructed by legal counsel and decided upon by the lofty stroke of judicial decision. Undoubtedly, the inhospitable atmosphere of what may be called formal, professionalised calculations and practices of justice has something to do with the survival of, and a continued search for, more congenial, informal 'alternatives' (Auerbach 1983). The disenchantment required to sustain a rational, codified law has itself generated a disillusion, this time in the form of despair.

In an attempt to ward off the apathy that often accompanies dejection, the following narration enquires into the promise of a different justice, beyond the professionalism of the courtroom. It provides an analytical diagnosis of the relatively recent calculations and practices of community justice indicated by an illustrative case study of community mediation in one particular dispute resolution arena; namely, in the Canadian province

1

of British Columbia. Its diagnosis extends an existing critical discourse around the topic by redrawing a theoretical map to reassess the perils and possibilities of community mediation. Does community mediation empower individuals locked in dispute? Is it merely a ruse for expanding and intensifying state control? Or does it signify a more complex mode of regulation? In responding to such questions, the narrative maps community mediation as part of an emerging political logic, a governmental rationality, that alters the ways in which disputes are regulated under postmodern conditions. Construed in this way, the analytical problem is silhouetted against several calculations and practices that today claim the mantle of justice.

As a sign, *justice* occupies a place of privilege across discursive environments and is often amongst those elite traces erected at the frontiers of meaning horizons, those foundations for enunciations within discourses that simultaneously buttress challenges from without. Consider the common question asked of the social analyst: what is the importance of this or that project, position, research programme, discipline? The simple response, 'justice', is often sufficient to silence sceptical questions, and to erect an accepted boundary between the voices within a discourse and that which lies beyond. Justice is capable of this, some say, because it is so intimately connected with our very being, our happiness, the 'good society', the goals of human aspiration (equality, fairness, liberty) and the processes by which to achieve the latter. Even so, justice is calculated in various ways and such calculations claim legitimacy by appealing to wider epistemic auspices at given historical locations. To put the matter crudely for the moment, under modern discursive conditions where grand images such as universal reason, freedom and progress prevail, only a subset of all possible rules for how to use the sign justice are likely to be viewed as legitimate. Here justice typically assumes the form of a unified entity whose presence is placed within the limits of universally valid principles grounded in a reason that promises human liberty and social progress. Equally, following this line of reasoning, were modern epistemic assumptions to rupture in a fundamental way, one might expect previously legitimate rules for using the sign to face a crisis of legitimacy, resulting perhaps in the emergence of different rules and traces, bidding for legitimacy under altered auspices. Under postmodern conditions, say, the quest for a peculiarly modern justice may well be out of place because the underlying auspices no longer license calculations of a singular justice founded on one conception of reason. The rules for its use under modern conditions have been significantly challenged and are in the process of being recast in light of the altered auspices of postmodern conditions.[1] In such an ethos, as we shall see, justice is fragmented into many coexisting calculations and practices, providing discursive conditions favourable to the elaboration of 'alternative' dispute resolution (ADR) formulas, including community mediation.

Against this discussion, the rise of community justice in British Columbia is explored as a recalculation of justice that licenses dispute resolution techniques (e.g. mediation) in the 'community' and outside of the state's court system. Although the analysis and its formulations are excavated from the particularities of a case study, much will be apposite to other western dispute resolution contexts. In any case, the recalculations have involved 'deinstitutionalising' so-called minor disputes, because community justice (together with other alternative dispute resolution techniques) promises to remove cases from the state's court system, which was deemed unable to deal with the volume of community disputes.[2] The courts' ineffectiveness is touted by judicial reformers as obvious from the enormous case-loads 'clogging' up the professional justice system, making litigation costly, time-consuming, alienating and unresponsive to those for whom it is designed (e.g. Emond 1988, Blair 1988). Moreover, these reformers argue that adversarial techniques place people in relations of confrontation and, therefore, divide rather than unite individuals in a 'community' (Hogarth 1974, Becker 1975). Because the adjudicative methods of litigation impose decisions based on guilt and innocence, or degrees of liability, without due concern with restructuring 'damaged' relations between people, disputing parties often remain locked in conflict when they leave the courtroom. This leaves disputes unsettled, which, so the argument goes, limits the possibility of creating consensually functioning communities.

In response, one group of advocates in the alternative dispute resolution movement, on whom I shall here focus, argue that minor disputes between people with ongoing relationships should be dealt with informally in the community, using hospitable mediation techniques to settle their disputes. For these advocates, mediation provides a voluntary, individually empowering way of resolving disputes in a congenial forum. It encourages disputants to work out acceptable settlements with the help of a neutral third party from their communities. Mediation is seen to be a voluntary process that sustains individual choice in the context of dispute resolution by encouraging individuals to take responsibility for their lives without deferring to central state interventions (Shonholtz 1993, 1988/9, 1987). So, when successful, mediation is deemed to be an informal alternative to the courts that empowers individual disputants, strengthens communities and restores peace to troubled relationships.

Although critics of community justice in Canada are conspicuous by their virtual absence, critiques of community justice in other contexts (e.g. the United States, Britain, Australia) are directly relevant. The central theme of early critics' writings is that any analyst ought to be deeply suspicious of a movement within the state's professional justice system that is sanctioned by the very forces it is designed to replace. For them, community mediation, despite its rhetoric, does not resist state control; instead, it is an insidious development because it expands and intensifies state regulation into more areas of individual life while deceptively claiming to do the opposite.[3] Although this contention is an important one, it has led many thinkers into somewhat of a sterile impasse that encourages political apathy. An exit from the impasse is difficult so long as one continues to construe the 'problem' in narrow state expansionist terms. In a broader formulation of the problem area, 'new informalist' critics direct their analyses at specific community mediation programmes in order to evaluate (rather than assume) their regulatory effects in context (see Matthews 1988). This allows them to avoid the advocates' seemingly wide-eyed optimism without falling prey to the extreme pessimism of early critical formulations. The ensuing analysis takes its cue from this position as it proceeds to address these questions. First, what sort of theoretical map will permit an analysis of community mediation in a specific context without succumbing to absolute responses of either protagonists or early critics? Second, and following from the answer provided to the previous question, what sort of political logic (rationality of governance) and model of power does community mediation embrace? Third, how does this political logic relate to the modern liberal state's formal legal model of power under postmodern conditions? Finally, what are the implications of this relationship for formulating an alternative politics of the dispute resolution domain?

Responding to each of these questions provides the *leitmotif* of the following text. In brief, community mediation is not viewed as a voluntary, empowering alternative to the crisis-ridden court system, as some advocates allege. Nor is it depicted as a mere expansion of state control, if by that one means mediation is instrumentally reducible to the state's political logic. Rather, I try to develop a grid of intelligibility to diagnose community mediation as a mode or regulation that has become possible in light of changes to the dispute resolution arena in which justice is fragmented (rather than unified, universal, modern). Here, community mediation is approached, not as an expansion of the state, but as part of a process by which the liberal (and latterly neo-liberal) state is governmentalised under postmodern conditions. At this point, the narrative spirals out of certain compelling themes raised by new informalist thinking and articulates these to a particular interpretation of Foucault on governmentality. In particular, the importance of Foucault's 'technologies of self', in conjunction with disciplinary techniques, to the analysis of community mediation is noted. The latter how it embraces a logic of government with a 'pastoral' model of power directed at individual disputing selves in the communities of postmodern conditions. In British Columbia, this model of power is closely articulated to the liberal state's 'sovereign-law' model as indicated by community mediation's constitutive relationship to the state's legal system – both seek to complement one another in the pursuit of dispute settlement. Having traced the links between these models of power, one is better able to assess the regulatory effects of their conjunction. In particular, my narrative characterises the governmentalised British Columbian state as an outcome of close articulations between pastoral and sovereign-law logics which produce a mode of regulation that I term *remote control*. The latter concept allows one to glimpse certain dangers associated with community mediation's implicit calculations and practices of justice, and indicates ways in which resistance to these dangers may be understood.

APPROACHING CRITICISM OR CRITICAL APPROACH?

More strictly: one must admit nothing that has being – because then becoming would lose its value and actually appear meaningless and superfluous.

Consequently one must ask how the illusion of being could have arisen (was bound to arise).

(Nietzsche 1967: 708)

The proposed endeavour strikes at the heart of a prescriptive question of value: what sort of justice should community mediation further? Devoid of absolute auspices, the postmodern ethos in which I develop the account renders absolute, prescriptive statements problematic. Yet, with questions of justice, one is bound to confront the abyss of prescription in one form or another. Although the following does not place itself within prescriptive discourses as such, it offers a tentative allusion to a justice that is unlike the professionalised and bureaucratised justice of the courtrooms. It considers justice as no more than the 'promise', a clumsy grasp beyond historical limits of associative patterns rendered untenable by profoundly troubling events. The involuntary jerks of a body as its life fades into death, caused let us say by the weapons of an unwelcome army, will almost certainly evoke an immediate sense, a trace, of injustice in the eye of a sympathetic bystander; a trace that will likely occasion reflection on the limits of a mode of being, a lived present, that produces such shocking events. So too might the oppressive effects of given limits on particular identities occasion a search for different patterns of association. Congruent with certain emerging formulations, justice is evoked as the search for an infinite aspiration beyond what is, a promise of otherness beyond the limits of that which is present (Derrida 1992). It is calculated in various ways, and different practices are licensed in specific times and places by calculations. Community justice is one such calculation, and it licenses various mediation practices in its name. But, as we shall see, its aspirations typically seek to fortify, to 'complement', professional justice rather than to, say, 'listen' to the aspirations of those who are subordinated by given associative patterns (Lyotard and Therbaud 1985, White 1987/8).

Clearly then, I do not try to address (place) the substantive question 'what is justice?' as if one could absolutely circumscribe its (absolute? essential?) ontological form. The following narrative's initial disruption is to refuse this question, to take a different strategic tack, to seek out horizons excluded by such questioning. Concretely, to ask the usual substantive question is to locate oneself within conventional metaphysical patterns of discourse, to seek ontological unity and descriptive closure at all costs. This is so even for the reconstructionist critic who ventures down the alluring metaphysical path. Such a critic may be concerned with correcting the mistakes of a given order, of reconstructing dominant ideas of justice. S/he might offer a definition of justice that runs counter to dominant liberal views, and then compare emerging patterns of community justice with this definition. Though the critical impetus of such a strategy may be considerable in the hands of a skilled critic, its parasitic proximity to metaphysical discourse places telling limits. In a search for unity, for ontological clarity, this critical strategy is hamstrung by a quest for synoptic, singular universal statements. It must delineate what justice really *is* across specified times and places, must articulate signs around questions of its essential character. By thus emphasising processes of exclusion, of rendering absent, to reconstruct another presence (what is), the constructionist critic is more or less orientated towards banishing those chains of reason considered problematic in order to construct an alternative view. When dominant images of justice are persuasively re-ordered, this sort of criticism may well have attained its apogee. Yet what is outside the bounds of such forms of criticism is the sustained search for reasons that are silenced by exclusion; those reasons of the 'other' marginalised by rhetorical strategies of exclusion that establish what is (ontology). The critical genre of reconstruction is therefore not orientated towards a search that *deconstructs* existing traces by focusing on the margins of discourse for the purposes of possible transgression of the existing order. To reconstruct an order is to elevate the precepts of one line of reasoning above all others, under the auspices of true essence. In the process, one seems bound to a form of imperialist logocentrism that – in the pursuit of a purified reason – either colonises fragments of the other's reasons for the purposes of domestication (under the 'unity of reason'), or reduces them to irrelevant silence.

Another critical strategy, for those who prefer not to lose sight of the other's reasons, is to attempt the deconstruction of the grids of intelligibility that b(l)ind us to the other within given chains of reasoning (Critchley 1992, Levinas 1989). The deconstructive impulse searches from within the constraints of contingent auspices, and locates aporias that try to render the familiar strange. It tries to point to the contingency in the so-called necessity of being. Against those who see community justice as a necessary development, I want therefore to expose its contingent, contextual and unessential nature. But mine is a form of criticism employed not

in the search for formal structures with universal value, but rather as a historical investigation into the events that have led us to constitute ourselves and to recognise ourselves as subjects of what we are doing, thinking, saying.

(Foucault 1984: 46)

Such a criticism must continually scrutinise the limits of our social identities, established by power-knowledge-subjectivity relations, in an effort to diagnose where these are in danger of subordinating particular subject positions and classes of people (Laclau and Mouffe 1985). In other words, it must reflexively examine our existence through an historically situated diagnosis of the perils implied by our historical identities. It could point to the techniques by which oppressing or oppressed groups are created and sustained, thereby problematising identities that might previously have been regarded as unproblematic. Criticism is there to expose the potential pitfalls in specific modes of reason and their associated power arrangements at particular times.

I do not, however, pretend to be an isolated iconoclast, an enemy of my age. Instead, what follows is the narrative of a critic who cannot be separated from the margins of a particular ethos, but who tries to chart some ways in which subjugation in a given power-knowledge-subjectivity formation is produced. Mine is a critical interpretation, an attempt at a 'connected' critique, an ontology of ourselves as we exist in a particular moment in history (Walzer 1987). Of course, this conception of genealogical criticism raises an immediate question: if knowledge implies power, then in what power-knowledge formation is the ensuing critique located?

One response is to suggest that the discourse of this book is located in an amalgamation of erudite and local knowledge that tries to provide an 'historical knowledge of struggles' that is 'tactically' useful (Foucault 1980: 83). This stance incorporates a notion of 'effective history' because it refuses to separate theory and practice, recognising that the process of theorising *is* a practice and locating this practice 'alongside those who struggle for power ... A "theory" is the regional system of this struggle' (Foucault 1977a: 208). As such, the theory tries to 'resist and refuse what is. Its use should be in processes of conflict and confrontation, essays in refusal. It doesn't have to lay down the law for the law. It isn't a stage in programming. It is a challenge directed at what is' (Foucault 1989: 114). Thus, to answer the questions at hand, the ensuing narrative's conclusions are no more than strategic evaluations designed to diagnose the possible dangers of specific identities and to chart a map of their constituent power-knowledge-subjectivity relations. It is in many ways a fiction that might, in particular sets of circumstances that are not easy to predict, be accepted as a wider truth, and not only as an enunciation located at the margins of existing power-knowledge formations. Regardless, it aims to 'reactivate' minor knowledges that are silenced, ignored or trivialised by dominant discourses (Foucault 1980: 85).

The point here is, of course, not to detach truth from power but to deconstruct the truth of a power formation that privileges the calculation of a 'professionalised justice' and equates the 'law' with justice (Cain 1988). This calculation of justice as an ideal type: conceals its class basis; defines the origins of conflict very narrowly by treating disputes in individual terms (i.e. it ignores the structural basis of conflict); appeals to specified and mostly universal rules of procedure; uses experts and professionals to resolve immediate manifestations of conflict; and places designated authorities in its bureaucratic networks. The aim of such justice is the maintenance of 'law and order' where it is assumed that society is consensually driven and free of gross inequities, justifying its perpetuation (D. Miller 1974). It ignores the harsh injustices that many people must endure on a daily basis as a result of socially imposed identities, and the impediments such issues place on the formal equality of law. It seems, for instance, quite oblivious to the added alienation that dispute resolution forums impart to participants who do not have the means to secure adequate representation. The following text issues a series of challenges to the hegemony of professional calculations and practices of justice by critically examining the claims of a recent 'alternative'; namely, community justice. What follows is not so much an attack on the contents (or even the methods) of philosophy or jurisprudence as it is an onslaught on the effects of the forms of power out of which dominant calculations and practices of justice emerge.

CONCEPTS, CONCEPTS, CONCEPTS

Any narrative that articulates itself to several discourses will encounter the equivocation that concepts attract as they float between contexts. Perhaps equivocation is what makes floating possible. In any case, the following story borrows concepts from elsewhere, but uses them in fairly particular ways. Let us here try to render explicit the uses of four key concepts that were initial orientating focuses for the narration.

Community mediation

Soon after commencing research into the topic of this book, I realised that the mutating identity of 'community mediation' is best unravelled as a series of shifting patterns, a changing movement with multiple facets. Far from its having a fixed, rigid or absolute being, the community mediation movement materialised as a contingent 'event' with shadowy outlines, fashioned by relentless antagonisms and struggle. These dynamic and ongoing processes annulled any attempt to clasp a presumed 'essence' in the grip of a simple, static concept. What I had come up against is the sheer contingency of our associative patterns, which implodes the stasis implied by consummate enunciations of existence; it exposes the relations required to sustain the mirage of a given social formation (Laclau and Mouffe 1985).

With this in mind, I use the sign 'community mediation' with some trepidation, avoiding the temptation to allow the sign's singular linguistic demeanour to gloss over the plurality and dynamism of relations that sustain the identity at hand. My focus is on the effects of these relations that have deployed a particular kind of community mediation under a discursive rubric of community justice. Stated differently, the practices of community mediation have been deployed in and through calculations of community justice that seem to evoke images of 'a genuinely popular justice as one that is locally controlled, non-professional and informal, and that envisages a renewed community and decisions made according to community norms' (Merry and Milner 1993: 3). The spirit of bringing justice back to the community is very much part of calculations that claim the various mantles of 'community justice', 'informal justice', 'popular justice' and 'neighbourhood justice'. And such calculations have licensed particular mediation practices that also assume various titles: 'community mediation', 'neighbourhood dispute resolution', 'conflict management', 'minor dispute resolution', 'mediation', and so on. So long as one understands that this book deals with a plurality of events, calculations and practices that define certain activities as community disputes between people with an ongoing relationship amenable to 'resolution' through 'mediation' that is external to formal court procedures in British Columbia, the particular choice of sign is not crucial.

Discourse

In what follows, the notion of discourse is not used to capture immutable truths about the world, as if its language were capable of attaching unchanging phenomena to absolute and rigid concepts. If Wittgenstein is correct, the meaning of concepts is highly variable across social contexts; the same words are put to quite different uses in different places (1983). If Foucault is right, discourses emerge through complex relations of power and knowledge, and are involved in creating the very entities they purportedly denote (Foucault 1977a, 1978, 1980). Both theorists urge us to see definitions in terms of their use in given (socio-political) contexts: they are not passive reflections of an assumed 'reality' but, rather, ostensive decrees enunciated from within given social contexts and expressing underlying relations of force.[4] As such, 'discourses' are dynamic linguistic formations in which signifiers are related to one another through rules governing their use, as shaped by power.[5] Identities, such as community mediation, are produced through rules that situate 'elements' of language in relation to one another in specific power-knowledge relations (Laclau and Mouffe 1985: 105–114).

These 'elements' are the raw materials of discourse and comprise any fragment of language. They are organised, or dispersed, within a discursive formation through processes of articulation that supply rules for how given elements are to relate to one another, and define what are reasonable, acceptable, appropriate or permissible uses of statements.[6] Laclau and Mouffe refer to such recomposed elements as 'moments', to distinguish them from those 'elements' that remain disarticulated from particular discourses (1985: 105). The identity of anything is established when a discourse colonises an element and, through processes of articulation, specifies how it is to relate to other moments. As such, to state what is by now fairly commonplace, identity inheres not in the sign, or signified, but in the discursive practices that specify rules for the 'acceptable' use of elements.

Now, to associate the two previous concepts, the identity of 'community mediation' emerges in particular contexts from the rules of dispersion erected through articulatory practices that, say, distinguish it from the formal procedures of the courts, or construe it as an 'alternative', etc. However, it is important to recognise the contingency of this identity, for articulatory practices are ongoing and never completely decided. Indeed, these practices are no more than the terminal effects of continuing power struggles. As we shall see, power and knowledge imply one another directly because the moments of discourse are erected and sustained through underlying relations of force, just as they are, in turn, used to justify particular forms of power. Therefore, changes to accepted calculations of justice imply transformations of underlying practices of justice and vice versa. As such, the identity of community mediation is contingent because its moments are never completely, or rigidly, articulated to a discourse. They are never fixed because elements are 'floating signifiers' that entail a degree of openness from whence the contingency of identity, and discourse, derives (Laclau and Mouffe 1985: 113).[7] This is significant because one of the aims of the present study is to work towards creating an identity for community mediation not as a mere complement to professionalised justice practices, but that attends to some of the latter's pressing failures.

Postmodern conditions

There is another issue that requires clarification, for it betokens a fierce debate that I would prefer to skirt. I am here, of course, referring to questions of whether or not the modern world has been fundamentally displaced by a postmodern one, and, more specific to the purposes of this book, whether the modern auspices of justice have been replaced by postmodern assumptions (B. Smart 1993, Bauman 1992, McGowan 1991). Few today would deny that significant changes have occurred in the ways that we talk about, legitimate, our use of signs, our knowledge (Bauman 1992, Giddens 1991, Touraine 1989, Hebdidge 1988, Lyotard 1984). Yet there is considerably less agreement on how to characterise changes to underlying epistemic patterns. There have been protracted and raging debates over whether such changes, bred from wider economic (industrialism-postindustrialism), political (modernism-postmodernism), cultural or social (modernity-postmodernity) transformations, indicate a shift from modern to *post*modern conditions (Featherstone 1991). My reluctance to engage these debates in this narrative stems from an agreement with Beck *et al.*'s assessment that the 'debate about modernity and post-modernity has become wearisome and like so many such debates has produced rather little' (1994: vi). In any case, they have been rather extensively canvassed elsewhere.[8] Yet for all this, it is probably useful to locate the following text in relation to that debate, if only to clarify my use of certain terms.

To begin with, the following text does not employ Beck *et al.*'s characterisations of our historical placement as one of 'reflexive modernisation,' or indeed of a globalising 'high modern' society (Giddens 1990, 1991). Nor does it simply assume that we now live in radically 'new times', that the sands of modernity have been entirely reshaped by the rising tides of the postmodern (Baudrillard 1983). Instead, I suggest that although the conditions in which we now live are different enough to mean that sociological analysis cannot proceed with its 'business as usual', and that knowledge claims are made on altered bases, it may be premature to declare a completed epochal discontinuity (Bauman 1992: 105). The difference is a relative one that has to do with significant alterations to the *conditions and the ethos* within which we live (B. Smart 1993, Lyotard 1984). These conditions comprise a complex association of past and newly emerging traces that defy simple distinction. For that reason, I have elected to speak of them as *post*modern conditions, indicating thereby the continued presence of modern themes that have been transformed by their uncomfortable and even untenable associations with notions that extend beyond modern auspices. The consequences of such thematic amalgamations have been profound in all areas of life, including in western academic environments with their notable dissensus on which underlying criteria should license what is to count as knowledge. As grand (modern?) approaches to legitimising knowledge claims have faced significant challenges, so the spaces for alternative discourses have been cleared. The outlines, the silhouettes, of these are still in the process of emerging. And it is the trace of the emerging ethos in which discourses and their alignments across social spaces are being rearranged, a relative (rather than epochal) product of the modern, that in the following pages will bear the name of postmodern conditions.

Neo-liberal regulation

The focus on community mediation in the following pages has a direct bearing on a more general drift towards community regulation in many western societies. Under postmodern conditions, the governmentalisation of the state takes place through a neo-liberal quest for community purportedly beyond the clutches of the liberal, welfare state. Liberalism is sometimes understood as a critique of state regulation that sought to develop clearly limited (private), self-regulating domains (Burchell 1991, Pateman 1988). In this light, liberal governance may be described as 'an historically specific ensemble of discursive, legal administrative, and institutional practices, which erases and seeks to co-ordinate dimensions of the state, philanthropy, households, and the economy, with the objective of promoting particular forms of conduct of life' (Dean 1992: 218). Liberal government, that is, 'identifies a domain outside "politics", and seeks to manage it without destroying its existence and its autonomy' (Rose and Miller 1992: 180). In the context of the welfare state, this domain takes the form of the social, a private arena that aims to encourage a specific type of personal autonomy (Donzelot 1991).

Neo-liberalism, by contrast, provides a reformulation of modern liberalism by returning to certain classical liberal themes (McBride 1992, Bonner and du Guy 1992, Weinstein 1991, Rothenburg 1984). As Vikki Bell puts it,

> Against a backdrop of welfarism, neo-liberalism appeals against too much government intervention, poses 'the market' as the solution and befriends the family, suggesting it has been downtrodden by welfarism and needs to become both independent and responsible once more.
>
> (1993: 395)

The neo-liberal critiques of the welfare state creating a 'culture of dependency' seek to restore choice, autonomy and responsibility to agents (individuals, families, corporations, communities). The aim here is to instil an 'enterprise culture' into as many aspects of social life as possible. This entails breaking down social welfarism, visible state intervention, bureaucratic empire building, collective provision of social security, and so on. By this logic, 'the individual producer-consumer is in a novel sense not just an enterprise, but an entrepreneur of himself or herself' (Gordon 1991: 44). The individual becomes an important element for choosing lifestyles, for taking out private insurances to secure that lifestyle, and for improving his or her way of life. It is the individual choice of the *homo economicus* that will ultimately bring about improvements to family and community.

In British Columbia, the ties to neo-liberalism (also referred to as 'neo-conservatism') are strong, especially through a prominent neo-liberal think-tank, the Fraser Institute (Resnick 1984, 1987, Marchak 1985, 1986, Magnusson *et al.* 1984). Many of the Social Credit Party's policies developed while in government from the mid 1970s to the early 1990s were shaped by the thinking of this institute (e.g. Bennett 1978). Its 'restraint programme' of the early 1980s sought to implement a version of neo-liberalism under the various guises of privatisation, deregulation, state minimalism, and deinstitutionalisation (Pavlich forthcoming). Much of this was done in the name of redress, of rectifying the fiscal and legitimacy crises facing most welfare states during the early part of the 1970s (Cohen 1985, Abel 1982a, O'Connor 1973). If some radical social critics held notions of community as a basis for utopian transformations, neo-liberal reformers in British Columbia colonised it as a weapon in their quest to install a minimal and deregulated state with restructured (privatised) social service sectors (Callahan and McNiven 1988). Community, for neo-liberal thinkers, provided a convenient symbol for extending liberal critiques of the state, a means of conceptualising an escape from the clutches of a growing therapeutic state and evoking a nostalgic sense of spontaneous, nativist forms of association (Gordon 1991, Butcher 1985, Cohen 1985).

There are several salient points for the ensuing narrative. For instance, neo-liberal governance has deployed a different mode of regulation through its emphasis on an amorphous 'community': state-centred policing is complemented by community policing components; state psychiatric hospitals are now largely replaced by community psychiatric and psychology efforts; social work increasingly becomes community work; parts of state correctional services – including prisons – are privatised and community sentencing/correction takes root; state responsibility for health promotion is increasingly delegated to community or private health initiatives; and so the list goes on. The move to community control implies what one might see as transforming modes of regulation; of what is regulated as well as of what regulation itself entails (Harvey 1991, Jessop 1990, Jenson 1990, Hirsch 1988, Cohen 1985, Lipietz 1984). Let us look at each of these in turn.

First, the quest for community regulation has fundamentally altered the spaces within which governance outside the state takes place. As noted, neo-liberal thinking spurns the culture of dependency that the social arena of the welfare state purportedly encourages, and instead nurtures the formation of an amorphous, multifaceted regulatory space to replace the social. The quest for community control has occasioned a splintering attack on the social domain (and its social control), which is seen to be the binding element for modern welfare states and their *social* democracies. In this respect, at least, the modern, liberal foundations of the social welfare state have been fundamentally challenged by a persistent neo-liberalism that seems determined to fracture the social domain and replace it with a particular vision of community that is not incompatible with its enterprise culture (Gordon 1991). It is, of course, highly revealing that the 1995 meeting of the American Sociological Association should declare as its theme 'a community of communities'. Is sociology, which was very much part of constituting the social, thereby indicating an acceptance that it is poised for radical reconstruction? The question is rhetorical, but it implies other issues, including the changing forms of the individuals who comprise society, and perhaps the enterprising self of contemporary consumer cultures (see Bonner and du Guy 1992).

Secondly, the nature of regulation has shifted. Much of what follows is an elaboration of this point, but let me here merely observe that with the splintering of the social domain into communities in neo-liberal political environments comes an alteration in the nature of regulatory practices. No longer is the preservation of the social domain predicated upon containing individuals who threaten it in geographically separated control institutions (the prison, the psychiatric hospital, etc.), as though physical removal would expunge dangerousness. Of course, traces of such disciplinary practices continue, but increasingly neo-liberal regulation is deployed within communities by volunteers and private, social service entrepreneurs. Now the controllers are invisible to 'societal members' not because they work behind institutional walls but because the semblance of altruism ascribes to volunteers (and private, non-state agents) an identity that masks the stealth-like spread of local authorities throughout the community. In short, one might say that the liberal welfare state and its modern modes of regulation are facing challenges with the increasing deployment of neo-liberal forms of community regulation to secure particular (postmodern?) patterns of association.

SIGNPOSTING THE NARRATIVE

I have organised my discussion in the following way. After this, the introductory chapter, *chapter 2* explores justice as an element that is calculated and practised differently as the discursive auspices of a modern ethos give way to emerging traces under postmodern conditions. The consequent fragmentation of justice provides a basis from which to understand the rise of such 'alternatives' as the calculations and practices of community justice. *Chapter 3* is mainly descriptive, detailing the calculations and practices of community mediation advocates in British Columbia. It leads into *chapter 4* which looks at early critical responses to the advocates' images of community justice. The analytical *chapter 5* evaluates the previous discourses from the point of view of more recent new informalist critics. It aims to provide an extended critical map of community mediation as part of a governmentalisation of the (neo-)liberal state under postmodern conditions. *Chapter 6* takes heed of the previous chapter's guiding orientations to develop an account of the political rationality embodied in practices of community mediation. It outlines the 'pastoral' model of power by which community mediation governs individual disputing selves in communities, using techniques of discipline and self (especially confession). Finally, *chapter 7* returns to a more general level of analysis by detailing the mutually constitutive articulations between the pastoral power of community mediation and the sovereign-law model of (neo-)liberal legality in British Columbia. The account provides a glimpse of how a governmentalised state regulates actions through a certain 'remote control'. The effect of the latter is considered, especially with respect to an alternative politics of dispute resolution that rescinds the hegemonic grip of professionalised calculations and practices of justice. The narration breaks with an invitation to use its precepts as a means of phrasing the promise of a justice outside the limits of that which is present.

2

THE FRAGMENTED AUSPICES
OF COMMUNITY JUSTICE

To the extent that community justice is cast as an informal, popular, *alternative*, it contests the hegemony of formal, professionalised legal institutions. It is placated as the law's rival, especially when it comes to the effective resolution of particular 'community' disputes. Without commenting on whether the antagonism is a ruse, as many critics suggest, I shall in this chapter examine the discursive bases of the apparent rivalry within many western dispute resolution arenas. In this respect, it seems important to explore the discursive means by which modern law legitimates its claims to providing true justice, before showing how competing claims to its justice have proliferated over the past few decades. No longer, that is, can one easily locate a metanarrative whose purpose is to reconcile calculations of justice in singular terms, or to centralise dispute resolution practices exclusively within the rule-regulated bureaucracy of the courthouse. Universalistic notions of justice, or just procedures, have been replaced by an ethos that licenses the simultaneous presence of diverse calculations and practices of justice. Justice, in this sense, has been fragmented, and our task here is to understand that change, particularly as it pertains to the rise of 'community' calculations of justice.

Of course, such a broad issue could be tackled in various ways, but my specific tack here addresses the auspices, the 'epistemic conditions', that legitimate particular discourses on justice (Foucault 1973). This chapter's narrative begins its complex path with a brief look at how the sign 'justice' has typically been located in western discursive spaces along a continuum that defers to universal principle (philosophy) on the one hand and universal practice (jurisprudence) on the other. It concentrates on the former, not only because of my own interests but also to make the task at hand more manageable. Yet it could be shown that both discourses defer to a modern metanarrative in which social progress is deemed to be the product of the universal application of a reason deemed intrinsic to all human beings (Douzinas and Warrington 1994, Bell 1994). The central theme of this chapter is that, whereas the ethos of modernity has promoted a rigidly demarcated search for justice as a single, universal, reason-based entity

16

designated by principles that all reasonable individuals will grasp, contemporary postmodern conditions will license no such search. Under postmodern conditions, with a characteristic 'incredulity' towards the auspices implied by modern metanarratives, justice is fragmented into a plurality of different calculations without a clear means of privileging any one of these (Lyotard 1984). This leaves the articulation of justice less rigidly bound to modern auspices, and invites bids to contest the validity of modern calculations of justice. And it is here that one can apprehend the shifting auspices of justice that have licensed challenges, such as the 'alternative' postulated by community justice (see chapter 3). Through such altering auspices, that is, one glimpses the fissures that have ruptured the smooth surface of modern discourse to permit diverse calculations of justice, including those offered by proponents of community mediation.

ENUNCIATING JUSTICE: TWO HORIZONS OF MEANING

> [S]ince justice cannot be fortified, we justify force so that justice and force go together and we have peace, which is the sovereign good.
>
> (Pascal 1962: #171)

Even if one were to contest Pascal's statement, there is in it traces of two different discursive horizons within which the element *justice* has been colonised as a moment in western thought. On the one hand, Pascal's allusion to failed fortification may be taken to denote philosophical discourses that seek apodictic grounds for making claims to justice (Cullen 1994). Despite numerous versions of justice, philosophical debate continues to associate the sign with diverse calculations, some of which achieve respectability and legitimacy (transient fortification?) at particular moments in history. An early example of the attempt to capture the essence of justice can be found in Plato's formulation of justice as embodied in principles deriving from reasoned analysis (e.g. *The Republic* and *Gorgias*). For Socrates, justice is an entity whose form (*eidos*) can be grasped only through right reasoning. Whether Plato is successful in developing his approach is debatable (Douzinas and Warrington 1994, Heller 1987), but he does initiate an understanding of justice as something singular, timeless, unchanging, fixed, absolute and intrinsically tied to notions of the Good derived from right reasoning (Havelock 1978). Thus, in *The Republic*, Socrates places justice within a higher order of ideals, an *a priori* realm of the good, that should be approached through rigorous philosophical reflection. For him, justice cannot be an empirical summary of practices carried out in its name; it is an ideal concerned with higher aspirations to the good life, to living out a noble existence in accordance with universally true principles. As is well canvassed, Plato sees the philosopher King as the appropriate vehicle for extracting just principles capable of rendering the ideal practicable. Ignoring for our purposes the details of Socrates' intricate arguments, one might view his dialogues as enunciating justice as something universal, unchanging, absolute and essential. Plato's doctrine of forms sets apart apodictic knowledge of real, unchanging essences from an everyday belief in the changing appearances (*doxa*) and locates the truth (as opposed to appearance) of justice as one of the virtues derived from notions of the Good (1973: 180 ff).

On the other hand, there is the justice of jurisprudence, of lawyers advocating particular enforcement practices in the name of a justice that need not (and often does not) accept the moral calculations of philosophers. The focus on either natural law or the legal positivist's concerns with procedure, equity, access, equality before the law, and so on, is a jurisprudential bid to secure bases, *sui generis*, for justifying the enforcement of law (Bell 1994). Such uses of the sign justice too have a history, including the justice that Homer's *Iliad* evokes as procedure. For instance, after losing an important race meeting, where the status of both men is placed on the line, Menelaus accuses Antilochus of cheating. In the ensuing exchange, one glimpses Menelaus' conception of justice. He says, 'Here: I'll conduct the case and not one man will take exception; it will be justly done' (Bell 1994: 23.566). In this context, the sign justice is used in either the singular (*dike*) or plural (*dikai*) form, and as either a noun or a verb (Havelock 1978: 134–135). Justice is understood as a performance, usually uttered out loud, that can take on diverse forms. It is a variable application 'in between both parties without favour' at an appropriate forum (e.g. an *agora*). Disputants are required to state their 'justices' directly to a public and must persuade others of their plausibility. Diverse 'managers of justice' are appointed in context. The Homeric depiction offers an early formulation of justice that emphasises procedural intervention appropriate to context. Justice is the legitimate procedures that help disputants settle their conflicts without recourse to individual violence in the first instance. The focus on process implies a spacial and temporal performance that is accepted as just in context. As such, just judgments, the applications of justice, are variable, applied to different heres and nows.

This relativisation of justice is also present in various post-Homeric formulations, including that of Thrasymachus of Chàlcedon who leaps dramatically into an otherwise genteel dialogue on justice with his assertion: 'what I say is that "just" or "right" means nothing but what is the interest of the stronger' (Plato 1973: 18). He awaits in vain for applause, but – though he could not have known it then – might have consoled himself with the knowledge that his enunciation helped to ensconce into the trace a version of justice as appropriate performance in context. Aristotle's *phronimos* too recognises the importance of time and place in practices of justice, as does Pascal's mocking pronouncement: 'we see no system of justice or injustice which does not vary from one country to another like the climate . . . A comic sort of justice that has a river for its boundary! Truth on this side of the Pyrenees, error on the other' (1962: #108). The sign continues to be associated with the relativism of the early uses; for instance, in legal positivism where justice is depicted as a matter of opinion that is best spoken of as 'law', where law means no more than 'the law of a particular community' (Bell 1994: 117).

Despite significant variations and overlaps within and between the bifurcated horizons of justice as principle versus process, the division does appear to serve as a possible candidate for a core 'binary opposition' around which the presence of justice continues to be placated under modern conditions (Cullen 1994, Jenkins 1980). Stated somewhat differently, these horizons stand as dichotomous poles of the trace, as the absent deferrals that have been etched into the very fabric of debates around justice under modern conditions. Of course, the precise formulation of appropriate principles and processes of justice has differed widely in often turgid debates, but the more general strategy of deferring to, or even trying to reconcile, the two horizons remains a prominent feature of the sign. With this in mind one can try to apprehend the relations between enunciations and the auspices of justice under modern conditions, between the calculations/practices of justice and the metanarratives that are drawn upon to legitimate these. Let us initially explore certain core auspices of a modern discursive ethos, before turning to how they are mobilised to legitimate very particular approaches to justice.

APPROACHING JUSTICE IN A MODERN ETHOS

Who would dare to declare with confidence an absolute formulation of the modern, modernism or modernity? Is the modern an epoch located in time and space, distinct from those before it in key ways, or a far less specifiable 'attitude' (Foucault 1984: 39)? The equivocal uses of the 'modern' and associated signs (modernisation, modernity, modernism) are by now notorious, requiring some thought of their use in the present context (see Beck *et al.* 1994, Giddens 1990, Featherstone 1988). Kumar argues that 'modern society is industrial society', noting that processes of modernisation and industrialisation are inextricably linked (1988: 3). Dramatic demographic shifts, vast population increases, urbanisation, the rise of bureaucratic administrative patterns, immigration, technological developments, mass communication, and transformations of the ways in which people view themselves in the world are all significant modernising processes that have altered the pace of life. Moreover, as Berman notes,

> These world historical processes have nourished an amazing variety of visions and ideas that aim to make men and women the subjects as well as the objects of modernisation, to give them the power to

change the world that is changing them, to make their way through the maelstrom and make it their own.

(1988: 16)

Coterminous with modernisation is what Weber (1976) succinctly calls a certain 'disenchantment of the world' and the associated development of new frameworks by which everyday existence is rendered intelligible. Stated differently, the maelstrom of modern life, the rapid movement of its pace, the vertigo of knowing that history is open-ended, occasions the rise of a specific ethos that finds expression in different aspects of society – social, cultural and political. This ethos was developed and guided by an overarching narrative that 'eliminates all superhuman and supernatural forces, the gods and spirits, with which non-industrial cultures people the universe, and to which they attribute responsibility for phenomena of the natural and social worlds' (Kumar 1988: 21). One need only recall Cartesian doubting, or indeed the famous *querelle des anciens et des modernes*, to connote the extent to which the elimination of past traditions was contemplated. In the process of revoking auspices handed down from the past, modern thought begins to establish different auspices by which to legitimate its particular narratives of the world. And it is the bastion of reason that is evoked as a foundation for the project of modern scientific and philosophical thinking (B. Smart 1993).

There are three particularly salient features of the ensuing modern ethos that bear directly on our project here. First, insofar as modernity emerges as an overt rupture with past tradition, it brings into prominence a time sequence that distinguishes the past from the moving present, and the present from its possible future. The postulated release from the 'tutelage of the past', which Kant (1990) heralds as a laudable feature of modernity, entails a recognition of the contingent and fleeting passage of time.[1] And this introduces its own anxieties for, as Smart puts it, 'The absence of timeless or universal criteria meant that modernity, constituted through a process of disarticulation from antiquity, had to confront the problem of grounding itself, or creating its own criteria of normativity' (1992: 148). In trying to create such critieria, the modern ethos seeks an absolute order and develops an 'attitude' that Foucault, reflecting on Baudelaire, argues,

consists in recapturing something eternal that is not beyond the present instant, nor behind it, but within it ... For the attitude of modernity, the high value of the present is indissociable from a desperate eagerness to imagine it, to imagine it otherwise than it is, and to transform it not by destroying it but by grasping in it what it is.

(1984: 39 and 41)

As such, modern attempts to recapture the eternal have produced narratives that place emphasis on the universality of processes deemed intrinsic to specified events. In most spheres of modern society, it is through the universal that the eternal is approached and the minatory presence of contingency placed to one side. In this discourse, a just order is deemed attainable through universally true principles or laws.

This leads into the second directly relevant aspect of a modern ethos; namely its rising secular rationalism (Weber 1976). Modern societies problematised the legitimating narratives of religious orders as a growing faith in a particular version of reason developed under the cover of emerging secular metanarratives. This modern ethos appeared to declare with some confidence: 'Reason will clear up the mess that superstition, revelation, faith (the devils of the rationalist) have piled up here on earth' (Brinton 1963: 110). In different Enlightenment projects, this declaration located reason as the solid bedrock upon which a society could found progressive change and reach out to a future that would be more enlightened than its past (Smart 1992, Bock 1979). Here reason is carved as an Archimedean point against which human progress could be measured. The greater the degree to which reason is inscribed onto a given social environment, the more 'advanced', 'progressive', 'enlightened', 'emancipated' that society is likely to be. Implicit here, of course, is a unilateral conception of reason with universal applicability – it provides us with a glimpse of the eternal through its truthful enunciation.

Finally, as the postulated rational laws of nature are associated with those of a human nature, one detects the expansion of a humanist dimension within the modern ethos (Brinton 1963). Here, the human being emerges as an entity *sui generis* and is located in a privileged discursive space. As Foucault points out, under modern conditions, 'man' emerges 'as a primary reality with his own density, as the difficult object and sovereign subject of all possible knowledge' (1973: 310). Women, by contrast, are accorded a density, but their capacity to assume the mantle of sovereign subjects is deemed limited by modern thought (Nicholson 1990). Even so, the modern humanist revolution had the effect of placing human nature as a sovereign entity in and of itself, and not pliable matter in the hands of an infinite deity (Foucault 1977a). Like nature in general, human nature is deemed to be intrinsically rational, and thus under the most advanced conditions will operate according to rational laws, not according to superstitions. The human sciences sought to clarify these laws with the ultimate aim of releasing individuals from the yokes of past tradition – the Cartesian idea of building a new house of reason is ensconced in, for example, Kant as a means of obtaining individual freedom and enlightenment (1990: 83–86).

Even if these three aspects of a modern ethos have here been separated for heuristic purposes, they are inextricably related to one another in an

21

overarching modern metanarrative. In a succinct statement of this, Bauman notes that, under modern conditions,

> Universal was to be the rule of reason, the order of things which would replace slavery to passions with the autonomy of rational beings, superstition and ignorance with truth, tribulations of the drifting plankton with self-made thoroughly monitored history by design.
>
> (1994: 13)

And, to continue our narrative on the auspices of modern thinking, the universalistic, rationalistic and humanistic themes of this modern ethos have licensed, no privileged, particular discursive strategies above others. But what sort of strategies are at issue, particularly with reference to philosophical enunciations of justice? Perhaps the most eloquent and explicit reflection on the strategies is to be found in the work of a thinker who has been described as 'the most perfect expression of modernity': Immanuel Kant (Douzinas and Warrington 1994: 409). In the *Foundations of a Metaphysics of Morals*, Kant overtly explores – as the title indicates – the auspices of his discursive strategies in the moral arena. And, since his influence on the modern ethos has been profound, it is not surprising that the suggested discursive strategies for apprehending moral being should be found in various modern conceptions of justice. Thus, let us first turn to Kant's postulated strategies, rooted as they are in a modern ethos, before then referring to his influence on various modern theories of justice.[2]

Kant's moral foundations

In the previously mentioned text, Kant lays the foundations for explicating moral traces. I shall focus on three core strategic moves by which the text identifies moral traces that rely upon the modern ethos outlined above. First, drawing legitimacy from the modern quest for universality, Kant demarcates the practical domain and tries to capture its essential – and therefore universally applicable – features. Here general principles constitute the backbone of the moral domain and govern the maxims that specify the nature of moral action. Secondly, echoing an Enlightenment faith in reason, Kant argues that in order to expose the nature of moral principles it is necessary to use pure practical reasoning. The underlying assumption is that moral principles are intrinsically reasonable. Finally, having focused on principle, Kant recognises that the means by which these will be followed in specific contexts lies ultimately with the rational human being. His humanistic position is that the basis of all moral action derives from the ability of rational human beings to apply moral principles to their everyday actions (1990: section III). Let us say a little more about each of these strategies in turn.

In Kant's discursive strategy we hear echoes of previous attempts (e.g. Plato) to reconcile universal, necessary moral principles and processes that correctly apply these to contingent situations. The universal, which always reaches beyond the particular, is nevertheless articulated to the particular, but leaves an absent trace, a promise of those aspects of the moral that are not yet realised. Kant (1990) begins his analysis by asking how we might know whether a given act is moral (or, by extension for our purposes, just). His overall response is to accept that the realm of morality is never arbitrary, but governed by universal laws, moral principles, which determine whether an act is moral or not. These laws must be universal if they are to be necessary, and they must be necessary if they are to distinguish absolutely between good and evil. In this, he clearly wishes to avoid equating moral precepts with natural laws without suggesting that the practical domain is intrinsically relative to time and place. Here Kant furthers the modern ethos's quest for a secularly defined universality in the realm of morals, and he does so through a series of analytical moves (1990: 3–8).

To begin with, he distinguishes the practical domain of morality from the physical realm of nature, arguing that the former is governed by its own practical (rather than natural) laws. Then, he tries to specify the precise form that practical laws assume: mostly as imperatives directed at the human will (expressed by 'ought' or 'shall', as in 'thou shall'). Kant holds that an imperative is less determining than the dictates of a natural law, but is nevertheless an objective principle, a universally applicable rule. How so? Because, Kant explains, it is 'valid for every rational being and the principle by which it ought to act, i.e., an imperative' (1990: 37 footnote). A truly rational entity, that is, will *ipso facto* have to follow the dictates of a rational imperative if it is to be true to its nature. Given, however, that the imperative is not as determining as a natural law, moral agents will have to use appropriate methods to calculate and discover universal moral laws. Because such laws are objective and *a priori*, they cannot be derived or inferred from the transience of empirical evidence. They can be established only through non-empirical, logical analysis as it operates in the practical domain (1990: 24, 43–44).

This sets up the conditions for Kant's second strategy; a strategy that is legitimated by a further feature of modernity: rationalism. In this context, Kant argues that calculations to establish universal moral principles must rely on the apodicticity of practical reasoning because, for Kant, 'all moral precepts have their seat and origin entirely a priori in reason' (1990: 27). Although he distinguishes between pure practical and speculative reason (which applies to nature), Kant insists on the unity of all forms of reason, arguing that 'in the final analysis there can be but one and the same reason which must be different only in application' (1990: 7). This presumed unity is crucial for him because reason is proffered as the absolute and unconditionally necessary bedrock of his philosophy. At the same time, however, this necessity cannot be grasped through reason.

Even if reason *qua* reason can seek an awareness of its own necessity, or attempt to become transparent to itself through critique (which distinguishes it from dogma), reason does face limits: 'Reason... restlessly seeking the unconditionally necessary, sees itself compelled to assume it though it has no means by which to make it comprehensible' (1990: 81). So, reason's ability to yield the unconditionally necessary, and by implication its own apodicticity, ultimately rests upon an assumption. As such, the spectre of faith lies at the very heart of a metaphysics of morals, and is possible because of a 'human reason generally'. The ground for such an assumption is that, although we may not grasp the necessity of moral imperatives, we do have a sense of their 'incomprehensibility'. And as Kant argues, this 'is all that can fairly be demanded of a philosophy which in its principles strives to reach the boundary of human reason' (Kant 1990: 82). In Kant's formulation of what is a fair demand of philosophy directed at the boundary of reason lies a tale of what is deemed epistemologically legitimate under modern conditions. But what we have so far gleaned from the strategy is the attempted pronouncement of moral action as something that is both indicated in, and guided by, universal principles calculated through a reasoning appropriate to the practical domain of life. And these principles are unconditionally necessary because they lie at the limits of reason, as revealed by a critique pointing to their incomprehensibility.

If Kant's discussion up to this point is concerned with outlining the foundations of moral principles, the third strategy is concerned with enunciating how human beings located in specific temporal and spacial locations are capable of performing moral actions governed by principles. Here, as noted, Kant tries to reconcile his idea of moral principles with processes that show that human beings are capable of moral action. His famous 'anthropology' is the basis of this humanist aspect of his strategy. By locating reason in humanity, Kant begins to make the transition from the general realm of universal moral principles to the contingent realm of moral action in particular sets of circumstances. He aims to reconcile the problem of applying necessary, universal principles of morality to particular sets of circumstances through his conception of subjective freedom. For him, moral laws define good and evil, and these are founded on a reason that is intrinsic to human beings. So, the ground of all universal principles of morality is reason, which serves as an Archimedean point of morality not because it is God given, or emanates from an *a priori* Platonic Good, but because it is a general feature of all rational beings. Hence, the source of morality is ultimately human, in that it emerges from the rationality that is deemed common to all rational beings. By grounding moral laws in practical reason, Kant ties the imperatives of moral action to a reason that directs, and yet is an intrinsic part of, a rational human being. At this

24

point in western thought, reason ceases to be an ethic (a guide to life), but is formulated as a distinctive and rigid 'nature'. Reason becomes the criterion by which to demarcate the human from the non-human being. In the process, the rational subject becomes both subject and object of moral principle; when a subject's will guides specifically moral acts, then it must be governed by maxims that are, in turn, universalisable as necessary practical laws. That is, as his famous categorical imperative states, 'Act only according to that maxim by which you can at the same time will that it should become a universal law' (1990: 38). Such an imperative, we should note, licenses a process that permits a very particular set of practices; i.e. those that can be universalised as principles.

Kant's strategies, located as they are in wider auspices of a modern ethos, provide an important orientation for subsequent modern discourses on justice. Indeed, Kant's thinking provides a moral orbit within which many modern calculations of justice revolve (Young 1990, Campbell 1988, Miller 1974). It offers a foundation for specific theories of justice that develop around notions of universal principle based on a reason that is deemed to be intrinsic to all human (rational, morally capable) subjects. One could refer to a number of specifically modern approaches to justice that operate within this canon (Cullen 1994). However, let us single out but two theorists for the specific purpose of illustrating common applications of Kant's strategies in modern theories of justice, and thereby point to the manner in which philosophical calculations of justice depend on the auspices of a modern discursive ethos for legitimacy. The two texts I have selected for the very limited purposes of the present analysis are Rawls (1973) and Reiman (1990).³

Two modern theories of justice

Rawls offers a theory of justice that openly declares an intellectual debt to Kant (1973: ch. 4). Since its publication, this book has had a marked impact on philosophical discourses on justice.⁴ Without claiming to do justice (as though that would fortify my exegesis) to the specifics of Rawls' theory, it is still possible to orientate oneself within the broad parameters of his language-game. His is an ambitious venture: to provide a theory of justice that would offer an Archimedean point from which to judge whether or not the structures of a given society are fair or not, outside of utilitarian thinking. So, for Rawls, justice has to do with the 'fairness' of social structures, and especially with ways in which a society distributes its primary resources. Underpinning this approach is the openly declared assumption that most people share an underlying notion of 'justice as fairness', and that justice is a moral quality to be understood at a societal level.⁵ A theory of justice would do no more, or indeed no less, than elaborate upon the bases upon which common notions of justice rest.

25

Rawls' attempt at providing such an analysis starts by evoking a thought experiment. Consider, he implores, the situation where sane, reasonable individuals assemble to develop moral principles to produce a just society. There is a further condition: such individuals are placed under a 'veil of ignorance' in the sense that they are aware of their own interests but do not know where they would be located in such a society. This theoretically 'original' position provides the opening from which Rawls seeks to formulate universal principles of justice, founded on the common agreement of sane, rational human beings. In general terms, these principles of justice are 'those that free and rational persons concerned to further their own interests would accept in an initial position of equality as defining the fundamental terms of their association' (1973: 11). From this general point, Rawls develops two specific principles (1973: 60 and 83), which are refined through the course of his analysis.[6]

Another version of justice explicitly influenced by Kant, and indeed by Rawls, but which tries to extend these, is found in Reiman's (1990) more recent formulations. Betraying his underlying allegiance to modern discourses, Reiman offers the following definition of justice: 'Justice is the set of principles regulating behaviour that it would be reasonable for all human beings to accept to best protect themselves against the threat of subjugation each poses to the others' (1990: 4). The quest to articulate a universal set of principles takes Reiman through a complex analysis that begins with his attempt to ground a version of a social contract as something that is necessary ('natural') and 'built into each individual's reason' (1990: 20). This provides the basis for offering two principles (embodying both a critique and an extension of Rawls' principles) that are founded in 'natural justice' but that imply a version of social justice. The quest for such universal principles to denote justice is deemed absolutely necessary to avoid the implicitly intolerable: 'Unless truths of morality can be identified by reason, moral conflicts are only clashes between people with unverifiable beliefs. Then, victory goes to the side of power ... to prevail, and right becomes indistinguishable from might' (1990: ix). The ghost of Thrasymachus haunts Reiman's text, which seeks to expel the nagging worry that process will out over principle. He does this by repositioning a faith in 'the natural reasoning faculties of human beings' (1990: ix). Reiman argues that justice – which is deemed to have 'primacy over other moral ideas' – is 'reason's answer to subjugation' and furthermore that 'only reason can require in a non-subjugating way' (1990: 7–8). Here, reason is viewed not as an abstract notion of how propositions relate to one another, but rather as a 'faculty of rational thought' and a 'capacity to make correct inferences from propositions' (1990: 9). The link between justice and reason is deemed fundamental, such that '[t]he fate of justice is tied to the fate of reason' (1990: 10).

There is enough in these brief remarks on both thinkers to indicate the continuing presence of Kant's strategies, and the legitimising threads of a modern ethos against which Rawls' and Reiman's enunciations are silhouetted. In both theories, justice emerges as a discrete entity whose presence is enunciated through universal principles: justice might be deferred to qualities such as 'fairness', 'equality', etc., but its essence is purportedly reflected (discovered) in principles. Drawing on Kant's strategy, both describe these principles as *a priori* and universal because they are assigned a daunting moral task: to decide absolutely between the just and specious claims to the just, regardless of parochial/cultural context. Such principles therefore occupy a special position in modern discourse in that they simultaneously indicate the form of justice and serve as moral imperatives to guide social action. So long as individuals act according to the imperatives of the principles, their actions are likely to be just. These principles serve as a stable, fixed, Archimedean point against which actions in the flow of life can be evaluated. As such, the principles should reflect the essence of justice, focusing on what is common to (what unifies) all contexts of justice.

Given the role assigned to principle in this framework, the need to establish the impartial, independent, necessary and absolute truth of any postulated maxim is critical. Like Kant, both Reiman and Rawls locate the apodictic grounding (and hence independence) of the principles entirely in reason. That is, a particular (Enlightenment) conception of reason is evoked as a means of fortifying the idea of justice as principle. Recalling Reiman's statement, 'the fate of justice is tied to the fate of reason', one is able to glimpse the undaunted faith that is placed in reason. Justice itself is rendered contingent upon a very specific conception of rationality. The principles of justice have to be calculated, but the sole basis for that calculation must be the precepts of a reason (rather than, say, empirical science or religious dogma) that any rational or sane individual would be compelled to accept. The final credibility of this point rests upon the use of reason in a dualistic sense. On the one hand, Rawls and Reiman offer their principles by way of systematically reasoned argument that presents the ideas as rightful claimants of the truth. On the other hand, both thinkers tell us that their principles are universally valid because no reasonable individual would possibly reject them. Finally, and related to this point, both theorists – following Kant's strategy – locate reason in the natural capacity of a free subject who under appropriate conditions (e.g. under a veil of ignorance, free-thinking individual) is capable of grasping the tenets of pure reason. The universality of this reasoning is assured in that that capacity to reason is located as something innate to all sane human beings.

In relying on Kantian strategies, such philosophical narrations of justice *ipso facto* ground themselves within a modern ethos whose 'metanarratives' champion the universal principles over particular enunciations, and placate reason as a unified grounding of all morality located in the human subject.

The just (progressive, enlightened, etc.) society is one that embraces such metanarratives and creates an ethos in which claims to justice are fortified by the auspices of modern discourses. So much then for philosophical renditions of justice. What about modern narratives (mainly in jurisprudence) that are concerned with 'practical justice', or justice through processes? That is, what of modern justifications of force that claim the rubric of justice? In various formulations (natural law, discursive theory, utilitarian theories, etc.) of justice as that which is justifiably enforced, one can also detect the auspices of the modern ethos; the force required to impose a reasonable and just order over free individuals entails a process that, too, claims legitimacy from modern auspices. Although beyond what I wish to accomplish here, let us at least tentatively indicate how this might be so.

Referring to lawyers' conceptions, Bell argues, 'It is a central theme in much writing that justice involves the impartial application of legal rules without bias and in a way which treats all subjects of law equally and entitles them to state their point of view' (1994: 127). This statement points to the quest for a universal process that is fair, equal and metes out justice with impartiality. It highlights the recognition that 'in modern society the typical conception of justice is first and foremost universalistic in nature' (Arts and van der Veen 1994: 149). One could locate the quest for the universal in codified rules of procedure deemed essential to the equal and disinterested application of a 'rule of law'. Even if she is the nemesis of many accused persons preparing to meet their doom, the blindfolded Themis holds scales of justice that symbolise a quest to apply collective laws impartially to all who come before her modern agora – the courtroom. She declares the institution's disinterested processes that either deny, or license, a series of impositions upon those pronounced not guilty, or guilty, respectively. Like its philosophical counterpart, this conception of justice implicitly appeals to the modern emphasis on universality as a glimpse of the eternal. Equally, the power of legal reasoning and the claim that judicial processes be founded upon reason provide explicit *ratios* for decisions reached. Furthermore, the 'reasonable' individual as the bearer of rights and duties assumed by many courtroom processes relates directly to the humanist dimension of a modern ethos (see Fitzpatrick 1992a, Barron 1990). The idea that justice implies 'access' to individuals to vindicate their rights implies a process that reinforces – rather than coercively robs – an individual's free will (Garth 1982, Cappelletti and Garth 1981).

So, even from these brief enunciations it seems conceivable to locate discursive strategies of legitimation in both philosophical and legal calculations of justice that appeal to three common auspices at the heart of modern thinking. With this in mind, were the common auspices to change, one could well expect calculations (together with discursive strategies used to create and legitimate these) to undergo alteration. The following section explores recent calculations of justice that are incompatible with, and do not appeal to, the modern auspices outlined above. I take this, in the section following the next, to be symptomatic of a wider crisis of faith in modern auspices and as a signal to a rising alternative, postmodern, ethos with different auspices. The main effect of the latter is to have fragmented justice, to have licensed calculations that do not cling to a singular, unified notion. In what follows, the implications of the altered postmodern auspices are considered, as indicated by Derrida and Lyotard, before indicating how such changes provide a background to the rise of community justice.

JUSTICE TALK IN THE INTERREGNUM

Despite the continued influence of modern conceptions of justice, notable challenges have been mounted against their foundational precepts and strategies. For instance, Walzer (1983) speaks of justice, not as a unified entity but as a more ephemeral notion that assumes different forms in the different 'spheres' in which it operates. He explicitly rejects the view that there is a singular, universally applicable set of principles that can identify what justice *is*. Rather, he tells us, 'the principles of justice are themselves pluralistic in form', and this reflects only that society itself is not homogeneous because it contains diverse 'spheres' that have marked different understandings of social goods and how these ought to be distributed (1983: 6). His point here is that any calculation of justice is bound to context, and that the currencies used in such calculations are the products of 'historical and cultural particularism' (1983: 6). As such, he argues, the distribution of socially created goods does not occur via a universally shared standard: 'There is no single standard. But there are standards (roughly knowable even when they are controversial) for every social good and every distributive sphere in every particular society' (1983: 10). His formulation of justice uncharacteristically concentrates on the nature of specific spheres (e.g. welfare rights, money and commodities, office bearing, etc.) in which calculations of justice are made.

Enunciating justice in this manner involves discursive strategies that are quite different from those employed by Rawls and Reiman. Certainly, one of the fundamental Kantian precepts is transgressed in the search for plural instances of justice, with an underlying assumption that justice may not be a unified, universally applicable entity. Justice, in Walzer's formulation, is segmented into different more or less autonomous spheres. Moreover, the autonomy of these spheres is fundamental enough to question whether a singular rationality could found all the different calculations of justice. This particular issue is elaborated upon by MacIntyre (1988), who argues that, in contemporary contexts, 'different and incompatible conceptions of justice are characteristically closely linked to different and incompatible conceptions of practical rationality' (1988: ix).[7] He sees in modern concep-

29

tions of justice an Enlightenment project that has failed and left us in a particular historical predicament: 'We thus inhabit a culture in which an inability to arrive at agreed rationally justifiable conclusions on the nature of justice and practical rationality coexists with appeals by contending social groups to sets of rival and conflicting convictions unsupported by rational justification' (1988: 5–6). For him, modernity is responsible for this situation because of its attempts to *replace* tradition with an Archimedean point, namely reason. His 'post-Enlightenment' plea is to place reason and justice within particular traditions, and to recognise that there cannot be an independent point outside of history. All that we have, from this point of view, is the weight of traditions to curtail the minatory presence of extreme relativism. But traditions will always have limits that silence or fail to consider the perspective of another; they are never entirely universalisable. Hence the need to ask, 'Whose justice? Which rationality?'

Fisk (1989) also questions the auspices of Enlightenment rationalism to which modern theories of justice appeal. In particular, he directs an attack on the notion that one reason can found universally valid principles of justice. His neo-Marxist orientation declares as archaic the quest for *a priori* principles, seeking instead to understand social justice as arising from definite socio-historical conflicts between groups located in different positions within global and local economies. 'Official' state justice, he argues, is placed in the contradictory position of having to articulate and enforce (limited) patterns of justice that allow the state to claim legitimacy without eroding the structural bases from whence disputes arise in the first place. In contrast to the logic of official justice, Fisk notes that 'radical' justice refers to the values and norms that a state ruled by the exploited would adopt. In contrast to even modern Marxist interpretations of justice (e.g. Buchanan 1982), Fisk argues that justice cannot be universal (or based on one rationality) because capitalist societies place people in conflicting positions with incommensurable logics of interest and justice. Therefore, like Walzer and MacIntyre, Fisk sees the quest for universal principles of justice founded upon reason as doomed from the outset. Justice, for him, must be located in actual social existence as the outcome of struggles between groups with competing economic interests in specific sets of circumstances. As such, he joins the previously noted attempts to dissolve modern strategies that enunciate justice through universal principles founded in a single, human reason. And, by turning away from these auspices, all three thinkers appear to placate visions of justice as process that takes different forms in different spheres, traditions or struggles. Thrasymachus again? Perhaps, but certainly the contingency of time and place is elevated above approaches that seek sweeping, absolute and reason-based principles of justice.

Continuing this line of thinking, Iris Young (1990) refrains from presenting a metaphysical theory of justice *per se*. She openly acknowledges the socially situated nature of both justice and her analyses of it (1990: 5). Her attack on Rawls (and other theorists of justice) centres around a perceived oversight that emerges from his working within what she calls the 'distributive paradigm'. In particular, he fails to grasp that justice is about more than the mere distribution of social goods; it must, Young argues, equally be concerned with 'the institutional conditions necessary for the development and exercise of individual capacities and collective communication and cooperation' (1990: 39). She identifies domination and oppression as the major impediments to establishing such conditions, offering five 'objective' (but not value-neutral or independent) conditions as criteria for deciding whether a group is oppressed in a particular society (1990: 64). If a group can be shown to experience any one condition, then it is oppressed. Even though Young's version of critical theory appears to maintain a partial allegiance to elements of a modern discursive ethos, she situates justice within a 'politics of difference' that extends beyond modern political theatres. This type of politics does not cling to the idea that group differences are purely incidental, and that emancipation comes from discovering that which is essential to, and thus unifies, all human beings. Young recognises that she is here at odds with the Enlightenment vision where, '[t]he state and law should express rights only in universal terms applied equally to all, and differences among persons and groups should be a purely accidental and private matter' (1990: 157). Her alternative is to 'seek a society in which differences of race, sex, religion, and ethnicity no longer make a difference to people's rights and opportunities' (1990: 157). In order for (social) justice of this kind to be developed, Young argues that a concept of group difference is important for understanding the identities of people who must endure the yokes of oppression in given contexts. However, she insists any group differences should not be essentialised.[8] To do so would be to fall into the liberal humanist trap of positing an absolute existence to what are really specific constructs, or identities that have emerged as a result of specific historical sorts of relations between people (1990: 171).

In short, Young's work dislodges the modern attempt to locate reason as an essential feature of a homogeneously conceived (European?) 'man'. She implicitly deconstructs the modern quest to ground justice in an essentialised, rational person who would (could do no other than?) agree to the premises of the various conceptions of justice. The effects of this move are profound: it licenses a search for justice not as something founded upon an essentially reasonable human being, but as a notion that can be recovered from the 'otherness' that is excluded by essentialising humanist concepts. Her politics of difference is meant to locate the oppression that marginalises identities other than that placated by modern humanist themes, and to associate justice with attempts to overcome such oppression. In this way, Young not only emancipates justice from the shackles that bind it to a particular (white, western, male) conception of the human being, but also shatters the image of a singular essential vision of what it is to be human. The unity of the subject is fractured and justice is placed on the side of plural attempts to counter the marginalisation, and oppression, of otherness (Cadava *et al.* 1991). The importance of this move is indicated in analyses that explore the limits of essentialising strategies (e.g. Nicholson 1990, Butler 1990, C. Smart 1989), and by theories that articulate justice to various conceptions of otherness: Moller Okin (1989) with respect to women; Mohr (1988) with reference to homosexuals, and Vattimo (1992) on colonised people.

Despite vast differences between the above accounts, all seem to render problematic central elements of justice as it is formulated within a modern ethos. Consequently, the manner in which they use the sign *justice* has altered markedly as modern auspices have been challenged in various ways. First, they question the search for one version of justice applicable to all contexts, on the grounds that such an endeavour has eclipsed the signifi-cance of particular, local narratives marginalised or silenced by the quest for universalism. This critique overturns the importance placed by modern thinkers on locating *a priori* metaphysical principles of justice, and focuses on processes that would make ontologically possible – rather than exclude – the experience of alterity and difference. Secondly, their calculations of justice are grounded in specific contexts (however these might be defined), and not in the purported apodicticity of a human reason. Since the ration-alities of different contexts are explicitly endorsed, calculations of justice are unlikely to assume a singular form (even if many seem concerned about the extreme relativism that this might license). Thirdly, the texts implicitly or explicitly question the modern assumption of liberal humanist themes: if justice cannot be calculated using a singular form of reason, this is partially due to there being no single point of origin, no single identity, from whence reason could be said to derive (e.g. rational 'man'). All identities are historically contingent rather than ontologically necessary, and accounts of justice are consequently affected. In the end, one might say that justice as enunciated under modern conditions has been fragmented by different discursive strategies: the repudiation of necessary principles of universal applicability, the pluralisation of reasons through which justice is calculated and the death of 'man' as an ontologically privileged category. But how are we to understand this apparent fragmentation?

Declining modern auspices

During the course of the twentieth century, and especially in the post-war decades, the credibility of modern metanarratives has faced profound challenges.[9] Already in the late 1950s Mills had noted the scale of change facing a modern ethos: 'We are at the ending of what is called the Modern Age. Just as Antiquity was followed by several centuries of Oriental ascendancy ... so now The Modern Age is being succeeded by a post-modern period' (1959: 165–166). Notwithstanding my noted reluctance to speak in epochal terms, we are today familiar with a world to which Mills alludes: the consumer in search of pleasure in the structured spaces of the shopping mall; the gleaming lights that beckon and invite rampant consumerism; the lure of electronic wizardry; the deification of technology; the global expansion of economies; the niche markets in newly fashioned cobblestone lanes; the cultural worlds of multiple television channels; the lure of pastiche in architectural design and home decor; the talk of 'community'; the difficult task of coming to grips with a contingent world devoid of absolute certainties of a modern order; and so on.[10] These common images betoken shifts in economic (post-industrialism, post-Fordism), political, social and cultural arenas of many lives, some of which directly challenge the auspices of the modern ethos.

Simultaneously, the modern metanarrative that a society built upon reason will increase individual liberty and progressively advance its condition has fallen from its place of privilege (Vattimo 1992, B. Smart 1992, Lyotard 1984). In particular, its singular, Eurocentric version of reason as the basis of progress has been profoundly challenged. As Vattimo notes, the metanarrative implicitly says: 'Europeans are the best form of humanity and the entire course of history is directed towards the more or less complete realisation of this ideal' (1992: 4). But, he points out, the west is now experiencing an 'explosive situation', which has emerged because of a sustained rebellion amongst colonised people and oppressed minorities (the 'other') across the globe (Vattimo 1992: 6). It would be impracticable to list the ongoing protests and revolts that are occurring both without and within European societies, even as I write, but it is surely possible to note the considerable extent to which these have challenged unquestioned patterns of association, and continue to express differently conceived rationales for existence.

Lyotard speaks to one salient aspect of this challenge by arguing that western forms of knowledge have encountered a serious 'legitimacy crisis' in which 'the question of the legitimacy of knowledge is formulated in different terms' (1984: 37). Neither the speculative nor the emancipatory metanarratives of the humanities enjoy the currency that they once might have had in a modern ethos. Under contemporary, postmodern conditions, a prevailing 'incredulity towards metanarratives' requires that claims to knowledge seek different auspices, beyond the metanarratives of social progress and individual freedom through the universal application of reason. No longer is a linear view of history, and the enunciation of progress, exclusively formulated in Eurocentric terms. In the ensuing hunt for legitimacy, Lyotard sees that knowledge seekers increasingly rely on economic or technocratic metanarratives to substantiate their truth claims (1984: 45ff). I shall return to this insight later, but the crisis of which Lyotard speaks has had a number of effects on discursive practices.

To begin with, those practices predicated upon the assumption that real forms of existence are absolute, and fixed, are problematised. The growing acceptance of deconstruction in all its variants has challenged the (logocentric) foundations of attempts to 'discover' absolute essences of entities.[11] The proliferation of informational technologies has also problematised the very idea of one essential reality, or a single absolute existence, and indeed what representation might entail (Baudrillard 1988). In this emerging discursive environment, the 'being' of anything can never be taken as absolute. Rather, under the influence of such thinkers as Nietzsche (1967), some analysts viewed existence as no more than the outcome of historically situated processes that define being through discursive strategies that articulate rules for the use of signs (e.g. Laclau and Mouffe 1985, Foucault 1973). And, if the unity of being is rendered impossible, then so too are universalising practices seeking to sustain this very unity. To return to Lyotard for the moment, one might say it is no longer possible 'for anyone to establish her- or himself in a field and proceed to produce laws in a sort of universal language or generalised metalanguage, and then go on to extend these laws to all fields of language' (Lyotard and Thebaud 1985: 98–99). The inordinate walling up of silence, the elimination of local language-games that is necessary to sustain universal claims has certainly come at great cost to those silenced by the voice of necessity. But, in the deconstruction of the necessary, a different set of practices has emerged – the recovery of silenced chains of reasoning that were suppressed in enthusiastic, modern quests for grand, general knowledge claims.

Second, an important challenge has been directed at the modern view that a single form of reason ought to guide social progress. An uncoupling of one (Eurocentric, sexist, racist, class-based?) type of rationality from societal progress and emancipation has occurred in many different ways. Most notably, while the forms of rebellion to the multifaceted subjugations of western modernisation are extensive, the rising choruses of oppressed voices have fundamentally eroded a sustained belief in the purity of its reason (e.g. Vattimo 1992, Maffesoli 1990, Nicholson 1990). The 'blackmail' of Enlightenment precepts that require us to stay within a given (western androcentric, white, European) tradition of reason, or risk falling prey to the dark forces of irrationality, is no longer as persuasive as it once might have been (Foucault 1984). In the process, reason has been pluralised, and the rationalities of marginal voices not immediately rendered irrational by imperialistic decree. Furthermore, the blights of such atrocities as apartheid and the Holocaust, whose protagonists claimed to be well within the domain of rationalising their societies towards more advanced states, have demonstrated the sheer flexibility of reason. In the process, not only has one (Enlightenment) version of reason been uncoupled from societal progress, but its heterogeneous (dispersed) nature has also been exposed. In effect, however, this has rendered the continued faith in one form of reason as a guarantor of social progress implausible (see Pavlich 1995). As such, Vattimo argues that,

> With the demise of the idea of a central rationality of history, the world of generalized communication explodes like a multiplicity of 'local' rationalities – ethnic, sexual, religious, cultural or aesthetic minorities – that finally speak up for themselves. They are no longer repressed and cowed into silence by the idea of a single true form of humanity that must be realized irrespective of particularity and individual finitude, transience and contingency.
>
> (1992: 9)

This succinct formulation also points to fractures within liberal humanism, within the conception that the freedom imparted by liberal democratic states and their legal systems to individual citizens is unsurpassable (Fitzpatrick 1992a, 1988). The rationality of individual right, of governance by the 'people', premised on the notion of one true universal form of human being, embodied by each individual, no longer serves as a legitimising metanarrative (Cadava *et al.* 1991). Indeed, the claimed 'essence' to subjectivity has been implicated in the very means by which liberal forms of subjection are sustained (McNay 1992, N. Rose 1990, Foucault 1973). The modern subject, then, is not so much a pivot for human emancipation as it is a condition for the maintenance and extension of modern, rational-ised patterns of association (Miller and Rose 1990). The debasement of modern subjectivity, of its claimed essence, has unleashed under postmod-ern conditions a veritable 'cult of the self', which focuses on transient lifestyles defined through capacities and processes of consumption (Bauman 1992, T. Miller 1993, Edge 1994). The sheer variation in the choices avail-able to postmodern selves, the identities that are held 'on offer', indicates a different emphasis and set of techniques for self-formation than is evident in the modern, production-orientated 'cult of the individual'.

In tandem, the issues discussed above have altered the nature of academic discourse to the extent that modern strategies for mobilising the sign 'justice' are no longer as persuasive or pertinent as they once might have been. But there is a qualification. As we have seen in the work of Walzer, MacIntyre, Fisk and Young, strategies for mobilising the sign *justice* no longer seek universal principles founded upon a reason that is deemed innate to all human beings. Their altered strategies are explicable in view of the legitimacy crises that face a modern ethos under postmodern con-ditions. But these are theorists in an interregnum, not prepared to submit to modern auspices as they level their foundation critiques, but also not yet prepared to overthrow these auspices. Thus, although their formu-lations debase the auspices of a modern ethos, none seems prepared to release their visions from these auspices. Yet there are an increasing number of (deconstructionist) texts around 'justice' that not only repudiate the ethos of modernity but also begin to formulate uses of the sign under postmodern auspices.[12] Such texts aim neither to formulate a true and essential conception of justice, nor even to define it absolutely. Instead, to use Lyotard's image, there is no final point to such talk about justice, only the desire to participate in the language-games of the just (Lyotard and Thebaud 1985). This 'gaming' is predicated on auspices of an ethos outside of the modern, and for that reason let us examine one example of an attempt to articulate 'justice' to the changing auspices of postmodern conditions as a preface to the rise of community justice; namely Derrida.

Envisioning justice under postmodern conditions

As noted, a postmodern discursive ethos views with incredulity grand narratives that support notions of justice as a singular plenitude, a fixed entity amenable to apodictic, descriptive closure. Because being is 'always on the way', justice is never a final entity whose essence can be grasped for all time. Thus, as Lyotard puts it, 'no one can say what the being of justice is' (Lyotard and Thebaud 1985: 66). The search for its essential, universal qualities is out of place in this ethos. Nevertheless, as Derrida's considerations of justice suggest, although is may not be possible (or desirable) to jettison a concept of justice, it is possible to seek rules for the use of the term outside the ethos of modernity. There are a number of consequences that ensue for any attempt to address justice under postmodern conditions, within an ethos that does not expound privileged access to certainty.

Echoing Lyotard, Derrida tells us, 'one cannot speak directly about justice, thematize or objectivize justice, say "this is just" and even less "I am just", without immediately betraying justice' (1992: 10; emphasis in original). The unity of justice is fragmented, splintered into an infinite alterity. Derrida adopts a discursive strategy that is not designed to capture the essential unity of justice, its presence, but rather to address justice as a meandering sign that is articulated to all sorts of calculations made by those who aim to prop up, as well as those wishing to escape, the limits of a given ontology. The quest is not for universal principles that would indicate justice, but to try to apprehend justice as a promise located just beyond any particular form of being; a promise that entices some to look outside the limits of their historical ontologies. Justice as infinity lies beyond any particular form of human being, but is recalled to stand in the name of multiple causes, issues and cases. Derrida mobilises justice as a 'mystical' concept, an idea, that forever reaches beyond any incarnations that presently bear its name. The 'mystical' here is seen to be the moment where a 'discourse comes up against its limit: in itself, in its performative power itself' (1992: 13–14). But if justice is an idea that is never fully present, yet is not entirely absent either, then is it not merely an ideal that guides us? Is it merely a reworked Kantian transcendental idea? Derrida responds in the negative to both questions. For him, justice is neither a resolved 'messianic event' nor a projected or transcendental ideal. Rather, it is a vague idea of work that is done at the margins of that which is 'present', at the performative points where being of a specific kind is established. As an event performing such an extraordinary task, justice is little more than 'an experience of the impossible' (1992: 16). Justice is paradoxically located beyond given limits, but is part of the process through which such limits are addressed, sustained, challenged, enforced, etc.

Here justice is envisioned as an incalculable idea whose incalculability derives from its location in the contingent, in the chaotic, beyond any purported necessities of a given age. Justice relentlessly finds itself pushed into unarticulated discursive spaces. In this sense, or rather use of the sign, justice entails performances of founding events through which boundaries are established. The founding events highlight the contingent emergence of given limits and the ontological importance of justice. As such, justice shares something with practices of deconstruction; Derrida even goes so far as to argue that '[d]econstruction is justice' (1992: 15). That is, deconstruction points to the contingency that surrounds claims to order, to necessity. It is work done at limits but that indicates arenas beyond these. However, justice itself is not deconstructable because it is no more than a mystical idea that defies necessary calculations. It is, that is, purely contingent and thus not amenable to the impetuses of deconstruction. For Derrida, 'justice' implies sets of rules without stability, founded upon paradox in which it is trapped in differently placed distinctions between 'justice' as the incalculable and the exercise (enforcement?) of justice through historically specific systems of statutory regulation and prescription. As such, it falls within a moving interstice between polar opposite distinctions (i.e. between the infinite and the finite, the incalculable and the calculable, the present and the unpresentable, etc.).[13] It assumes the guises of various aporias that emerge from its paradoxical location. Derrida offers three examples of justice as aporia, all of which indicate its paradoxical foundations (1992: 22–29). To take one example, he notes that a just decision is required immediately and yet justice, as we have seen, is always 'on the way'. This implies a moment of decision, of judgement, that is finite (i.e. it cannot base itself on infinite or unlimited knowledge) yet claims to embody the infinite. The moment of decision involves a madness in which the violence of the present makes a version of the unpresentable (justice) present.

The aporia signals the paradoxical performance of having to venture beyond the limits of a present system in order to erect or sustain its limits.

This is a moment of 'madness' when unstable traces of justice quite literally entail an 'experience of the impossible'. As such, just performances glimpse alterity, the other, by requiring the performer to move beyond the language of his/her present. Yet, justice as 'the experience of absolute alterity is unpresentable, but it is the chance of the event and the condition of history' (1992: 27). Justice, the unpresentable, the incalculable, the chaotic, the 'chance of the event', is the means by which the historical limits of a given present are approached. As such, both the legitimacy of, and resistance to, these limits rest on calculations of justice, on the rationales for the founding performative acts through which the limits emerge. Therefore, as Derrida puts it,

> incalculable justice requires us to calculate ... Not only must we calculate, negotiate without the sort of rule that wouldn't have to be reinvented there where we are cast, there where we find ourselves; but we must take it as far as possible, beyond the place where we find ourselves ... This requirement does not properly belong either to justice or law. It only belongs to either of these two domains by exceeding each one in the direction of the other.
>
> (1992: 28)

These two domains noted in the above quotation, justice and law, resonate with older meaning horizons: principle and process. Justice as principle has become a mystical idea devoid of the certainties once accorded to it. Law, as the hegemonic process of justice under modern conditions, is problematised as is the connection between justice and law. But still we must calculate, and our calculations have not entirely extricated justice from its deeply entrenched meaning horizons. Nevertheless, as indicated in Derrida's text, the auspices of the discursive strategies and calculations of justice that emerge under postmodern conditions are radically different from those that have gone before them.

No matter what one might make of Derrida's text, it reconsiders justice without deferring to modern auspices. It is a recent example of a trend that over the past four decades has placed justice at a distance from modern theories. Derrida's analysis is, one might say, a consolidation of various discursive moves away from a dependence upon, and perhaps a despair with, modern metanarratives. As such, reflecting backwards as it were, one can glean much from his approach. Certainly it highlights that, under postmodern conditions, the 'principle' horizon of justice has been de-emphasised, becoming no more than an instance of the paradoxical attempt to calculate the incalculable. The modern formulation of necessary principles of justice founded upon reason are no longer sustainable, replaced by the notion of justice as aporia. Even so, this has not relinquished us from the responsibility of calculating justice, because we are here dealing with the very knowledges and practices that render our historical existence possible. But under postmodern conditions, if the principle horizon is significantly problematised, attention has shifted towards processes of justice. And its calculations of just processes do not defer to universality, a single rationality or essential human subjects; instead they seek to address plurality in different contexts. Justice is in search of idioms appropriate to context, guided if at all – and assuming Lyotard (1984) is correct – by a series of technical metanarratives.

JUSTICE IN SEARCH OF IDIOMS: THE RISE OF MEDIATION

Alongside the de-emphasis of principle has been a concomitant explosion of debates on the most appropriate processes by which 'justice' is to be achieved. For one thing, under postmodern conditions, it cannot require the imperial enforcement of a single means of justice to reign supreme over all others; on the contrary, it seeks idioms to which different rationalities of silenced disputants can be articulated. As such, justice is fragmented into different processes that assume different forms in different contexts – the experience and expression of alterity are seldom uniform. Nurturing and preserving difference in processes of justice affirm the chaos that belies calls to order. The quest for the impossible, for that which lies behind what *is*, brings us face-to-face with the textures of silence dammed up in the founding acts that enunciate a particular conception of being (Bauman 1994, Critchley 1992, Levinas 1989). The attempt to sustain difference is an attempt to articulate these textures of silence, the rationalities within small narratives, and to maximise the narratives of an age (I. Young 1990).

Now, as Lyotard (1988) notes, this quest requires the formation of idioms that allow (rather than prohibit) the diverse voices of the 'other' (the oppressed, the marginal, the 'deviant', etc.). Justice is a prescriptive discourse different from the descriptive discourses in that it is not linked to the truth (Lyotard and Thebaud 1985: 16, 98). Moreover, in this prescriptive discourse we must judge, but 'one judges without criteria' (1985: 16). In the 'pagan' society of postmodernity, consensus cannot be the ideal because it would undermine plurality in favour of universal principles; a situation that 'does violence to the heterogeneity of language games' (1985: 99). So justice under postmodern conditions does not operate on the basis of consensus. Instead, as Lyotard puts it, justice under postmodern conditions requires that we try to find idioms to redress the imbalances of the so-called *differend*. This *differend* occurs 'whenever a plaintiff is deprived of the means of arguing and by this fact becomes a victim', as in the case where resolving their dispute 'is made in the idiom of one of them in which the wrong (tort) suffered by the other signifies nothing' (Lyotard 1984: 24–25). It occurs, that is, 'when the "regulation" of the conflict which opposes them is done in the idiom of one of the parties, while the injustice suffered by the other is not signified in that idiom' (1984: note 12).[14]

The emergence of the ADR movement internationally, in some of its forms at least, indicates an example of the attempt to locate idioms that not only phrase the inequities of the *differend*, but also try to find alternative forums to achieve 'justice'. Ingram phrases the general impetus, or perhaps intention, here rather well in suggesting that, under postmodern conditions, 'justice demands only that one judge without prescribing, that one listen for the silences that betoken differends so as to finally let the suppressed voice find its proper idiom' (1987/8: 299). By permitting the voices of the marginal, by exposing the subordinations of the unheard, such justice is better poised to open cracks in present discursive limits and expose discursive horizons beyond the limits of the present. Of course, addressing this issue is by no means entirely new; indeed, well-developed 'access to justice' debates indicate precisely the opposite (e.g. Pound 1922, Galanter 1981, Shapiro 1981). But what is different in more recent attempts is their deliberate search for 'justice without law', and without deferring to the auspice of a modern ethos (Auerbach 1983). In jurisprudence this search was partially conditioned by the critical impetuses of legal realism (Frank 1970), and later the Critical Legal Studies Movement (Unger 1983, Kairys 1982). Through various critiques of adversarial litigation, especially with respect to its universal application, one can identify traces of the quest for alternative dispute resolution mechanisms, especially with respect to 'minor', 'community' disputes (Ford Foundation 1978, Sander 1977, Becker 1975, Hogarth 1974).

The despair with modern auspices of justice simultaneously licenses a search for alternatives to universal procedures of litigation. It opened a space within which legal anthropologists could contest the universal value of western law by pointing to the social significance and standing of 'customary law' and 'customary jurisprudence' (Nader and Todd 1978, Comaroff and Roberts 1977, Hamnett 1977, Gluckman 1965, Bohannan 1957, Schapera 1955). Simultaneously, the way is paved for 'legal pluralism' and its sustained attempts to dissolve the rigid boundaries that modern, state law had erected around itself (Merry 1988). In this contested environment, community mediation assumes a place amongst various alternative dispute resolution mechanisms and finds itself within a discursive ethos where it is construed as an undervalued technique whose time has come. In the early 1970s, following the ascending incursions by legal anthropologists on modern processes, the noted scholar of law Lon Fuller (1971) openly declared the value of mediation as a potentially viable dispute resolution technique, and even touted its promise over litigation in specific cases.[15] The theme was continued in the United States with the influential articles by Danzig (1973) and Fisher (1975), calling for decentralised dispute resolution systems, and explicitly endorsing such techniques as mediation to 'complement' or 'replace' existing court services, respectively.[16]

From here the expansion of community mediation programmes into numerous contexts and countries bears witness to the alerted ethos that licenses different calculations of justice. In the search for idioms without appealing to modern auspices, or to rational principles, justice has been fragmented, cast adrift from the secure shores of an essentially unified courtroom process. And it is this fragmentation that provides the discursive space for the rising tide of alternatives, claiming as they do to operate in the name of justice – be it popular, informal, community, restorative or neighbourhood justice. This chapter has offered one means of grasping how community mediation alternatives have acquired a discursive licence to offer their calculations and practices as claims to justice. And it is through the call to let silenced voices speak that we can understand the claims by some community mediation programmes to empower individuals, to provide contextually sensitive (informal) dispute resolution settings and to deploy flexibility processes that allow disputants to develop their own settlements (Shonholtz 1993). The justice is local, focused on tackling local rationalities as they pertain to different disputants in a particular dispute. Gone are the necessities, the principles and the grandiose metanarratives of modern justice; gone too is the wistful promise of massive, progressive societal change through one law. And it is in the emerging ethos that we continue our narrative, diagnosing, with reference to the British Columbia case, the perils and possibilities of the emerging shape of dispute resolution arenas under postmodern conditions.

3

CALCULATING COMMUNITY JUSTICE
Mediation in British Columbia

The previous chapter explored how current discursive legitimacy crises have altered the auspices upon which calculations of justice have come to rest. Under postmodern conditions, notions of justice have been fragmented, and recalculated without universal precepts derived from singular notions of human reasoning capacities. In turn, different claims to justice have emerged in diverse settings, including the calls for 'popular', 'community', 'informal' or 'neighbourhood' justice. Despite the plethora of terms, and the notable absence of explicit definitions, all appear to invoke images of a justice that is 'alternative' to the professionalism of state legal justice. The quest seems to be for a popular justice, a form of justice where overt coercion is absent, and where immediate, voluntary and consensual dispute settlement is the order of the day. By implication, such voluntarism requires the active contribution of local participants, and idioms that are sensitive to contextual nuance. Yet the emergence of community justice should not be seen as an event that completely reverses the spirit of state law. Professionalised justice is neither miraculously replaced overnight, nor tossed as a sealed package and summarily discarded. Rather, the very form of state law seems to be in the process of alteration, even as it continues to play an inordinate part in managing the fluid and diverse transformations within various dispute resolution arenas.

With this in mind, where community justice advocates have managed to obtain a footing they have mostly done so through the stealth of disquiet and enterprise rather than through the spectacular force of open defiance. This serves as an early signal to recognise that, as the fragmentation of a universal justice develops, there will be many paradoxical and uneasily aligned practices. Indeed, reflecting on one such paradox, Fitzpatrick (1992a, 1993) alleges the very 'impossibility' of a popular justice that develops comfortably alongside, and appeals to the mythical symbols embedded in, formal state justice. Even so, advocates of community justice continue to enunciate and develop their calculations of justice, licensing an array of practices outside the courtroom. Yet, in view of the fragmenting formulations of justice under postmodern conditions, it may not be sustainable to seek a general description of such calculations. Instead, more modest attempts to delineate local conceptions by tapping into particular discourses on community justice seem more appropriate. This is not to say that there cannot be overarching resemblances across contexts, for plainly there are many replications and faithful renderings of favoured models. But, to assume generalities in advance, and then to uncover these as 'essences', is likely to eclipse the contextual nuances, the differences, that breathe life into the fragmented justice of our times, our places.

In such circumstances, there is perhaps much value in narrating particular case studies, to provide descriptive glimpses into the 'grids of intelligibility' that render particular social practices meaningful (Yin 1989). The aim is to provide some indication of a given context's conceptions of community justice and the practices that bear the name of this new justice. To do so is to add to an existing series of case studies that detail various elements of the San Francisco Community Boards Project, a community mediation project heralded by many as the model *par excellence* of community justice (Merry and Milner 1993, Fitzpatrick 1992a). I have studied a local context closely over a period of some three years (especially from 1989 to 1992) and then at a distance since then; namely, community mediation in British Columbia, Canada.[1] The choice of location is always somewhat arbitrary, as is the designation of what is to count as a 'case' (Yin 1989). But, for all that, there are heuristic gains to be made from focusing on a particular context, particularly when justice is no longer calculated in universal terms.

THE CONTEXT: A SOCIAL FIELD EMERGES

The rise of community mediation in British Columbia should be silhouetted against a more general interest in the value of alternative techniques to litigation that emerged in diverse disciplines, including legal anthropology[2] and jurisprudence,[3] and a growing alternative dispute resolution movement in such countries as Britain,[4] the United States[5] and Canada.[6] Notwithstanding its history in labour disputes, mediation – specifically – is currently used to 'settle' numerous local conflicts, including: victim-offender reconciliation; family conflict; community (neighbour) disputes; commercial disputes; criminal disputes; environmental disputes; First Nations issues; and school-based conflict (Canadian Bar Association, Task Force Report, 1989, Peachey *et al.* 1988). However, one of the first community mediation programmes to emerge in British Columbia developed out of law reform efforts under the auspices of a Justice Development Commission (JDC). This Commission established an experimental Small Claims Project in the summer of 1975 as a response to 'justifiable criticisms' of the Small Claims Court.[7] The project was designed to provide a feasible option for managing disputes, and apparently met with some success:

The use of 'mediation' as an integrated part of the court process was successfully demonstrated to the satisfaction of both the public and the judiciary. Mediation can be used to increase the perceived quality of 'justice' while complementing the present role of the courts.

(JDC, Courts Division, 1976: 46)

Such unequivocal acclaim helped to clear the space for the increasing emergence of a particular set of community mediation practices (see Pavlich 1992a, Edwards 1990, Peachey et al. 1988).

Although the form (and number) of mediation programmes is in constant flux, rendering synoptic sketches vulnerable to becoming outdated, the foundations of its identity seem rather more constant. For that reason, I have elected to focus on the relations that sustain its identity, and the calculations of justice that help to support these. Certainly, by the early 1990s, this identity had assumed a particular form as expressed in the range of mediation services and networks available. For example, there were three active Community Mediation Centres, an International Commercial Arbitration Centre (BCICAC), a mediation section in the Better Business Bureau, Victim Offender Reconciliation projects, school-based mediation programmes and a well-endowed multicultural conflict resolution project. By June 1993, a national organisation's handbook listed eleven organisations and sixty-four people involved in ADR in British Columbia (Network, 1993/94).

In addition, mediators in the province had become involved in international (The Community Justice Initiatives Network), national (Family Mediation Canada established in 1985), provincial (Mediation Development Association of British Columbia) and even regional (Southwest Mediators' Network) mediator networks.[8] Moreover, several mediator training facilities emerged, with a growing trend towards certified training facilities, such that '[t]he pressure to certify mediators is increasing rapidly as changes in legislation expand the opportunities available to trained skilled mediators' (Burdine 1991: 7). This pattern has been reinforced by the interest that universities in the province have directed towards ADR (Sloan 1989). For example, in 1989 the University of Victoria's Law Faculty established an Institute for Dispute Resolution, which claims to be 'devoted to improving the ways in which disputes are resolved in our society' and aims 'to enhance awareness and acceptance of alternative dispute resolution (ADR) procedures in the community' (UVic Institute for Dispute Resolution, pamphlet). The deployment of such mediation services and practices indicates an expanding use of mediation in diverse contexts, and the growing sense that appropriately trained mediators provide a needed skill to resolve numerous kinds of disputes. In the process, mediation is granted an air of professionalism in the sense that training is advocated as a means to acquire the necessary expertise. For example, the Mediation Development Association of British Columbia has published standards and practices for the 'Certification of Mediators'.⁹ This important pillar of community mediation's identity in the province has continued to flourish.

Community mediation programmes in the province are not neatly divided into state-based or agency-based services because many programmes receive funding and case referrals from both public and private sources. In addition, there are individual mediators who offer services independently of particular programmes. In ideal-typical terms, though, programmes that target commercial, consumer, divorce, family, school, landlord-tenant, and small claims disputes tend to receive direct funding from various state departments. By contrast, programmes directed at victim-offender reconciliation have attracted funds from both justice departments and church organisations (e.g. Menonite Central Committee; see Bowler 1993/4), while innovations, such as school-based mediation programmes and multicultural (or intercultural) conflict resolution programmes, have attained funds from private foundations (e.g. The Canadian Donner Foundation; see Lotz 1994, Kalpatoo 1994 and Edwards 1990). Even so, there is marked overlap in the overall thinking of the various programmes, and indeed if a difference is perceived it is typically seen to exist between programmes and private individual mediators who charge a fee for their services. Thus, as one advocate puts it,

> The objectives of a Community Conflict Resolution Centre differ from those of private mediators in that the major mandate is to educate the public about conflict resolution and to provide mediation for individuals at the low end of the economic scale.
>
> (Dussault 1993)

In any case, there is much support for the various forms of mediation within the legal establishment. For instance, the Canadian Bar Association established a Task Force (centred in British Columbia) to examine alternative dispute resolution in Canada and one of its key recommendations was:

> That the Canadian Bar Association recognise credible and responsible ADR organizations and programs as a valuable aspect of the Canadian Justice system and that appropriate institutions be urged to give the necessary support, on a long term basis, to enable these organizations and programs to develop, improve and maintain the quality of ADR services.
>
> (CBA Task Force Report 1989: 75)

In addition, legislation actively supporting mediation has been in place for some time now; e.g. the Divorce Act, 1985, S.C. 1986, c. 4. This Act imposes a duty on lawyers to tell clients involved with divorce proceedings of the possibility of trying mediation and of known mediation services in the area. A federal government guide to the Act describes this duty in these terms: 'A lawyer consulted by a person seeking a divorce must point out the advisability of negotiating support, custody and access matters. The lawyer must also inform the client of any appropriate mediation services that are known to the lawyer' (Canada 1986: 24). In British Columbia, a study commissioned by the Attorney General's Office to find ways of maximising access to justice in the province produced a report (Hughes 1988) and a government response (Smith 1989), both of which fully endorsed the role and value of using alternative dispute resolution alongside the court system. Thus, with greater or lesser acceptance of the quest for 'alternatives' to court-based dispute resolution, the legal establishment in British Columbia has provided a tentative seal of approval for the use of mediation in particular circumstances.

In state-affiliated and agency-based programmes, as well as with mediators in private practice, one can identify proponents of a community justice discourse, the foundations of which were erected with the deployment of early programmes. And it is to the calculation of justice within, and the practices licensed by, this discourse that we now turn. Let us turn to practices before exploring the discourse.

COMMUNITY MEDIATION IN ACTION

There are diverse practices that now occur in the field of action that has been deployed in the name of community mediation in British Columbia. The initial flurry of activities centred around the actual deployment of particular mediation programmes (Pavlich 1992a: ch. 1, Turner and Jobsen 1990). Sustaining and developing such fields of action, however, implies the ongoing presence of various activities: fund raising; training and coaching mediators; setting up and maintaining the administration of 'cases' (i.e. 'case management'); forging regional (e.g. the Southwest Mediators' Network), provincial (e.g. the Mediation Development Association of British Columbia) and even national (e.g. the Community Justice Initiatives Network) support networks; marketing community mediation through public awareness ventures; and, of course, mediating so-called community disputes (see Pavlich 1992a: 31–34). Despite the range of these activities, I shall here focus on the practices of mediation licensed by calculations of community justice.

As we shall see, in contrast to courtroom procedures, mediation is considered to take different forms in different contexts. It is designed to be a flexible process, which must be so if it is to perform the informal, facilitative, individually empowering, settlement functions attributed to it. However, this is not to say that the discourse does not offer general 'rules of thumb', and even a framework, for stages of a dispute resolution process that can be viewed as mediation. For the most part, the discourse is orally communicated through education forums,[10] practically based programmes[11] and in-house training sessions.[12] It is also now common to find texts that offer practical tips on how to mediate effectively.[13] There were two particularly influential texts of this genre amongst participants of this case study: many legal mediators were aware of Landau *et al.* (1987); social mediators, by contrast, seemed to rely heavily on a text written by a local instructor at the Justice Institute of British Columbia's Conflict Resolution Certificate Programme (Burdine 1990). Since so many mediators in the province have attended this training course and use Burdine's four-stage model, it is perhaps instructive to examine her text. But I shall infuse the precepts of the text with a hypothetical case (structured out of observations) to write up the practices as I read them out of the text. My analytical construction may fruitfully be viewed as an empathetic Weberian 'ideal type' of the mediation process.[14]

To help construct the type, let us consider a hypothetical dispute between Lara and Pete. The end of a busy work week finds Lara lying on her sun-deck, reading a novel and enjoying the booming sounds of her music. The solace of the setting is brought to a sudden halt by the screams of Pete, an obstreperous neighbour, who threatens to destroy the source of the 'noise' unless there is complete quiet. Since it is early afternoon, and since Lara has recently endured, without complaint, an extremely noisy party at the same neighbour's house, she decides to ignore the threat. Even so, it is not long before Pete hurls a stone through a small lounge window in protest. After the initial shock of the event, Lara is angered by Pete's sheer audacity, not to mention the damage caused. The situation escalates into a raging conflict in which reciprocal insults are hurled, ending with Lara withdrawing to contact the local police. By the time the officers arrive – several hours later – her fury has subsided somewhat, leaving her without any real desire to lay criminal charges against Pete. She does, however, expect an apology as well as material restitution for damages and for the inconvenience involved. What courses of action are open to her?

Were we, for the sake of argument, to step back into the opening years of the 1970s in British Columbia, one could envisage a number of possible responses. For example, she could confront Pete again, simply 'lump' the case, call for third-party intervention (e.g. a church), or file a writ in the Small Claims Court. If the last of these options were selected, legal counsel would probably have been solicited to negotiate the case through the formal procedures of the court system. No doubt, this might have entailed considerable cost, and delay, offering Lara and Pete little control over the outcome of the dispute. Some twenty years later, in the early years of the 1990s, over and above these, there would also be the option of seeking help from a local community mediation programme. Suppose Lara calls a local Community Mediation Centre; the resident case manager is likely to obtain some rudimentary details and assess whether the dis-pute is suitable for mediation. If considered appropriate, both parties are invited to attend an informal, legally non-binding, mediation session, which is described to both as a voluntary process to help work out their own settlements under the guidance of trained mediators. Mediation is depicted as a 'nothing to lose' option that allows disputants to work through conflicts in an informal way, but that does not exclude the courtroom as a final option if no settlement can be reached. It is touted as inexpensive, quick, convenient and confidential.[15] Assuming both parties agree to mediate, the Centre calls on the services of a senior mediator and a co-mediator (usually volunteers) and arranges a convenient time for all concerned.

At the appointed time and place, the senior mediator introduces everybody and attempts to 'break the ice' by creating a casual atmosphere. Turning to Burdine's first stage, mediators are implored to 'set the tone' of a given mediation. They are encouraged to put disputants at ease by providing a non-threatening setting, facilitating relaxed conversation, and using congenial introductions. The differences between mediation and litigation are emphasised, that is, by ensuring mediation assumes an informal format. The aim is to entice people into discourse around a dispute that is familiar to their everyday lives. Lara and Pete are informed that the aim of mediation is to find an agreeable settlement – it does not try establish who is guilty or who is innocent. It is not a blame-orientated process, parties are told, but a confidential environment in which disputants try to resolve conflict. Although mediators might jot notes down (with the permission of disputants), no formal notes of what 'goes on' in the session are kept. The flexible nature of the mediation process is explained, reinforcing the idea that disputants are the owners of their conflict and that the settlement thereof is entirely in their hands. The mediator underscores her or his role as a mere facilitator, someone who will help them to reach a solution. Some basic rules of the process are then made explicit; e.g. no abusive language, name calling, threats, one person to speak at a time, speak to each other rather than the mediator, and so on.

At this point the mediator tries to ensure that disputants are 'committed' to the process. This commitment is regarded as a key ingredient to the success or failure of mediation, for without it disputants are unlikely to take its precepts seriously. As if to reinforce its importance, mediators are encouraged to obtain an 'Agreement to mediate', which disputants are expected to sign. Having obtained a signed commitment to mediate from both parties, s/he requests that Lara convey her side of the dispute and indicate possible ways to resolve the matter. With this, we move into the second stage of Burdine's model, called 'generating the agenda'. To ensure that Pete has understood Lara's point of view, he is asked to paraphrase the concerns raised, and Lara is given an opportunity to comment on Pete's summary. Then Pete is asked to give his version and the paraphrasing process is reversed. Throughout the session, the mediator encourages the disputants to speak directly to each other and focuses discussion on possible areas of 'common ground' between them. A common means of establishing some common ground is through a technique called 'reframing'. This involves restating an idea in a way that 'focuses' the dispute on particular issues, which are phrased in a 'neutral' way. As Burdine puts it, when reframing a dispute, '[t]he mediator changes the frame of the communication by eliminating the harshness, the confusion or the glare, thus allowing the communication to reach its intended receiver' (1990: 41). Another commonly used technique when trying to set the agenda is 'probing', or the use of relevant, specific and directed questions that help disputants to identify common ground. Thus, mediators constantly check that their formulations are accepted by direct questions ('Are you comfortable with that, Lara?'), in introductory phrases ('Tell me if I'm wrong, Pete, but I hear you saying . . .') and well-timed summaries of the enfolding narrative flow ('Let me summarise where I see both of you are at . . .'). The mediators repeatedly emphasise areas of agreement and try to ensure that the disputants see themselves 'in the same boat'.

Let us continue with the mediation; assume that Lara wonders whether she could ever agree with Pete, given his sheer rudeness and recalcitrance. Her anger surfaces in an outburst where she cannot contain herself in the face of what she takes to be blatant lies. Pete responds with equal abuse and the generally cordial atmosphere of the room is sharply interrupted. Curiously enough, the head mediator reacts quite calmly, and with some humour, by calling a 'time out' and then acknowledging the respective sources of the anger, but firmly emphasises that, if the dispute is to be resolved, it is necessary to adhere to the rules of the process agreed to at the outset of the session. The intervention calms the situation somewhat as both agree to cease interrupting and swearing at one another. The mediator summarises the main points of the dispute, which seem agreeable enough to all, and this paves the way for Burdine's third stage (i.e. 'establishing' and elaborating upon the common ground between parties).

This stage involves clarifying positions, needs and interests through such techniques as those already noted – reframing, skilful questioning, probing. In addition, by this point in the process, the mediator would probably have identified critical stumbling blocks to settlement and have started breaking large issues into smaller, more manageable components. For instance, with continued questioning, it may become clear that Lara had not considered many of the effects her actions have had on the quality of Pete's life. He is a chronic insomniac and sleeps in the afternoon, a pattern that is often disturbed because of the way Lara's hi-fi speakers are positioned. Conversely, Pete discovers, with some surprise, that Lara was in fact at home on the night of his party, and that the guests had indeed made a lot of noise. Reciprocal apologies on these matters begin to pave the way, despite initial impressions, for both to see some common ground in the dispute. Indeed, as the mediators clarify more fundamental interests behind the positions that each disputant has taken (e.g. Lara's desire for peace and quiet at night, and Pete's desire for the same by day) and show how these might bear on the possible resolutions of the conflict, both parties begin to see aspects of the problem that they had not considered previously.

At this point in the process, both disputants may well agree with the mediator's suggestion that the 'core' of the dispute revolves around Lara's desire for restitution and a formal apology, as opposed to Pete's desire for future consideration of his insomnia. Once the core of the dispute has been enunciated to the satisfaction of all parties, the final stage of Burdine's model requires that a settlement that is feasible, fair and satisfactory to all (including the mediator) be sought. If successful, mediation will build on the unfolding consensus between disputants to identify specific conditions that each party is to uphold and thus resolve the dispute. This stage employs previously used techniques, but introduces some others as well. For instance, disputants are requested to 'brainstorm' for possible solutions to the dispute. The co-mediator is often the one who writes all suggestions on a flip-chart in point form. Each point is considered in turn, focusing on what they might mean in practical terms and assessing the degree to which either party agrees with them. Using the agreed-upon aspects of this discussion as a base, the leading mediator provides various possible combinations for an acceptable agreement. In the end, the co-mediator suggests the following possible settlement: Lara agrees to accept payment only for replacing the window (not for cleaning up the broken glass); Pete pays the sum requested; both apologise to each other for their respective 'mistakes'; and both agree to reposition their stereo speakers and to be more considerate when playing music – day or night – in the future. As a settlement acceptable to all, it is drafted in the form of a written statement with specific conditions (e.g. how much is to be paid, by when, etc.), and ways for evaluating whether both parties have complied with these. At this point the 'dispute' is deemed to be well on the way to being 'settled' – all that is left is to make sure that the conditions of the agreement are upheld. The mediation process is deemed to have closed the dispute when this occurs (a situation that is usually checked some weeks later by case managers).

As should be evident from Burdine's model, and the hypothetical case, the quest for community justice here is rendered synonymous with the effective settlement of conflict. Thus, Burdine's model, in contrast to modern thinking, does not equip mediators to practise a profession in accordance with universally specified principles of justice. Nor does the model identify how community activists might effectively agitate against, or resist, unjust social structures. Instead, the practices licensed in this model are of a qualitatively different order. The flexible and diverse rules of thumb and tips that Burdine offers to mediators are designed to restore peace to communities. Effective mediators should acquire diverse skills that allow them to engineer a social environment conducive to settling disputes between individuals. The more technically astute a mediator is, the more likely she or he is to settle disputes in context. Thus, the ideal is to deploy through each mediation session a unique social field in which the conflict between individual disputants is 'voluntarily' transformed into an agreement to comport themselves harmoniously in the community. This raises an immediate question: by what discourse are such practices of mediation licensed? No doubt, this question bears directly on the issue of how advocates calculate community justice, and how they view community mediation as a means of deploying their vision in practice. Thus, let us turn to the advocates' calculations of community justice in context.

CALCULATING COMMUNITY JUSTICE IN BRITISH COLUMBIA

For the most part, early advocates of community mediation argued the need for dispute resolution contexts outside the courts on two related grounds: first, they challenged the courts' ability to provide adequate justice for common community disputes; and, second, they pointed to the courts' unresponsiveness to the 'community'. Turning to the first issue, most early advocates of community justice portrayed the state's justice system as an anachronism that was simply unable to respond to the new times of the 1970s. As an influential report of the time argued,

> Generally, the courts show all the signs of a system which has been denied adequate financial support, has failed to keep pace with an ever changing and growing society and has failed to make use of modern methods and technology to adapt to these changes. The result has been the loss of public confidence and respect for the Court process.
>
> (Justice Development Commission, Courts Division, 1974: vi)

This position is echoed in various other texts, but the main point seems to be that courts no longer are able to deliver justice as a result of several inherent failures. To begin, researchers working under the auspices of the Law Reform Commission of Canada (LRC) attacked the courtroom's adjudicative processes as being unsuited to resolving all forms of dispute resolution (Becker 1975, Hogarth 1974). Pointing to research in jurisprudence (Fuller 1971) and legal anthropology (Fisher 1975, Danzig 1973) that had identified mediation as a promising mechanism of dispute resolution for minor disputes (and which we encountered in the previous chapter), the LRC noted in one of its reports:

51

As research throws more and more light on what actually happens in the name of criminal law, it became clear that the court and correctional processes are not able to deal with many of the cases brought to their doors. The adversary processes of the courts are not able to deal with cases that require mediation or settlement.

(LRC 1975a: 23)

This text concludes that mediation and/or conciliation ought to be used in so-called minor cases involving complex emotional processes with people in 'continuing bilateral relationships' (Becker 1975: 226). The courtroom should be reserved for 'serious' disputes, not those commonly found in the community. As such, the LRC indicated its commitment to find 'solutions which minimise the traditional adversary process and maximise conciliation and problem settlement' (1975a: 1).

In this discourse, and indicating another purported failure, the court system is criticised for administrative inefficiencies that affect the kind of justice it can deliver. Its procedural inflexibility is deemed costly, time consuming and inhospitable, resulting in serious problems for a society promising unhindered 'access to justice'. One report on this issue offers a comprehensive list of the major flaws of the court system as perceived by its critics:

> *Unreasonable delays* in both criminal and civil proceedings
> *Unnecessary costs* in criminal and civil proceedings
> *Procedural complexity*, particularly in civil proceedings
> *Outmoded methods and procedures* for court administration
> The lack of adequate and appropriate *court facilities*
> Insufficient numbers of properly trained court *personnel*
> Inhuman *lockup and remand facilities*
> *Improper use of police officers* in the administration of courts
> The lack of *statistical information* and information systems.
> (Justice Development Commission, Courts Division, 1974: vi)

Calls for greater flexibility are then postulated as a way of redressing such failures and simultaneously making the courts more responsive to their clients.

This relates to the second ground for the advocates' attack on the court system, namely its unresponsiveness to the 'community'. Legal reformers in the province had long pleaded that justice must be seen to be done in the eyes of ordinary citizens. In the early 1970s, therefore, the province's New Democratic Party government established a series of Community Resource Boards designed to involve communities in the formation and execution of all government policy (Clague *et al.* 1984).[16] With specific respect to justice enforcement, a Justice Development Commission (JDC) was established, headed by the then Deputy Attorney General David

Vickers. Its aim was to create 'more local autonomy, and active community participation in the affairs of social justice in the community, and the formation of a justice system which is coordinated with the police, courts, corrections, legal services and members of the community in an effective system of social justice' (JDC 1974b: 6). Some sixty-four local Justice Councils were established in seven regions of the province to implement this policy (Pavlich 1992a: 157, Lageunesse 1976a, Cossom and Turner 1985, ff). In such a discursive environment, there is little reason to doubt the salience of a report by one such Justice Council: ' "Bringing justice back into the community" is the motto of today' (Capital Region Justice Council 1977: 13).[17] As part of the general ethos indicated by the motto, community mediation advocates touted their programmes as a response to a 'need in the community'. In the words of one interviewee, community mediation was deployed because 'we were hearing about all these problems in the community that didn't seem to have a logical place to go ... to be resolved' (interview, 12/09/91). Or, in the words of another advocate, 'Citizens in various communities decided there had to be another way to resolve conflict and bring harmony to the area where they live', and so community mediation may be seen as 'simply a modern restatement of the pursuit by all Canadians for social justice and peace' (Brown 1991: 1 and 2).

It is, however, important to note that this common view of mediation as a community-driven initiative (echoed by most people I interviewed) is contradicted by other parts of the advocates' discourse. For one thing, most community mediation programmes complain of a paucity of cases, which raises an important question that a prominent member of a funding agency expressed thus: 'If mediation is so magical, why aren't people clamouring for the services? Because that's not what is happening. In fact, the opposite – when community mediation programmes open, there's trouble getting clientele' (interview, 29/01/1991). This point is confirmed in an article that suggests that '[m]ediators in B.C., including the Mediation Development Association of B.C. ... have bewailed the dearth of clients and the general lack of information and knowledge about mediation in our community' (*The Mediator* 12, 1987: 1). In this light one can better understand the spirit of this jocular poem entitled, *The Mediator's Lament*:

> Mediate, not litigate
> Cooperate, not obliterate
> Facilitate, not vindicate
> AND HOPE TO GET SOME BUSINESS
> (*The Mediator*, June, 1985: 13)[18]

Undeterred by the apparent contradiction in portraying their attempts as a response to a 'need' in the community, and yet finding a dearth of cases to mediate, advocates explain the discrepancy as being no more than a problem arising from a lack of 'public awareness'. Consequently, most programmes emphasise the importance of 'educating' the public, or 'marketing' mediation, and are often active participants in local events (e.g. law days, public lectures, education forums, radio and television programmes).[19]

Another example of where the community-driven view of mediation flies in the face of other elements in the discourse is the role assigned to the entrepreneurial activities of volunteer mediators. For example, oral accounts suggest that an early mediation programme, Westcoast Mediation Services, was founded as a result of the active input of volunteer members on the Board of the Westcoast Mediation Services Society (e.g. interviews 15/01/1990, 26/09/1990, 12/09/1991). It is said to have emerged in the wake of a successful practical mediation course run through the Justice Institute of British Columbia. Those who completed this course had no easy outlet for their newly acquired skills: 'Out of our training here a number of the people that had taken some of our courses said, "Where do I now go to get some experience in mediating community disputes?" ' (interview, 12/09/91). In direct response to this appeal, the Westcoast Mediation Services Society (in association with the Justice Institute) was constituted by a Board of some four volunteer members who drafted proposals for the development and funding of a non-profit mediation programme. The role of these volunteers (as opposed to, say, the 'clients' of mediation) was clearly critical to the formation of community mediation programmes, raising significant questions about what specific needs of which community were being met. In sum, the apparent lack of demand for mediation services from disputants in the community, together with the indication that programmes were deployed by key mediators, contradicts the idea that community mediation was autochthonously deployed as a response to a general need in the 'community' to which it is directed.

In any case, the two grounds for criticising the court system provided community mediation advocates with a discursive space within which to advocate very particular calculations of community justice. That is, their calculations rest upon the assumption of a court system whose procedures do not foster (and may even hinder) the resolution of 'community disputes', are not freely accessible to many people and are not sufficiently responsive to the needs of the 'community'. In the discursive space that such assumptions opened, advocates enunciated community mediation as an efficient (in terms of cost and time) and accessible alternative procedure that encourages disputants to 'resolve their issues in a less formal, less structured, less expensive and more satisfying way' (interview, 26/09/1990). In their eyes, community mediation became the idiom *par excellence* for the practical accomplishment of community justice, and hence definitions of mediation are formulated in such terms as: 'Mediation is a voluntary process where an impartial third person, the mediator, maintains a respectful environment for two or more people to resolve a dispute' (pamphlet, Westcoast Mediation Services); or, 'Mediation is a voluntary process during which people in dispute resolve their problems with the assistance of an impartial third person called a mediator' (pamphlet, Dispute Resolution Centre of Victoria); and even, 'Mediation is a voluntary, confidential approach to conflict resolution. It offers, that is, people a legal, peaceful, informal alternative to the adversarial system. Mediation, so we are told, brings people together in a neutral setting to discuss their situation and find a lasting solution to it' (pamphlet, Surrey/White Rock Mediation Services Society).

But what sort of justice do these advocates derive from such auspices? What is involved in their calculations of a specifically community (as opposed to, say, legal or social) justice? The questions are seldom explicitly addressed by advocates, but remain a constant presence guiding and helping to shape their approach to dispute resolution. There are key nodal points, assemblies of elements colonised as moments, that provide a relatively stable assumptive framework readily mobilised to explain particular mediation practices. As noted, the advocates defer to images of a community justice that is deemed different from the justice to be found in the courtroom. The former is touted as a means by which disputants can resolve conflict through informal, individually empowering and community-enhancing methods that also yield lasting settlements. In this discourse, community justice is constituted as a residual entity, an open place holder, which is the outcome of a voluntary (non-coercive) dispute resolution process. Mediation is closely articulated to images of community justice in as much as it is deemed to be an appropriate vehicle for restoring peace to communities and is particularly lauded as an informal process that empowers individual disputants to take control of settling their disputes (somewhat congruent with Bush and Folger 1994). At the same time it is said to strengthen community ties by its conciliatory (rather than adversarial) approach, which nurtures peace in localities that would otherwise be fraught with conflict. From these brief statements, one can identify certain nodal points in the advocates' calculations of community justice, but three stand out as common reference points: community mediation as a voluntary, informal alternative that empowers individuals; community strength; and restorative justice through effective settlement.

An empowering informal alternative

In the advocates' discourse, community justice is closely linked to the presence of voluntary, informal processes for resolving conflict. Mediation is situated as an important means of deploying such a process because it 'is dedicated to the principle that we all have a right to be actively involved in determining the outcome of our conflicts' (pamphlet, Surrey/White Rock Mediation Services Society).[20] What is at stake here is the view that just outcomes to common community disputes do not require the heavy-handed, coercive sanctions of a courtroom. Indeed, by taking responsibility away from individuals, courtroom processes deprive people of the 'right' to become active participants in finding appropriate settlements. In court, so the argument goes, disputants become passive recipients of an unfolding process over which they have very little control.

As a result, community justice advocates focusing attention on finding an idiom that allows disputants to regain control over the process of resolving conflict. Since mediation is a flexible and informal method that demands the active participation of disputants, it has become a crucial element in the discourse. Advocates see mediation as returning choices to disputants, in that '[t]he decision to enter into mediation is voluntary and any agreement realised must be voluntarily agreed upon by both parties, thus maintaining control over the decisions that effect them' (pamphlet, Surrey/White Rock Mediation Services Society). Such voluntarism is deemed crucial to ensuring lasting settlements to community disputes because agreements that disputants work out themselves are more likely to be followed than those that are imposed by judicial decree.

Here the discourse counterposes mediation against the courts' adversarial methods by contrasting its non-alienating, relaxed, informal and casual format with rigid courtroom procedures. Thus, the discourse emphasises the informality of mediation and its use of 'a cooperative rather than an adversarial approach' that is 'private and confidential' (pamphlet, Westcoast Mediation Services). In addition, mediation is held to be an effective, inexpensive and cost-effective process that 'can usually be scheduled within a short period of time, avoiding court delays' (ibid). But even if these characteristics are used to distinguish mediation from the courts, advocates do not suggest that it should replace the existing justice system. Instead, most conceive of mediation as a complementary alternative; in the words of a proponent, 'There are a lot of disputes out there and there are more than enough for ADR to exist *within* the justice system as a *complement* to the justice system' (interview, 26/09/1990). Echoing this sentiment, Turner and Jobson recommend that 'legislative assistance should be made to facilitate mediation as a mainstream justice service' (1990: 46), and Brown notes that (small claims) courts and community mediation should not be 'pitted one against the other' (1991: 2).[21]

Involvement in mediation has, for advocates, the tangible benefit of 'empowering' individuals to take control of their search for community justice. Reflecting this nodal point, one mediator asserts, 'our goal is to help people to be empowered to resolve their own disputes whenever they can' (interview, 12/09/1991). This claim implies the common perception that mediation is an empowering process because it returns to people their 'right' to remain active participants in working out just resolutions to particular conflicts. A spin-off effect of such empowerment, so we are told, is to educate individuals how to resolve potentially disruptive conflicts cooperatively, rather than resorting to confrontation and possibly violence. Mediation, that is, teaches 'problem-solving skills' that 'strengthen relationships and improve ongoing communication' (pamphlet, Westcoast Mediation Services). Armed with this knowledge, individuals are able to deal with conflict, increasing their autonomy from state controls and reinforcing their capacity to act as independent members of a community. As such, individual empowerment is a core nodal point in the advocates' calculation of community justice: autonomous, free individuals are necessary elements of the search for local, community justice. A functioning link between individuals and the community is deemed to be vital for empowering disputants; i.e. individuals are able to exercise their independence from the state in the immediacy of the community.

Community strength

In somewhat of a recursive conceptual loop, advocates also argue that individual empowerment is crucial for strengthening community ties, because it helps to build peaceful, harmonious and conflict-free communities (see Shonholtz 1988/89). In this sense, mediation serves to 'improve the quality of community life through more direct citizen participation, reduced community tension and increased community problem-solving skills' (Peachey and Tymec 1989: 43).[22] If sufficient numbers of disputants resolve their disputes through the active processes of mediation, it is possible to counter individual apathy and commence the task of rebuilding communities (Dussault 1993, Shonholtz 1984).[23] Mediation, that is, 'reduces anger and sets the stage for future cooperation' (pamphlet, Surrey/White Rock Mediation Services Society).

Here, the advocates' discourse targets various specific groups of people who are likely to benefit from mediation; e.g. in cases with 'racial/ethnic or religious tensions', neighbourhood disputes, room mates, landlord and tenants, employers and employees, consumers and merchants, victims and offenders, and so on. In addition, mediation is said to be useful for dealing with disputes between spouses and/or other family members, and is effective in working out custody, access, divorce or separation agreements (pamphlet, Westcoast Mediation Services Society). There is even a strand within the discourse that conceives of community justice as helping to redress the subordination of particular groups. For instance, the informal processes of mediation are thought by some to be beneficial for advancing the position of women in the community (Whittington and Ruddy n.d., Scambler 1989, Rifkin 1984).[24] As Turner and Jobson put it, '[f]urther thought should be given to mediation as a process that is more receptive than the adversary system to women's values' (1990: 46). Others, it should be noted, are much more sceptical of the purported 'empowerment' that mediation can provide to women in certain cases (e.g. spousal abuse), who enter mediation sessions carrying the burden of structurally based oppression that cannot be diffused by individual mediation sessions (Lerman 1984).

In all cases, however, advocates premise their calculations of community justice upon structurally intact communities. However, they do not offer a clear or precise conception of the 'community', even in the specially orchestrated forums and social fields, ranging from conferences, seminars and symposia to public education programmes, where their visions of community justice are articulated. Perhaps this indicates the extent to which advocates rely on a flexible notion of community to deploy various types of mediation programmes. Even so, there are a number of ways in which certain truths of this 'community' (what it is, what it ought to be, etc.), and its relation to calculations of justice, are implicitly declared. For the most part, the community issue is tackled obliquely; for example, through references to the 'community disputes' that mediation is supposed to target. The Canadian Bar Association Task Force Report defines such disputes as follows: 'Community disputes can be defined as those disputes involving persons with an ongoing relationship because of a community connection' and this 'connection' 'may be geographical, social, family, religious or other similar type of relationship' (1989: 42). If this definition indicates the sheer range of disputes considered amenable to effective resolution through mediation, it also gives an implicit conception of the community. In particular, the 'community' is designated as a physical and metaphysical 'space' within the social domain that has not yet been colonised by the state (hence the above reference to social, church, family, etc. relationships). But it is not synonymous with the social domain. In many ways, the community is seen as something more local, an element of the social. If the advocates' calculations have fragmented totalising concepts of justice, then so too has their vision of local community shattered the overarching unity of the amorphous social domain. One might infer that the discourse is here addressing the neo-liberal reforms that have rolled back *social* welfare. No longer is the social domain promulgated as the most immediate associative pattern; now it is the amorphous community that is primary, and peaceful relations between communities produce a secondary social order (Callahan and McNiven 1988).

In this discursive arrangement, the community is conceived as a gentle, non-alienating domain of freedom. It is a comfortable arena that contrasts with the cold, hostile impositions of the state's court system. In many ways the advocates seem here to be displaying a 'profound nostalgia' for a Golden Age in which communities resolved their disputes endogenously (Cohen 1985: 117–119). The discourse is deeply ingrained in the symbolic use of the 'community' as a way of gaining a respite from estrangement, disorganisation and homelessness – the negative outcomes of life in a modern society with expansive state forms. As such, the community emerges as an icon for the familiar, hospitable and 'informal' arena outside of the state's tutelage that allows empowered, free individuals to resolve their disputes. The apparent 'freedom' of the community is offered as a mark of its separation from the tutelage of state imposition (i.e., free from state control). Similarly, the heightened differentiation between court adjudication and mediation, which we have already spoken of, is clearly symbolic of the attempt to ascribe to the 'community' a quality of a non-imposing domain of freedom, of being a 'total comfort zone' for participants. This image credits the community with a spontaneity that advocates portray as the basis of specifically 'democratic' states. In this respect, many mediators see themselves as agents for social change, and see mediation as a 'life skill' that is crucial for revitalising democratic coexistence in the community (interviews, 12/09/1991, 15/01/1990). For them, if democracies are to take heed of the 'people', they must return to the 'community' to listen to its needs. As implied above, there has been a great impetus in British Columbia to identify the community as a viable domain from which to gather information when formulating justice policy: the state from individuals and *vice versa* (Butcher 1985, Cossom and Turner 1985).

In the advocates' enunciations, then, community justice is calculated as something more immediate to local participants than is professionalised justice. As should by now be clear, the logic is along these lines: empowered individuals who strengthen community relationships by taking responsibility for resolving disputes have a more direct affiliation with justice than those who turn to the state's courtrooms for coercively enforceable solutions. Of course, embedded in this conception is a view of the ideal community as a consensual domain of freely shared, common values that is largely free of conflict. As noted, it is precisely because people share a common background that they can find and draw upon the common ground to resolve their disputes. In this sense, the community is founded upon consensus, and conflict erodes its integrity as a viable entity. The consensus, moreover, is spontaneously developed when people interact in the absence of state intervention (Shonholtz 1978, 1984, 1988/89). Clearly, in such a vision, conflict is viewed as abnormal, unhealthy and destructive, and so must be resolved because it threatens the very stability of spontaneous, consensual community cohesion. It creates distances and destroys the harmonious communality that secures lasting peace and order. It is therefore – and here is the link with the final nodal point – important for disputes to be effectively resolved in order to restore peace to community existence.

Restorative justice and settlement

At this point in the discourse, community justice is calculated as a very particular form of 'restorative', rather than 'restitutive', justice. Advocates such as Umbreit (1994), Zehr (1994, 1986), Wright and Galaway (1989) and Peachey (1989b) offer detailed calculations of a justice whose emphasis is to 'restore' peace and harmony to communities. This nodal point is especially well developed in the victim-offender reconciliation field of mediation. The main concern is to heal the wounds that naked conflict causes, not to secure the principles of a *lex talionis* (an eye for an eye, a tooth for a tooth) that dominate calculations of repressive justice. The general tendency is to calculate justice as 'the restoration of right relationships, the healing of broken relationships' (Lederach and Kraybill 1993: 360). If mediation is to fulfil the aims of restoration, it must settle conflicts effectively. Thus, to tap directly into the British Columbian discourse once again, mediation must bring about 'an understanding of the real dispute, an understanding of the dispute that leads them to settle . . . The commitment to settle is really key, and you have to keep testing for that again and again' (interview, 26/09/1990). This emphasis on settling disputes is related to a pervasive trend in the discourse that equates the success of mediation with its ability to produce the tangible result of 'resolving disputes' (Merry 1982). In this respect, mediation is sometimes even described as 'a settlement conference that has many advantages over the normal discovery procedure [of the courts] . . . You can sound [the other disputant] out about settlement in a way that isn't possible within the confines of the litigation system' (interview, 26/09/1990).

But how precisely do advocates conceptualise the 'settlement' of a dispute? For the most part, it is conceptualised in terms of agreement: if both parties voluntarily agree to a 'reasonable' resolution, then the matter is considered settled. In other words, settlement entails 'something mutually acceptable agreed on by both parties; and that could take the form of something written which they then sign and agree to abide by, it may not – it may be verbal' (interview, 15/01/1990). This is thought to bring about 'dispute closure', which permits disputants to continue their relationship without the tension of conflict. The basic message here is that an acceptable agreement is one that is made 'voluntarily' by the (usually two) disputants involved in a conflict. As such, settlement is defined within the extremely narrow confines of a specific dispute between two parties: if both parties are satisfied with the outcome of their dispute, and agree to abide by its conditions, then the dispute has to all intents and purposes been settled (assuming the people do actually abide by the conditions; interview, 26/09/1990). The overarching discursive image is one of harmony between individuals where peace is restored to communities by expunging conflict. The 'restorative' aspects of community justice are emphasised so as to help disputants 'better understand each other (i.e. developing communication skills) and work towards healing some of the damage done (e.g. mostly things said or done)'.[25]

Settlement thus conceived is rendered central to calculations of community justice. Finding lasting agreements that are acceptable to disputants and that restore peace to communities are posited as important features of this community justice. In the process, calculations of justice are associated with technical considerations of efficiency and the quest to settle individual cases quickly, inexpensively and with minimum recurrence. Undergirded by a concern with administrative efficiency, advocates tout the technical ability of mediation to resolve conflict as crucial to securing community justice. So important is this nodal point that the 'success' of particular mediation programmes is mostly identified on this basis. As one interviewee described, 'funders say, "Okay, how many cases have you done?" And they will base their funding on how successful that list looks ... it's easier to count heads' (interview, 12/09/1991). Clearly, in such an ethos, questions of the aetiology of conflict (e.g. wider inequalities deriving from race, class and gender), or the capacity of a dispute resolution idiom to articulate difference, are subordinated to the more technical measures of case settlement, narrowly conceived in statistical terms.

If the previous discussion gives some indication of the core nodal points in the advocates' discourse, it says rather little about an actor whose presence in the field is crucial to achieving the goals of community justice: the mediator. Not only are mediators centrally involved in the mediating disputes, but many have influenced the identity of community mediation in British Columbia. But who typically becomes a mediator? Are mediators united in the kinds of practices they espouse? How do mediators conceptualise their roles in the process of mediation? Since mediators are central players in the advocates' discourse, let us round off the case study by briefly considering these sorts of questions.

THE 'NEUTRAL' MEDIATOR?

To begin with, the advocates' discourse usually evokes bifurcated images of mediators as professionals on the one hand, and yet ordinary everyday community members on the other. Thus, in response to questions about who mediators are, the following represents a common response: 'Our mediators are professionals from a variety of backgrounds who have special training in conflict resolution' (joint publication, Surrey/White Rock Mediation Service and Westcoast Mediation Services), or 'A member of your community, who is fully trained and assessed by the Centre' (pamphlet, Dispute Resolution Centre of Victoria). The dichotomous formulation of ordinariness versus professionalism is indicative of two contrasting tendencies between the requirements to remain sensitive to local communities while providing services deemed legitimate (hence the quest for professionalism). That these contrasting tendencies should be at the forefront of this section of the discourse hints at an underlying struggle between two different types of mediators.

This division is not always acknowledged, as is evident from the following bland description provided by a local mediation network (reflecting its diverse composition): 'In British Columbia, mediation is provided by counsellors, educators, lawyers, psychologists, social workers or trained volunteers in either private practices or family counselling agencies, community mediation centres or Family Court Counsellors' offices' (pamphlet, Mediation Development Association of B.C.). However, the division in context is clear enough; it revolves around mediators in private practice who charge a set fee for their services, as opposed to volunteers who do not get paid (or receive only token amounts) for services. Typically, this split coincides with a cleavage between lawyers who include mediation as one of various legal services offered as opposed to people with non-legal backgrounds (mainly 'social science' or church-associated) who have trained as mediators. Although the motives of the lawyers may include altruism, the expectation of pecuniary reward separates them from volunteers who are involved in mediation because of a vision and a desire for 'social change', and who 'really feel the need to help people' (interview, 11/01/1990). Even so, as a prominent mediation advocate perceptively put it,

> What I find intriguing in this field is there's a struggle between who's going to dominate it. Is it going to be the lawyers (and judges and court system) or is it going to be the human service people and community-based people? . . . That's the same all over North America. There's always an interplay between these two groups.
>
> (Interview, 12/09/1991)

For the sake of clarity, I shall refer to the latter as 'social expert' mediators and the former as 'legal' mediators. Many social expert mediators are located in the so-called 'new middle class', or are former social services employees who were retrenched (or disaffected) and have become private agents in a state-ordered social service contract market (see Howlett and Brownsey 1988, and Callahan and McNiven 1988). As outsiders to the legal establishment, social expert mediators tend to advocate community-based versions of mediation that are complementary to, but outside of, the legal system. A fear common to them is that, were mediation to fall under the exclusive jurisdiction of lawyers, non-lawyer mediators would soon be excluded from the informal justice domain. If the social experts are reasonably united on this score, lawyer mediators seem rather more divided: some support the social expert vision of community mediation; others oppose the use of mediators who are not formally trained in law;[26] and still others are simply indifferent, so long as no untrained mediator spoils the 'professional' reputation of the mediation process.

One consequence of this division within the body of mediators is a pre-eminent concern with devising and implementing standards of practice for mediators.[27] With certificate (and other) courses, social experts can entrench their credibility as mediation experts while lawyer mediators – in the field of family law – can extend their insurance coverage into mediation, provided they have completed an accredited course (CBA, Task Force Report, 1989). But, even here, the division in question surfaces again in the courses that people elect to attend. In particular, social experts (and their lawyer supporters) tend to favour the Justice Institute's Conflict Resolution Certificate Programme, whereas lawyer mediators favour courses and practicums offered by the Continuing Legal Education Society of British Columbia (Sloan 1989) or the BCICAC. Moreover, mediators in the different 'camps' revealed a rivalry that influenced the kind of recognition accorded to these different courses. For example, in one interview (and confirmed in others), a social expert derided the Continuing Legal Education programme as a 'Mickey Mouse' course, especially when compared with the more rigorous training offered by the Justice Institute. Equally, in a revealing omission, the CBA completely ignores the Justice Institute's programmes in its overview education in the ADR field (CBA, Task Force Report, 1989: 45). In sum, then, these various observations suggest that mediators are not a homogeneous group, but rather are split into various groups that include 'volunteers' versus 'paid mediators', a division that closely mirrors 'social expert' as opposed to 'legal' mediators.

In all cases, however, the mediator's role is portrayed as no more than a passive one that opens closed channels of communication between disputants. Mediators do not enforce settlements, or coerce people into resolving their disputes; nor do they make decisions, offer legal advice, assign blame or establish guilt and innocence. The mediator's role is depicted as no more than a facilitative one, working to open communication channels between disputants that have been closed by conflict (see Sloan 1992). As one mediator put it, 'Our goal is to help people to be empowered to resolve their own disputes whenever they can' (interview, 12/09/1991). S/he, that is, uses various mediation techniques to set 'ground rules' and assist 'parties to come to their own solutions' (pamphlet, Dispute Resolution Centre). But the mediator does not impose decisions in the attempt to be no more than a neutral third party who builds a 'safe' environment from which to secure an acceptable resolution (Burdine 1990).

Interviews with various mediators indicate that there are differing conceptions of neutrality and the possibility of ever entirely achieving this. However, for most, a core issue is captured in the following statement by a prominent mediator apropos her understanding of mediator neutrality: 'What I would like to see happen does not become an issue in this mediation. I have to step back and recognise that it's these two people trying to resolve a problem and I'm here to help them' (interview, 11/01/1990). In practical 'role play' training sessions for prospective mediators (i.e. simulated mediation sessions where other trainees assume the roles of disputants), a qualified 'coach' underscored this conception of neutrality by encouraging mediators to focus on the 'process of interaction' in a given mediation context and to avoid getting 'caught up' in the details of what disputants had to say. The general theme here is not so much that mediators ought not to intervene in a given dispute (on the contrary, they are encouraged to keep control of the session) but rather that their interventions should only further the task of facilitating a settlement acceptable to the parties involved. The advocates' focus on mediator neutrality no doubt addresses the possible objection that community mediation is too partial a process to deliver fair settlements. At the same time, it distinguishes mediation from litigation because the mediator, unlike the judge, does not impose a judgement on disputing parties. Indeed, by assuming a degree of common ground to exist between disputants, advocates require no more than the 'neutral' assistance of a mediator to recover the consensus lost through conflict. At a slightly more reflexive register, one might even say that the idea of 'neutrality' in this context is predicated upon the assumption of a primordial 'community' consensus that supersedes any conflicts that may arise between individuals – hence the call for mediators to adopt a neutral role.

COMMUNITY MEDIATION: A POSTMODERN IDIOM?

Neither the practices of community mediation typified above, nor the associated calculations of community justice, involve appeals to universal principles founded on human reason. In its attempts to engineer informal social fields that will promote settlement, community mediation requires the flexibility to be responsive to the differing demands of the various contexts in which it operates. It does not appeal to fixed auspices for legitimacy, except perhaps to images of its technical efficiency at settling disputes. That is, it seeks to settle local conflicts to the satisfaction of disputants with maximum efficiency and cost effectiveness. Following on from the logic of the previous chapter, what seems clear from this is a shifting allegiance away from the auspices of speculative or emancipatory metanarratives of a modern ethos. In its place, appeals to a technical capacity to resolve disputes, to get the job of restoring peace done, loom ever more prominently on the informal justice horizon (see Lyotard 1984). Questions around the effects of restoring peace to 'communities' that harbour structured discrepancies between oppressed and oppressor fade almost imperceptibly from the discursive horizons that speak to this emerging idiom of justice.

Indicating perhaps their location within a postmodern ethos, without the certainties of absolute and clear auspices from which to make confident declarations, community justice advocates nevertheless contest the unity (singularity) of modern justice and make a bid for their particular calculations. The nodal points of their discourse demarcate the grounds for this claim, and offer justifications for deploying mediation as a suitable idiom to house its visions. In the process, community justice advocates help to fragment justice into openly different and sometimes competing logics, and so give a different identity to the emerging dispute resolution arena and the provision of justice(s). The quest for locally relevant justice(s) disowns the imposition of one essential unity to all forms of justice, such as a single, universal rule of law. As but an instance of numerous calculations, community justice centres its claims around an idiom that is said, as we have seen, to be familiar (informal), voluntary and individually empowering, and to nurture community strength by restoring peace. Yet are their claims as sanguine as their discourse would appear to suggest? Even if, as noted, the advocates' formulations in British Columbia have not attracted much critical analysis, there is a fairly well-developed critical discourse directed towards calculations and practices of community justice elsewhere that is directly pertinent. Positioning the discourses of advocates and critics in relation to each other would seem to be an important way in which the present narrative might diagnose the perils of mediating community disputes under postmodern conditions. It is, therefore, to the critical discourse that I now turn.

4

THE CRITICS RESPOND
Dark shadows of courtroom justice

Beware the Rulers Bearing Justice.
(Cohen 1988: 203)

If community mediation advocates offer community justice as a dignified escape from formal court procedures, critics are far less sanguine about the purported 'empowerment' it offers those involved in 'minor', community disputes. As Matthews (1988) indicates, the optimism of advocates was rapidly matched by a growing pessimism amongst critics, whose discourse appears to have developed in two successive waves: a variously formulated critique focusing on community justice as little more than a residual feature of state justice; and a less totalising critique that seeks to confront community mediation directly, highlighting both its perils and possibilities. We shall examine the first developments of the critical discourse in this chapter and leave the more recent formulations to the next.

The initial critiques of community justice were mostly developed in the United States, and to a lesser extent in Britain, but its precepts pertain directly to the case of British Columbia. From the outset, the critics' discourse has been heterogeneous, with perhaps two overall points of agreement. First, most reject the advocates' claim that community mediation is a 'community' response to an overburdened, expensive and time-consuming court system. Second, critics repudiate the view that community justice is an independent 'alternative' to the state's justice system that promotes individual emancipation. Instead, they see it as a way in which the state expands and intensifies its control over individuals. In the words of a prominent critic, through such mechanisms as community justice the state is said to be growing in an insidious way because, '*it is expanding through a process that, on the surface, appears to be a process of retraction*' (Santos 1982: 262; italics in original). Although early critics emphasise different aspects of this complex theme, most see community mediation not as a mechanism to increase individual participation in disputes but as a means of making 'individuals' more accessible to state control.

66

Despite similarities, one can identify at least three different points of emphasis in the early critics' discourse on community justice.[1] First, there are critics who challenge the coherence of the advocates' calculations, depicting these as little more than ideological masks for reforms in the state's provision of justice.[2] Another group of critics, operating within broadly conceived neo-Marxist and/or neo-Fordist discourses, focus on underlying structural crises within contemporary capitalist societies that render the emergence of such regulatory forms as community justice feasible.[3] Finally, there is a critical strand that conceptualises community justice as one element in the changing face of the capitalist state as it seeks to develop power arrangements to redress the crises of the post-war period.[4] Let us turn to each of these strands of the discourse in turn.

CALCULATIONS AS IDEOLOGY: CONTROL THROUGH CONSENSUS

The first series of critics direct their critiques of community justice to the apparent paradox of calculating a decentralised, local type of justice from within the state's centralised, bureaucratic justice system. Despite overtones of Marx in evoking notions of 'ideology', most critics in this camp owe a far greater debt of allegiance to Weberian thought. In any case, these critics view the advocates' calculations of community justice as a little more than a reform 'ideology' that has been created and implemented out of historically specific political struggles, and that has the effect of trying to engineer consent (and discouraging political dissent). As such, their discourse (i) describes and challenges the precepts of the calculations; (ii) explicates how this has emerged as an accepted ideology; and (iii) explores some of the political consequences of the community justice ideology.

As an instance of the first approach, Nader's (1988) review suggests that the calculations that license such practices as community mediation are best understood as a 'harmony ideology'. In advocating a shift away from confrontation and adversarial litigation to community-based, harmonious forms of dispute resolution, the ideology equates mediation with the peace, well-being and consensus of actively functioning communities. In this scenario, she argues, courtroom failures (alienation, cost, delay, etc.) are associated with the erosion of communities, and community justice with their redevelopment. Nader, along with several other critics, also argues that the ideological calculation is flawed because its claims are either contradictory or not confirmed by existing research.[5] And, to the extent that it has been successfully enunciated, the ideology has entrenched a series of misleading myths and distortions about the nature of informalism (see Tomasic 1982, Abel 1982b). One such visible deception is the advocates' portrayal of community mediation as a decentralised alternative to the formal courts, when mediation is clearly planned, developed and implemented in large measure by central state agencies (Abel 1982a: 9, Harrington 1985: 69).[6] This has implications for other aspects of the harmony ideology; e.g. what does this mean for the so-called 'expanded participation' that mediation is said to provide disputants? Or what is the nature of a voluntarism, or empowerment, that is extraneously granted by central planning (Abel 1982b, Harrington 1982)?

With such concerns in mind, the neo-Weberian critics in this camp question whether mediation is actually capable of relieving an over-burdened court system, since there is little evidence to suggest that it is less bureaucratic,[7] speedier, less costly, fairer, or more flexible than litigation.[8] Some even wonder whether there *is* a crisis within the court system (Nader 1988: 281). In addition, community mediation is not seen to be quite as 'voluntary', or non-coercive, as its advocates allege. Instead, it appears to complement formal legality, and is always bounded at its margins by the threat of legal sanction (Tomasic 1982: 225–229). In this sense, community justice provides a useful ideology to support a shift in the ways in which the justice bureaucracy is managed (Harrington 1985).

Also, by focusing on individuals in conflict, the community justice calculations help to individualise disputes that may have structural roots, thereby offering somewhat superficial resolutions (Abel 1982b: 286, Tomasic 1982: 222, Mica 1992). As such, the ideology supports a conservative model of conflict (Abel 1981), and reduces the 'potential for social disruption' through collective action (Abel 1982b: 288). Indeed, the ideology's focus on individual voluntarism may even militate against its purported quest to rebuild failing communities (Abel 1982a: 9, Tomasic 1982: 230–234, Cohen 1985: ch. 4) and question the notion that informal justice is a 'community-based' initiative. Abel (1982a: 8) and Tomasic (1982: 229–230), for example, argue that there is 'considerable' evidence to suggest that many members of communities prefer the authoritative decisions of the courtroom above informally reached settlements, not least of all because the former can potentially redress power imbalances between litigants.[9] Perhaps this partially explains the almost universal problem experienced by community mediation programmes in securing a steady flow of cases for mediation (Tomasic 1982, Turner and Jobson 1990). In sum, then, the ideology critics see these as some of the ways in which mediation, despite its advocates' exhortations to the contrary, helps to perpetuate the *status quo* and expand state control. After all, so these critics charge, if 'informal institutions render law more accessible to the disadvantaged, they also render the disadvantaged more accessible to the state; this latter consequence may be the more significant' (Abel 1981: 258).

Even if the ideology critics agree that the community justice ideology is not inevitable, 'natural' or a response to the community, they are divided on their views about how it did develop. The more radical amongst these critics argue that informalism is integrally related to crises in capital accumulation. For instance, Abel asserts that '[i]nformalism is a mechanism by which the state extends its control so as to manage capital accumulation and defuse the resistance it engenders' (1982a: 6). It is one of the 'endless projects of legitimation within the legalist paradigm' (1982b: 25) that seeks to maintain the legitimacy of state authority in the face of a 'rights explosion' where growing numbers seek to vindicate their rights in courts.[10] It tries to resuscitate the failing legitimacy of law by providing 'relatively new', 'untested' and peripheral experiments, which attract intense scrutiny and deflect critical attention away from the 'older formal institutions that lie at the core of the legal system' (Abel 1981: 256).

However, Abel argues that informal institutions also strengthen the state in other ways. For one, the ideology of informalism underscores the liberal state's focus on individuals by denying the class-based nature of any conflict: it relies on an individualistic and 'conservative' model of conflict that assumes that all disputes can be resolved individually (Abel 1981).[11] In addition, mediation takes little account of the wider social structures and inequalities that bring people to mediation in the first place, thereby denying the potentially liberating aspects of conflict. Hence, it helps to perpetuate the *status quo* and undermine non-state resistance (e.g. collective neighbourhood action) by defusing, or trivialising, legitimate conflicts. In short, informal justice defuses resistance to accumulation, resulting in the re-legitimation of the court system and a strengthened state. Moreover, the informal ideology benefits certain occupational groups over others (including judges, lawyers, mediators), and their interest in shaping it in a particular way has important effects on the eventual form of community justice (Abel 1982b: 301–304).[12]

Consonant with their pluralist, 'neo-Weberian' tack, Harrington and Merry argue that the reform ideology of community mediation, like other ideologies, is an outcome of struggles between social actors in given sociopolitical contexts (1988: 710).[13] Consequently, they explain the rise of an informal justice ideology as a product of political contests around such matters as 'mobilising funding', gaining institutional support, forging the necessary judicial connections, securing and maintaining case-loads and ensuring legitimacy (Harrington and Merry 1988: 710). Within these contested domains there are multiple struggles between a plurality of agents and interest groups (mediators, lawyers, judges, etc.), who try to impart a particular vision of community mediation and then colonise symbols to rationalise the implementation of specific kinds of mediation programmes. As an instance of this approach, Harrington (1992, 1985, 1982) provides a detailed analysis of Progressive judicial ideologies and management strategies deployed at the turn of the twentieth century in the United States, and shows how they came to be replaced by those of informalism (see also Auerbach 1983). Her historically focused accounts discuss the importance of political contests in forging the ideology of community justice. For instance, she examines how the initial emphasis on 'effective justice' and 'rights' in discussions on the introduction of a Dispute Resolution Act in the United States was transformed into a debate concerned with matters of administrative 'efficiency' and how to ensure the creation of 'effective' institutions (Harrington 1985: 73–99). This occurred, she suggests, through a series of subtle contests in which dominant political agents managed to gain control over the development of the ideology, allowing them to define informal justice in terms expedient to an emergent judicial management strategy. They did this by selecting sympathetic agents to serve as core mediators, as 'experts', who then disseminated their preferred ideology (Harrington and Merry 1988). As 'experts', these mediators not only came to dominate the 'thinking' on mediation (at conferences and presentations, in articles and books, or through their organisational positions), but were also uniquely portrayed as competent to train other mediators. In this way, a truncated, and undoubtedly politically expedient, version of what 'proper' mediation ought to entail was dispersed.[14]

Finally, what are the consequences of the ideology from this perspective? Those who address this issue tend to see it as having profound effects on the notion of a popular justice. For instance, the ideology maintains a dubious separation between a voluntaristic community and a formal state through the use of rhetorical formulae (e.g. 'buzzwords', 'false comparisons'[15]) and other devices (e.g. 'folksy', informal procedures in hospitable settings[16]). This perpetuates a false dichotomy that masks the fundamental continuity between formal and informal controls[17] and even justifies the expansion of formal control. Thus, as one critic puts it, 'the shift from an adversary, formal ideology to informalism should thus be seen as a rationalisation of management style rather than a fundamental change in the processing of minor conflicts' (Harrington 1985: 171). As such, Harrington's particular (neo-Weberian) approach suggests that the ideology has facilitated the deployment of an 'administrative-technocratic' judicial management strategy that stifles genuine political discussion (Harrington 1985: 69). It links local control sites to centralised institutions in a 'decentralised unification' of the justice arena that evades politically contentious issues by reframing them as mere 'problems' of inefficient administration to be 'solved' by technical means. Thus, for example, questions pertaining to disputants' rights, or to the fairness of the mediation process, are considered only in the light of their possible effect on practical steps to implement 'workable' programmes. Politically contentious discussions on whether justice is measurable in cost-benefit terms, or whether mediation is really necessary to 'solve' administrative problems in the court system, are conspicuously absent from this discussion. By impoverishing the theatre of political debate in this way, informal justice encourages a 'consensus-based' politics in which the contingency of political choice masquerades as technical necessity (Harrington 1985: 64). To the extent that mediation seeks an assumed 'common ground' between its participants, it helps to further a politics of 'consensus building' and fosters complacency that erodes political dissent (Harrington 1985: 173).[18]

The overall effect of the emphasis on consensus is to license a unification of informal and formal control institutions and to increase 'the quantum of state resources devoted to social control' (Abel 1982b: 273). In the process, 'coercion, centralisation and dominance' are disguised, while the state looms as an ever larger Leviathan, regulating behaviours that previously escaped its social control network (Abel 1981: 262).[19] Consequently, the frequency and type of comportment subject to regulation are increased, and the measure of effective justice is translated into a capacity to settle disputes.[20] In parenthesis, one might here note the links between these critics' and Lyotard's (1984) observation that knowledge under postmodern conditions is increasingly legitimised in technical terms – calculations of community justice are said here to be legitimised by their technical capacity to resolve disputes more efficiently and effectively than courtroom litigation.

The ideology critics themselves have come under attack from other critics for not paying sufficient attention to the structural conditions of capitalist society within which community mediation has emerged. Even though some ideology critics allude to the 'structural roots' of conflict, none offers a detailed account of how such structures influence the relational patterns of society (e.g. Abel 1982b). The pluralist base of their accounts is deemed problematic because it does not encourage sustained analyses of the articulations between related domains of capitalist society (law, state, economy, etc.). For critics of various neo-Marxist persuasions, the articulations between these are more integral than a mere assemblage of conflicting 'interest groups' at particular contexts. There is, for the latter critics, a 'logic' to capitalism that is the force behind the rise of informal modes of regulation.

THE STRUCTURAL LOGIC OF COMMUNITY MEDIATION

Hofrichter's eclectic materialism

Hofrichter (1987) offers an explicitly materialist, capital logic account of 'neighbourhood dispute resolution'. He preserves the concept of 'ideology' in his narrative, but mobilises it as an attempt to merge Gramsci's notion of hegemony[21] with state-derivation theory.[22] This is not an easy theoretical project to accomplish, especially when one considers the ambiguity of Gramsci's concept.[23] Nevertheless, Hofrichter (1987: Part 1) uses it to ground his conception of 'neighbourhood dispute resolution' as part of the state's non-coercive mechanisms of control that aim to produce consent and secure hegemony in the social domain. He begins with the following

71

premise: capitalist societies may assume different forms, but they always develop in response to the logic of capital accumulation. This logic is founded on the continuous attempts of 'the social class that owns and controls the apparatus of production to increase the rate of capital accumulation and to maintain control over the surplus produced by labor' (1987: 4). As a result, there is an ongoing class struggle between capital and labour, which is 'formally' waged in the changing sets of relations referred to as the 'state'. Somewhat more contentiously, and in opposition to the contingency implied by Gramsci's conception of hegemony, Hofrichter depicts the state as a 'system of social relations that create order and maintain the rule of capital' (1987: 30). Its task is always to create and perpetuate certain 'conditions' for unhindered capital accumulation by regulating the social environment. It is, for him, a class-based set of institutions favouring one class (capital) over others. Paradoxically, however, the state's effectiveness is directly proportional to its ability to claim legitimacy from those that it does not represent (i.e. the working class).[24] Such legitimacy, however, cannot be won by constantly resorting to coercive repression. Hence, Hofrichter notes, '[i]n order to survive, capitalist rule must be secured and obscured without direct force and without the appearance of promoting direct class interests or indeed, any exercise of power' (1987: 33).

As such, the state seeks to organise the consent of the governed, to foster consensus through ideological regulation, by relying on consensus-based forms of control in 'civil society'.[25] Here, Hofrichter echoes Gramsci's contention that state power extends beyond the limits of formal structures to the cultural forms and 'moral imperatives' of everyday social life (Hofrichter 1987: 34). In other words, consent is mobilised in diffuse institutions (e.g. the church, mass media, schools, family), all of which seek to impart a particular view of the world through ideological education.[26] With this in mind, Hofrichter argues that community justice has been developed in an attempt to secure ideological 'hegemony' in civil society, not least of all owing to the declining significance of various traditional institutions in this arena (e.g. the church). It does this in a number of ways. For instance, mediation fragments the potential for collective labour opposition by individualising disputes. That is, because its 'cases' are defined in individual terms, mediation disallows collective responses to social problems (through unions, neighbourhoods, etc.).[27] Moreover, by preserving the appearance of everyday life in mediation sessions, neighbourhood dispute resolution masks the exercise of power by emphasising the values of consensus and agreement (Hofrichter 1987: 142). Its singular objective of settling disputes – regardless of disputants' rights or interests – helps it to reinforce middle-class norms (1987: 134–142). Should it fail, however, informal justice has the backing of coercive state apparatuses (e.g. the courts; 1987: 150). In Hofrichter's view then, although community justice may appear to be an open-ended process by which participants work out their own settlements, its mechanisms seek to organise the consent of the governed by promoting a 'predefined order' that serves to 'automatically suppress working class interests' (1987: 89).

This implies that neighbourhood justice is not – as its advocates allege – a community-orientated initiative; it is instead a valuable part of the state's bid to secure ideological hegemony. The argument is supported, we are told, by the significant degree to which neighbourhood dispute resolution programmes rely on local governments or other state agencies (or Foundations and Bar Associations), not only for their funding but also for case referrals. Through these ties, the state defines and develops, according to its priorities, the discourse, institutional structure and target population of neighbourhood justice (1987: 153). Consequently it is a state-planned form of social control that regulates more areas of society and expands the state's administrative network into new areas of social life (Hofrichter 1982: 228–229 and 1987: 94–100). Neighbourhood dispute resolution casts a larger, and more finely meshed, control network over social life in a regulatory arena created by the state, but which presents itself as an independent domain (1987: 89). The supposedly passive, congenial and voluntary arena of informal justice actually 'expands and intensifies' state power into areas of society that ordinarily exclude formal control. In other words, through this strategy, the state amalgamates centralised planning with decentralised community regulation to ensure the consent of those whom it governs.

But why, one may ask, has the community mediation movement emerged at this juncture in history? Hofrichter offers two related, but different, sorts of reasons. First, he agrees that the formal legal system is unable to deal with the scope of resistance produced by the recent crises of capital accumulation. Indeed, he suggests, '[l]egal rationality obstructs the ability of the courts to manage new forms of class conflict and economic dislocation arising from the irrationalities of capitalist production' (1982: 227). Presumably Hofrichter is here driving at the kinds of issues raised by Selva and Bohm (1987) and Spitzer (1982). For these writers, whereas the market 'anarchy' of competitive capitalism may have demanded the universality and predictability of a formal legal system to avert social dissent, the organised markets of contemporary monopoly capitalism require far more flexible control mechanisms that can respond to the particularities of accumulation crises in local contexts. From this view, informal justice is an essential part of the 'transformation of the political economy from the stage of competitive capitalism to the stage of late monopoly capitalism' (Selva and Bohm 1987: 43).

The second set of reasons Hofrichter offers for the rise of neighbourhood dispute resolution pertains to specific trends that he identifies in the United States. He refers to the social disruptions caused by the ascent of non-labour social movements in their resistance to the prevailing order (neighbourhood and welfare rights, consumer rights, women's and environmental movements, etc.). Resistance of this kind, he argues, complements labour's increased intransigence to the more 'direct' forms of exploitation associated with massive capital centralisation by monopolies. Also, many of these struggles have been waged in contexts of expanding urban problems (e.g. congestion, decay, unemployment). In tandem, such resistance has heightened an awareness of social disintegration and put a peculiarly social slant on contemporary accumulation crises, leaving the state to manage an acute series of legitimation crises. The Fordist state's response to these threats to social stability was to colonise more areas of social life, but this only exacerbated its fiscal crises and multiplied the points at which its legitimacy could be challenged. Over the past few decades, according to Hofrichter, the neo-Fordist state has altered its course by retracting its formal apparatuses from the social arena (including the courts), opting to regulate this domain informally (through, for example, informal justice).[28]

Hofrichter's perspective has been criticised in various ways, especially by critics who fear his account does not take sufficient notice of the contingency Gramsci ascribed to hegemonic formations. Thus, his perspective is seen by some to be unacceptably economistic and reductionist in its very formulation.[29] His assumption that community justice must always service the so-called 'needs' of capital and the state worries many. As one commentator suggests, 'Hofrichter's functionalist perspective presupposes more than it explains' (Gallagher 1988: 138). In other words, Hofrichter's narrative is said to presume in advance what it really ought to investigate, offering little empirical evidence when forging connections between mediation and the state (Gallagher 1988, Etheridge 1988: 234). Baskin, another structural logic critic, argues that Hofrichter's perspective is 'inadequate, since it views community mediation as a *fait accompli* in the ongoing attempt by the capitalist class to maintain its hegemony' (1988: 100). In response and in an attempt to 'historicise' the analysis by placing community justice in its late twentieth-century context, Baskin examines community justice as part of a mode of regulation, an emerging strategy of social reproduction, in neo-Fordist capitalist societies.

Baskin: Social reproduction and neo-Fordist modes of regulation

Although Baskin's narrative sees 'hegemony' as useful to understanding the place of community justice in capitalist societies, she emphasises the 'modes of regulation' by which 'social reproduction' is achieved. Drawing explicitly on regulation and state derivation theory,[30] she describes community mediation as an element in a changed mode of regulation corresponding to recent shifts from a 'Fordist' to a 'neo-Fordist' regime of accumulation.[31] She views community mediation as a 'process' aimed at reproducing the conditions from which the 'lived experience' of capitalist society can emerge. It is part of a changing strategy of 'social reproduction and regulation', a 'component process of social administration', which has emerged to cope with historically specific crises arising from the ongoing contradictions of capitalist exploitation (1988: 100).

For Baskin, a notable feature of the Fordist state, associated with the increased accumulation that followed the Second World War, was its capacity to extend the quantum and scope of 'commodity relations'. By penetrating into the heart of social life, the Keynesian welfare state had in effect subjugated other social relations to the dictates of wage labour and exchange (hence residential and employment mobility, the emphasis on work, and so on). One consequence was widespread social disintegration in which 'traditions and mediating institutions' were eroded by 'the process of commodification' (Baskin 1988: 101). The disintegration rendered social reproduction 'indeterminate', for, without the active influence of 'indigenous helping networks' (the family, the church, etc.) and other 'traditional helping institutions', social behaviour remained unregulated – a situation unlikely to secure the conditions for social reproduction. The state's initial response was to develop an extensive welfare system, but this fuelled both legitimacy and fiscal crises. The latter encouraged a different strategy in which the state increases its control over society but under the guise of diversification. Here, Baskin notes, '[s]tate, semi-state and private entities have been empowered to intervene into personal relations for the purposes of preventing, identifying, and/or correcting disruptive behaviour' (1988: 103). State expansion occurs through 'deregulation' (or community regulation) where private agencies are recast as agents of state control, and where one does not have to break a law to be ensnared by the state's ubiquitous, informal network of control.[32]

Baskin describes community mediation as one such reform implemented to 'expand regulation', 'neutralize conflict' related to social disintegration, and 'reinforce the commodity form' (1988: 102). It expands regulation by seeking to control aspects of social existence that were previously deemed to be 'private'; i.e. exempt from public scrutiny. By transferring regulation to the 'community', the state blurs the public/private distinction, thereby expanding its control network while making this expansion appear as a retraction. For instance, in mediation sessions, people are required to expose minute details of their lives pertaining to a dispute (e.g. attitudes, sleeping habits, how one feels about raising children) for the scrutiny of a mediator. This inserts regulation into the very fabric of social life, and produces a modality of control that encourages 'self-management'. Community mediation neutralises conflict by 'reducing social problems to interpersonal and individual ones' (1988: 105) and considers the structural bases of conflict (e.g. racism, sexism, poverty) as mere failures of communication or individual quirks.

Finally, Baskin describes mediation as an extremely efficient control mechanism because it simultaneously reproduces the social conditions required for capital accumulation and expands the circuits of capital.[33] By privatising the field of social regulation and encouraging private payment for social regulation, the state appears to be retracting from the private sphere, enlarges the exchange of commodities to more areas of social life (as 'services'), and entrenches the 'motivational patterns' of (i.e. the subjective orientations required for) capitalist production and consumption (1988: 107).[34] In short, under different pretexts, this process inscribes the commodity form into greater areas of the social arena and reinforces the basic motivations of existing modes of production and consumption, namely 'possessive individualism' (1988: 109). As such, informal justice simultaneously increases the number of circuits capital may traverse while bringing subjective dispositions closer in line with the requirements of capital accumulation.[35]

Even with her apparent attempts to rescind Hofrichter's reductionism, Baskin's focus on community mediation as a component process of a shifting regime of accumulation places significant strictures upon its contingent deployment as a mode of regulation. In this light, one might read Santos's (1982) focus on mediation as a contingently deployed form of power in late capitalism as an attempt to avoid the charges of reductionism without jettisoning the neo-Marxist problem entirely.

Santos: Community justice and power in the late capitalist state

Integrating various neo-Weberian and neo-Marxist strands in the critics' discourse, Santos (1982) argues that the emergence of community justice is related to changes in the forms of power within the legal system, which are, in turn, related to wider dislocations in the nature of the capitalist state. Like Hofrichter and Baskin, he views the state as no more than a historically specific set of structures and relations that respond to economic crises. It seeks to 'disperse' threats to the order by 'integrating', 'trivialising' or 'neutralising' conflicts through force and techniques of 'exclusion' (e.g. prisons; 1982: 251). As such, it assumes various forms to cope with the relentless crises that arise from structural contradictions in the 'non-state' (economic and social) domains.[36] Yet its ability to integrate, trivialise or neutralise conflicts in these arenas depends in large measure on its ability to preserve a semblance of neutrality in class struggle. It does this by granting a certain 'independence' to its legal system, thereby masking the fundamental symmetry of interests between state, capital and law.[37] In this account, the law emerges as a fragmented and pluralistic entity that bolsters the state's legitimacy by aiding its claims to neutrality in the class struggle.

Santos subscribes to a version of legal pluralism, viewing community mediation as but one manifestation of law. Structurally, for him, 'the law' is best seen as a heterogeneous complex that adopts three basic strategies through which decisions on particular conflicts are made and communicated: 'rhetoric', where judgements are made on the basis of socially accepted arguments; 'bureaucracy', where decisions are imposed through authorities that appeal to professional knowledge, formal rules, hierarchies, etc.; and 'violence', where decisions appeal to the threat, or use, of physical force.[38] He describes community mediation as part of a recent trend in which structures of rhetoric at the periphery of political domination are expanding at the same time as bureaucratic and violent structures at its core are becoming more pervasive. The symbols of increased participation, self-government, informalism and community participation may be used to distinguish mediation from the adjudicated coercion of courts, but both serve to expand structures of state control. In other words, although informal justice expands rhetorical structures by extending into peripheral areas of the legal domain, it does not hamper the dominance of formal bureaucratic and violent structures at the core. On the contrary, for Santos, in western contexts, the peripheral expansion of informalism actually facilitates a concomitant expansion of bureaucracy and violence at the centre of the legal system.[39] Yet, he adds, structures are never impervious to influences from other legal structures (hence, 'structural interpenetration'); indeed, bureaucratic and violent structures have expanded into the very form of rhetoric. Thus, peripheral structures (e.g. informal justice), while grounded mainly in legal rhetoric, have also become contaminated with the logic of bureaucracy and violence. (For example, mediators frequently allude to the court as the 'only other option' if participants fail to reach agreement, thereby invoking the threat of having to resort to the formal legal bureaucracy, and possibly the coercion of the state.)

In tandem, for him, these tendencies reflect a more general transformation of the way the capitalist state exercises power. Santos suggests that it typically exercises power in two complementary – but 'mutually exclusive' - ways: on the one hand, it exists as a centralised and hierarchical 'cosmic power' which operates through 'formal' institutions at a macro level; on the other, it is exercised through a less organised, but more diffuse, ubiquitous and flexible 'chaosmic power', that emerges 'wherever social relations and interactions are unequal, in the family, at school, on the street, etc. It is a micro power' (1982: 261). Even though these may appear in different institutional guises, and operate at different levels (i.e. macro and micro), Santos feels they have always cooperated to perpetuate the same basic inequalities of capitalist society.[40] But in early capitalism the residues of feudalism helped to sustain a genuine division between 'civil society' and the 'state', such that cosmic power was excluded from the former.[41] However, in late capitalist societies there is no 'civil society', for it is neither distinct from the state nor in opposition to it. At best, there is a 'secondary civil society', which is no more than 'state produced non-state areas of social life' (1982: 262 at note 15).

This reflects a fundamental shift in the nature of state power, in that closer links are being forged between cosmic and chaosmic power such that the latter increasingly carves out areas in which the former operates. As such, community mediation articulates cosmic power to aspects of chaotic power in its quest to exercise power in situations that previously did not fall within the ambit of state regulation; that is, conflicts between people involved in ongoing relations. It helps to expand state power while simultaneously assisting the state to cut back fiscally. Consequently, the state is expanding even though it claims to be retracting and leaving regulation to the 'community'. In the process of such expansion, the state and non-state realms begin to converge, resulting in a stronger and more pervasive, but also more flexible, form of the state.

Santos argues that this transformation of state power was prompted by the need to revive a bond between the state and the working class in a situation of stagnating accumulation. Hence, the state has expanded materially to absorb some unemployed people, but it also expands symbolically to neutralise the resistance that such crises evoke.[42] Community justice is designed to stabilise power relations and thereby deal with certain structural contradictions in capitalist society.[43] In as much as community justice deals with conflict by assuming the value of – and appealing to - 'consensus', it reinforces the *status quo* and achieves a dubious 'repressive consensus' (1982: 261). As such, it serves to disarm and fragment the working class in late capitalist society. Santos predicts that core areas of political domination are likely increasingly to assume a chaosmic form. In so doing, the distinction between core and peripheral will be blurred, leaving very little room for political contestation at the periphery. In this ominous Orwellian environment, the ubiquitous state will face all people directly as it shifts from formal institutions to 'informal networks'. The net effect of this, for him, is that '[s]ocial networks will then become the dominant unit for the production and reproduction of power – a source of power that is diffuse and interstitial, and therefore is as familiar as it is remote' (1982: 263).

APORIAS IN THE EARLY CRITICS' DISCOURSE

Despite their notable differences, as noted, the previous narratives share a common view of community justice as a means of expanding and intensifying state control (Cohen 1989). Were one to expand on this common theme in their discourse, it seems that community mediation is part of a process by which the state casts a larger, more finely meshed, control network over a regulatory arena that it has created but that appears as an independent realm of freedom (e.g. as is implied by the notion of 'community').

Depending upon which perspective is adopted, early critics examine this theme in relation to: ideology; accumulation-hegemonic or regulation structures; or power. As such, the central problematic of their discourse revolves around depicting community justice institutions in terms of a question that Abel summarises as follows: 'the central question must be: Do they expand or reduce state control?' (Abel 1982a: 6). As is evident by now, early critics respond unequivocally to this dichotomous question: the community justice movement expands state control and, ironically, it does so by denying that it does.[44] To the extent that community justice is understood almost entirely through the control functions it performs in its expansion of the formal state, these early critics subscribe, to a greater or lesser extent, to a 'reductionist' thesis that, in effect, denies that community mediation is, or can be, autonomous from the state in any important sense (Fitzpatrick 1988: 180, Matthews 1988: 15).

But such an approach can be seen to be founded upon a vexatious aporia. By describing community mediation as an 'expansion' of state control, the early critics implicitly assume that clear definitions of, and comparisons between, different modes of state control (e.g. past and present) are possible. A closer look reveals an aporia at the very heart of such an assumption. Consider, for example, the comparative precision required of a distinction between forms of state control that would allow one to assert with confidence that contemporary forms of state control have expanded on those of the past. The early critics' problematic is based upon the assumption that such precision is possible, and that a high degree of commensurability must exist between the entities being compared. Yet, the complexity of regulatory modes within a given spacio-temporal context, let alone across historically different contexts, seems to defy the precise descriptive closure that would be required to make the comparison in question.[45] This points to difficult questions about how to distinguish between one state form and the next, to compare these forms and to provide a basis for declaring that one form expands on another. In effect, an aporia lurks at the discursive moment where the early critics' enunciations of community justice as one element transforming complex control formations fly in the face of their clear-cut assertions about expanded state control. The formulation of a simple but appealing image of expansion cannot be reconciled with the complex descriptions of the changing processes of regulation. The formulation of regulatory modes as complex, continually mutating processes seeps through the grip of any absolute enunciation of expansion that promises simple descriptive closure.

The aporia leads to at least two difficulties for the early critics. First, in their bid to illustrate the state expansion thesis, they have focused on continuities between state (formal) and community (informal) forms of dispute resolution while largely ignoring possible discontinuities. This promotes a search for functional alliances between the state and community mediation at the expense of potentially non-functional dimensions of such a relationship. So, for example, although these critics often point to ways in which informal justice brings the state in closer contact with what were previously seen to be 'private' matters, they fail to examine how this very process renders state control indirect and indeterminate. Indeed, in as much as 'experts' act as relays to reconcile the goals of state authority with the immediacy of personal experience in mediation sessions, political domination becomes less direct and, at times, its outcomes are rendered less predictable.[46] The nature of resistance, therefore, needs to be analysed in different terms.

Secondly, and following from the previous point, most early critics' texts reflect a perplexing structure. Having rendered what appear to be decisive blows against community justice, most then conclude with a squeak of hope for its utopian, 'positive functions' (Santos 1982: 265) or its 'potentially liberating element' (Baskin 1988: 112).[47] The apparent incongruity between the bodies and conclusions of the texts is an outcome that might have been different if early critics had ventured beyond the limits of the state expansion thesis. In short, were community justice enunciated as something more than a residual feature of state expansion, then the discourse might have alighted upon nuanced depictions of idiomatic political or regulatory logics located within the deployment of particular community mediation programmes *sui generis*. Even if such logics may (and often do) intensify a state's regulation over everyday life, it is possible to conceive of situations in which these logics render state control indirect and unpredictable.

As Nikolas Rose usefully points out, regulatory innovations have 'frequently been made in order to cope, not with grand threats to the political order, but with local, petty and even marginal problems' (1990: 9). If nothing else, this serves as a sobering reminder not to exaggerate the importance of community justice to the modern state, and perhaps to seek articulations in a critical discourse at the margins of innovations. Without the latter, it is easy to see how critics can lapse into a 'despair' that engenders political apathy (see Matthews 1988). Ironically, it may even license an acceptance of adjudication by implying that 'the devil of formal justice whom we know may, after all, be better than his [sic] dangerously unfamiliar informal brother' (Cain 1988: 51). Stated somewhat differently, the early critics' calculations of community justice suppress a 'search for progressive alternatives' and may well encourage a capitulation to dominant calculations of justice (Matthews 1988: 17). Of course, this is not to condone the specious optimism of the advocates, but merely to endorse a more pragmatic assessment of the perils and prospects of community justice deployed under postmodern conditions. This is a point Harrington later seems to agree with when arguing that,

Rather than join those who would debate whether community mediation movements are autonomous from state control or not, what interests me about the politics of this movement is the simultaneous struggle for autonomy from the state and dependence on it for both legitimacy and clients.

(1992: 177)

And it is precisely this division between the dependence and autonomy, the mutual constitution of state and community justice, that requires further exploration. This is the 'problem' to which the following chapters are directed as they negotiate a theoretical path that tries to learn from the strengths of the early critics' discourse, and yet write out its paradoxical political pessimism.

5

REDRAWING CRITICAL LINES OF ENQUIRY
Foucault, power and community mediation

A second wave of criticism directed at community justice, initiated by various contributions to Matthews (1988), recasts the analytical problem to evade certain difficulties with both the advocates' and early critics' formulations. Designated as the 'new informalists', these critics explicitly renounce the advocates' unqualified optimism without falling prey to the pessimistic 'analytical despair' or 'adversarial nihilism' that flows from earlier critics.[1] Aside from the noted aporia, the existing debate has drawn a rigid battleline between those who are *for* and those who are *against* community mediation. And this, so the new informalists argue, has 'precluded the need for a detailed investigation of the political dynamics which were implicated in the expansion of informal justice' (Matthews 1988: 16). Consequently, critical discourse has opted for a certain political detachment, an apathy, and exonerated itself from confronting the perils and the political possibilities of contingently unfolding community justice calculations and practices. The upshot is an unduly state-conspiratorial view of community mediation that has promoted a 'chorus of despair' whose refrain is that nothing works (Cain 1988: 51, Matthews 1988: 17). In response to this situation, the new informalists analyse community justice in terms other than its being a necessary, functional elaboration of formal state legality. They try to distinguish (in a 'theoretically adequate way') between contingently located community mediation programmes on the basis of their contextual connections with state justice (Cain 1988: 51).

This move constitutes 'the law' in pluralistic terms that allow community mediation to be viewed as part of an existing dispute resolution arena, but amenable to independent, substantive analysis. Community mediation, then, may be viewed as a 'semi-autonomous' identity that is articulated to state dispute resolution mechanisms, but that also harbours autonomous dimensions. Its identity is a contested one, not inherently subsumed by state power, that could potentially resist specific calculations and practices of professionalised justice.[2] And this realisation, say the new informalists, is reason enough to 'take community justice seriously'. Notwithstanding the compromised form of its current deployment in many western countries, community mediation could, that is, assume a social identity directed at transforming rather than reinforcing inequitable professionalised judicial structures. The new informalists seek to conceptualise the political dynamics through which community justice is deployed in specific places, to grasp its perils and possibilities in context. Despite notable differences in the methods they use to assess danger, the new informalists all question the professionalised calculations of state justice and view community justice as neither inherently dangerous nor liberating. Instead informal justice is seen to be a contingent innovation of the 'social' domain that is itself a changing 'hybrid sphere which links up the "state" and "civil society"' (Matthews 1988: 18). Community mediation is located in the social domain, which is only partially regulated by the state and which serves to preserve the distinction between the state and non-state arenas. And it is from here that the new informalists develop their cautious engagement with community mediation. To gain some insight into the latter, it may be helpful to turn to Fitzpatrick's insightful accounts of informal/popular justice (1993, 1992a, 1992b, 1988).

FITZPATRICK: TAKING COMMUNITY JUSTICE SERIOUSLY

Fitzpatrick has conceptualised different aspects of popular/informal justice but, as with other new informalists, views it as neither an autonomous dispute resolution domain nor a mere residuum of state power. Apropos the former, his more recent work points to certain fundamental homologies between state and popular justice (1992a, 1992b, 1993). Despite claims to alternation, and even opposition, popular and formal justice share common mythical figures to which both appeal in the attempt to regulate action (1992b: 199–200). As such, there is a fundamental continuity between the popular and the formal to the extent that they appeal to core mythical figures, including the responsible, self-actualising individual and the natural pre-existing community. Such continuities militate against the advocates' claims to provide an alternative to state justice. Yet, Fitzpatrick insists, this does not mean that popular justice should be viewed as a mere expansion of formal state justice, as early critics allege. This is because the two forms of justice are 'interdependent but mutually and specifically resistant' (1993: 468).

But where does that leave the analysis? Fitzpatrick's response is to explore the division between the early critics and the advocates:

> I want to explore this divide, not to dismiss it or to dissolve it, much less to provide the resolution that it may seem to call for, but rather to see it and to see the work done around it as illuminating a key dynamic in modern modes of power.

> (1988: 182)

Both informal, popular and formal state justice are implicated in the operation of this power. Here he circumvents the advocate/early critics debate by re-conceptualising community justice as an emergent mode of power whose relations with existing patterns of state power require conceptual elaboration. For this reason, Fitzpatrick begins to analyse the sorts of power relations that comprise informal justice, and reflects on how these might link up with the power of formal (state) justice. Let us briefly canvass some insights from this essay, particularly as they pertain to the present text.

Fitzpatrick argues that informal justice is part of a developing trend towards informal, decentralised modes of exercising power in liberal democratic states.[3] In an effort to maintain its hegemonic dominance in the legal field, and thus to perpetuate a 'liberal social ordering', liberal legality has established a space for informal justice. This has become necessary because of a clash between the 'coercive authority' that grounds modern capitalist societies and the liberal democratic values that such societies espouse. As a means of avoiding legitimacy crises attracted by coercive enforcements of law, liberal legality increasingly relies on less visible forms of power; hence, the growing importance of confidential informal justice and the disciplinary techniques associated with it. Fitzpatrick draws on Foucault (1977b, 1978, 1980) to indicate the receding significance of hierarchical, centralised models of power that purport to emanate from a central force (sovereign) to dispersed subjects via the law.[4] Although not obsolete, the dominance of this model has been rivalled by disciplinary power of the kind embodied by informalism. This power operates in local, micro contexts to structure social fields within which individuals act. Fitzpatrick reworks Foucault's account of discipline to develop the latter's 'theoretically unelaborated' notion of resistance, and offers an account of the links between micro and macro powers. On the one hand, Fitzpatrick speaks of local, 'syncretic' powers, which take the form of ongoing, micro struggles. On the other hand, he points to a 'synoptic' power, which is the composite of syncretic powers seeking to 'unify component powers into a singular power' (1988: 188). Synoptic power produces a 'working map' of the complex struggles within and between component syncretic power relations at a given point in history. Such power is neither stable, nor static, nor a 'settled resultant'; instead, it is in constant flux, changing in tandem with the ongoing struggles and resistances in the multiple local contexts from which it emerges. There is a constitutive and recursive articulation of syncretic and synoptic powers, a link that is sustained through techniques of discipline and normalisation. The ensuing disciplinary power is not simply repressive, for, out of the relentless struggles, various positive social identities (e.g. law, community mediation) are produced.

Within this framework, Fitzpatrick characterises informal justice as a disciplinary mechanism that helps to preserve the synoptic hegemony of law. Informalism has developed as the 'dark side' of law since the law 'relies integrally on disciplinary powers to constitute a massive, non-rebellious normality' (1988: 190). That is, law is a synoptic power that emerges out of disciplinary mechanisms that link up component syncretic powers, and creates the 'general space' within which particular forms of informal justice operate (1988: 191). It does this, in part, because of its very constitution. Thus the law is not simply a negative mechanism of restraint on the natural, 'unbounded freedom' of the individual subject, as liberal conceptions may insist. Fitzpatrick does not accept that individual subjects are 'natural' in any primordial sense, but rather sees them as continuously crafted by techniques of disciplinary power. So, to the extent that law is predicated upon the 'unbounded freedom' of an individual 'subject', its very identity requires a space in which this may be produced. It creates an informal domain, an 'area of action in which the subject is "free" to accept the dictates of disciplinary power' (1988: 190). This domain is presented as one of 'freedom', self-realisation, non-power, and in so doing masks the disciplinary techniques used to create so-called 'normal' individuals.

Simultaneously, however, the informal domain bolsters the integrity of law by 'coming between' the syncretic and synoptic dimensions of law. It does this in order to buffer the contradiction that arises because the law presents itself as an independent and universal power yet it can do so only as a result of local disciplinary power. We have already alluded to ways in which informalism obscures the disciplinary grounds for the 'natural' and 'free' legal subject. But it also 'accommodates' the opposition between the universal and the particular aspects of law in two related ways: first, it reduces or 'disaggregates' collective challenges to the legal system and translates these into support for the law (1988: 193); and, secondly, it individualises conflicts and deals with them in informal contexts where they are unlikely to call the integrity of law into question. Furthermore, by counterposing itself to formal law, informal justice obscures the fact that it is a 'constitutive condition' of law. As such, the informal social field is seen to be integrally related to its legal counterpart. Indeed, they are deemed to be 'mutually constitutive' (1988: 190).

Clearly, then, Fitzpatrick presents informal justice as a site where the disciplinary powers integral to the continued existence of the liberal state and its legality are exercised. However, even if informal justice is partially constituted by the legal field, it harbours autonomous aspects, just as the legal field is never completely encompassed by the state.[5] As a buffer between the synoptic and syncretic dimensions of modern law, community justice resides in a definite space – even if unstable and transient – that is not entirely embraced by the state or law. As such, there is an 'unembedded' dimension to community justice that serves as a possible basis from which to resist the hegemony of formal legality. But Fitzpatrick is clear that such resistance is not evident in current calculations and practices of community justice, even in its more radical versions (1993, 1992a). What he has in mind is a more concerted attempt to develop a transformative politics of law out of the 'silences' of the unembedded dimensions of community justice. The point here is to unearth the subjugated discourses that are excluded by the enunciations of both informal and formal justice, of popular and state legal justices. He then tries to grapple with the requirements of a counter-power that will have to engage with present forms of power, but which sets the terms of its engagement outside of these (1988: 197).

The poignancy of Fitzpatrick's arguments render the text worthy of considerable attention. Consonant with the new informalist attempt to take community justice seriously, Fitzpatrick offers a useful exit from the limiting and paradoxical formulations of the early critics. By conceptualising informal justice as a key element in the shifting patterns of power-knowledge that comprise social being at a given moment, his approach licenses an analysis of the power relations established by community justice as well as the manner in which such power is articulated to state control. Hence, he considers informalism without reducing it to, or declaring it as necessarily independent of, state power. In turn, this allows him to offer a nuanced account of resistance to the patterns of power-knowledge relations that arise from the deployment of informal justice. It also permits a subtle critique of the regulatory patterns associated with community justice, and provides a map of its perils, indicating possible strategies to resist these. Aside from thus breaking the political apathy of early formulations, he has also forged a useful link between his version of informalism as a power beyond the state and Foucault's work on discipline. Yet, Fitzpatrick is sensitive to the notion that Foucault may have underestimated the continued importance of law in contemporary power-knowledge configurations, and takes account of this in his formulations.[6]

Achievements of this order are certainly formidable, especially in the context of a single essay. However, there are at least two areas where it might be extended in order to analyse the community justice power complex in greater detail. First, Fitzpatrick has clearly indicated the relevance of Foucault's approach to the new informalists' vision of the community justice problem, but his particular interpretation emphasises the so-called Foucauldian 'middle period' (see Bernauer 1990: 142–148). Were one to apply some of Foucault's later insights to the context of community justice, it might be possible to expand upon elements that are missing from existing analyses. For instance, given the confessions, or public disclosures, required of disputants in community mediation, there is a *prima facie* case for taking seriously the role of confessional techniques, and perhaps a wider 'pastoral power', in an analysis of the mediation process. As such, community mediation could be explored not only as a conduit for individualising disciplinary power, but also as a means by which political technologies to shape the self-identities of disputants are deployed (see Foucault 1982, 1981b, 1981d). As Foucault would later say in relation to his previous work on discipline,

> If one wants to analyze the genealogy of the subject in Western civilisation, one has to take into account, not only techniques of domination, but also techniques of self. One has to show the interaction between these types of technique ... What we call discipline is something really important ... But it is only one aspect of the art of governing people in our societies.
>
> (1981c: 5; see also Burchell 1993: 268)

So, the disputing subject of mediation is not only a product of discipline but also a result of the modes by which such individuals are encouraged to embrace particular subjective identities.[7] Analysing this dimension of mediation is likely to entail, as the above citation indicates, a focus on what Foucault terms the art of government and the deployment of particular technologies of self (see B. Smart 1995).

Secondly, such an analysis might be articulated to a series of issues that, somewhat more contentiously, extend both Fitzpatrick's and Foucault's analyses. Their investigations seem to accept that, under modern conditions, liberal political rationalities have legitimated the ascendancy of disciplinary power that came to displace the dominant political location occupied by the law and sovereign model of power in pre-modern societies (Foucault 1977b, 1980, 1981b). The rise of discipline in early forms of governmentality was the 'dark side' of a liberalism that maintains 'there is always too much government' (Foucault 1981b: 354–355; see also Gordon 1991, Burchell 1991, 1993). Yet, as Foucault later argues, power relations outside the state extend beyond the disciplines and indeed appear to be poised on the brink of further elaboration with the ascendancy of neo-liberal thinking and its attempts to 'extend the rationality of the market by proposing schema for analysis and suggesting criteria for decisions in domains that are neither exclusively or primarily economic' (1981b: 359). Crudely stated, the point I am driving at here is as follows: if discipline and/or some versions of government were legitimated by liberal political rationalities under modern conditions, then it might well be appropriate to consider neo-liberal rationalities as legitimating different political practices under postmodern conditions. Discipline remains important within neo-liberal government, but emphasis is also placed on deploying techniques of self to condition the self-identities of the individual consumers and their 'lifestyles' in a postmodern ethos (Turner 1994, T. Miller 1993, Bonner and du Guy 1992, Bauman 1992). This issue forces one to confront community justice as an element of a fragmented justice, whose calculations and practices embrace particular (neo-liberal) political rationalities and techniques under postmodern conditions. As indicated in chapter 2, devoid of the faith in universal principles, singular rationalities and indeed innately rational subjects, the calculations of justice become ordered around markedly different practices and idioms (e.g. community mediation).

In view of this, one might well extend critical discussions of community justice to contemplate the political technologies that its processes introduce under specifically postmodern conditions (e.g. technologies of self-formation). At the same time, it seems appropriate to draw out certain dimensions to the new informalists' diverse attempts to diagnose the perils of community mediation. No doubt, the quest to attenuate existing narratives in the two ways indicated above will require some reflection upon how to orientate the task of redrawing critical maps. That is, a reflexive theoretical task is required to orientate any analyst wishing to develop particular discursive spaces. By what grid of intelligibility is one to proceed? What pitfalls ought one to consider? What elements are to be colonised as moments? Such questions have led me to reconsider certain Foucauldian texts to clear particular spaces and orientate the analysis in ways that the final two chapters of this book follow. Thus, for the remainder of this chapter let us return to elements of Foucault's thinking to focus on ways in which to re-conceive the critical map, the 'grid of intelligibility', out of which substantive analyses of community mediation under postmodern conditions may emerge.

INTERPRETING FOUCAULT: METHODOLOGICAL PRECAUTIONS

A central tenet of Foucault's approach is its consistent refusal to equate power with centralised manifestations at a given point in history (e.g. the state; 1980: 95).[8] As he argues, 'power is not an institution and not a structure; neither is it a certain strength we are endowed with; it is a name that one attributes to a complex strategical situation in a particular society' (1978: 93).[9] Any strategic situation is transient, and never contained within the boundaries of a single, formal authority. This insight has prompted Foucault's thoughtful analyses of such political technologies as discipline, bio-power and government (1977b, 1978, 1979). In attempting to redraw aspects of the critical maps provided by early critics and new informalists, I shall mine the rich seams of Foucault's thought on such notions as discipline, techniques of self, pastoral power and government, especially as they pertain to community justice. My interpretation will be structured around five methodological precautions that Foucault offers as a way of approaching power relations (1980: 96–102).

Power outside the state

Since Foucault argues that 'power isn't localized in the State apparatus', he examines power as it operates at 'a much more minute and everyday level' (1980: 60). As such, and contrary to the early critics' formulations, if one is concerned with the power of community mediation, 'one cannot confine oneself to analyzing the State apparatus alone if one wants to grasp the mechanisms of power in their detail and complexity' (1980: 72). In other words, like the new informalists, Foucault warns against reducing power to its centralised manifestations.[10] The state is not to be regarded as an essentially unified entity from which all power derives; rather, it is a 'nominal' entity that is but a subset of all power relations in a given society. The implication here is that some power relations are qualitatively different from the formal state's nominally differentiated power relations, and it is this very difference to which Foucault directs his attention. Consequently, he asks us to look beyond the 'limited field of judicial sovereignty and state institutions, and instead base our analysis of power on the study of techniques and tactics of domination' (Foucault 1980: 102).

Foucault's exploration of power tactics 'outside, below and alongside' the state yields productive results. He notes that the tactics of pre-modern societies involve power-knowledge relations centred around a 'law and sovereign' model (1980; see also Gordon 1991 and Burchell 1991). In this model, the political problem revolves around an attempt to extract 'a single will – or rather the constitution of a unitary, singular body animated by the spirit of sovereignty – from the particular wills of a multiplicity of individuals' (Foucault 1980: 97). The law and sovereign model enunciates a political logic premised upon hierarchy: power emanates from the will of an absolute sovereign and is exercised over a principality or territory. In this configuration, power is exercised through law over citizens within a given jurisdiction with the aim of reinforcing the absolute strength of the sovereign. A central political technology in such societies is the spectacle, as instanced by public executions, through which the absolute power of the sovereign is graphically underscored (Foucault 1977b). By contrast, in modern societies, and in the wake of urbanisation, industrialisation, bureaucratic administration and rapid population growth, the dominance of the law and sovereign model is increasingly displaced by the spread of a political innovation that is both more efficient, and less visibly coercive, than spectacles. The innovation in question is, of course, disciplinary power, which Foucault (1977b) has so eloquently explored, and which has now attracted a vast secondary literature (e.g. Dreyfus and Rabinow 1982, B. Smart 1985, McNay 1992, 1994). In contrast to the spectacle, the object that simultaneously exercises this disciplinary power is the modern, live individual (i.e. a biologically rather than a legally specified entity). By subtly shaping the bodily comportments of individuals, discipline creates agents that are both economically productive and politicly docile – both regulatory products being most favourable to the continued expansion of capitalism and the development of 'the great administrative monarchies' (Foucault 1977b: 220–221).

Disciplinary processes directly imply the rationalising impetus of disciplinary knowledge and many of the problematics associated with liberal critiques of the law and sovereign model (Foucault 1981a). These processes were directed at regulating individual comportment outside of the visibly coercive mechanisms of the sovereign's legality and beyond the rubric of state power. Power here operates by rendering individuals observable to a hierarchical gaze that has the semblance of ubiquity only because its presence is never clearly visible. This quasi invisibility has the important political effect of allowing power to be exercised in a continuous, unobtrusive and thus efficient way. As discipline escapes the surrounds of its founding institutions (quarantining plagues; the army, the school, the prison, etc.), as its gaze comes to focus on more and more aspects of live individuals in their daily actions, so the pre-modern 'society of law' comes to be replaced by the carceral 'society of regulation'. The live individual of the disciplines is superimposed over the abstract citizen of judicial knowledge, and in the end comes to overshadow the latter. However, the disciplines continue to make use of the symbolic capital that can be extracted from the latter. As such, the language of law remains current even as the disciplines become more and more central to the preservation of the older language of rights. This is why, for Foucault, the disciplines constitute the 'dark side' of liberal law through which the requirements of the state and its liberties are secured (e.g. Foucault 1977b: 222–223).

Even if Foucault here focuses on 'micro processes' of power, he recognises that these political techniques beyond (but related to) the state tend to form wider strategic envelopes in given contexts (1978: 94–95). At first he refers to a 'carceral archipelago' of disciplinary power, but later offers a rather more precise analysis of generalised tendencies of modern disciplinary power through the concepts of bio-power within populations, and then to the notion of governmentality (1978, 1979, 1981a-d). With respect to the last of these, Foucault explores the ways in which sixteenth-century discursive concerns with 'security' directed at 'reason of state' in diplomatic-military knowledges and a 'police science' helped to generalise local tactics into an emerging pattern of liberal government outside the state (1979, 1981b, 1981d and especially 1981a: 240–241). Foucault notes the importance of the concept 'population' to this new generalised envelope, and shows how it attracts different power-knowledge relations directed at the size, wealth, health and welfare of given populations. In the process, the problematic of government is recast around the living, breathing individuals who comprise populations (cf. the strength of a sovereign *vis-à-vis*

90

citizens). Such government, however, is deployed under the guise of limiting state intervention, even if its techniques are designed to preserve the strength of the liberal state (1981b, 1981d, 1982). Over the centuries, as governmental envelopes have developed beyond yet alongside the state, the art of government has assumed an increasingly prominent role in contemporary societies.

But does this mean that the state, despite its apparent dominance in our everyday lives, is a decoy? Certainly, critics such as Poulantzas (1978) and Hunt (1993) argue that Foucault has prematurely 'expelled' law and state from existing power relations, and certainly there are passages in Foucault's work that will sustain this interpretation. Equally, however, there are moments that indicate a somewhat different reading where the state is rendered possible by virtue of an increasing articulation with technologies of power beyond the law and sovereign model (B. Smart 1985, Fitzpatrick 1988). For example, Foucault notes that:

> I do not want to say that ... the institutions of justice tend to disappear, but rather that the law operates more as a norm, and that the judicial institution is increasingly incorporated into a continuum of apparatuses (medical, administrative, and so on) whose functions are for the most part regulatory.

> (1978: 144)

In this sense the power relations of the formal state, modelled as they are according to law and sovereignty, are seen to undergo a fundamental transformation as the state is re-positioned within a modern, liberal political order. In such an environment, where disciplinary regulation prevails, the state's coercive apparatuses are limited in favour of those that promote 'normal' individual liberty. Foucault tries to elucidate the political techniques by which such normal individual freedom is produced in modern societies.

With this precaution in mind, one might well consider community mediation as an instance of power outside the state, but which is constitutively implicated in the latter's continued survival. Community mediation is one of various sites that create the 'empowered' individuals who are capable of choice and who strengthen the community. It is not a simple expansion of state power, but is rather more actively involved in changing the ways by which liberal power configurations are buttressed. One might therefore locate community mediation as one of many governmental powers that operate in the shadows, on the dark side, of the law and sovereign model. In this sense, Foucault is correct to suggest that '[m]aybe what is really important for our modern times, that is for our actuality, is not so much the State-domination of society, but the "governmentalization" of the state' (1979: 20).[11] Community mediation, then, is very much part of the governmentalisation of the state; it is one of several processes through which the art of government operates in contemporary society. But how are we to approach community mediation as a mode of governmental power outside the state? Here I turn to the second of Foucault's orientating precautions.

The power of government

Aside from arguing that power is not encompassed by the state, Foucault also offers a particular approach to power that suggests a specific way of viewing government. He develops a non-substantive, non-essential and 'bottom up' view of power as no more than the name that is attributed to complex and contingent patterns by which attempts are made to structure fields of action. In short, power is no more than the diverse attempts to regulate action by 'guiding the possibility of conduct and putting in order the possible outcome' (1982: 221).[12] Implicit in this conception is the notion that power can be exercised only over people who are capable of action. That is, it is exercised only over agents, 'who are faced with a field of possibilities in which several ways of behaving, several reactions and diverse comportments may be realized' (1982: 221). Thus power relations operate in fields in which they have several courses of action open to them, such as the purportedly informal domains of the community. This openness of action (relative though it inevitably is) and the continuous possibility of intransigence give to power relations the form of relentless provocations and reaction.[13] Although power relations may assume the appearance of stability, this merely indicates the relative success of given political patterns – yet these can always be upset by the possibility of actions that successfully resist existing forms of control.[14] This implies that power is not simply a repressive or negative phenomenon imposed from 'above' a society; on the contrary, it is rooted in local matrices of social relations. As such, it is much more 'productive' than 'repressive' for 'it traverses and produces things, it induces pleasure, forms knowledge, produces discourse' (1980: 119).

The power of community justice thus deploys various governmental practices that structure fields of action in such a way as to decrease hostilities between individual disputants to 'restore' peace to 'communities'. But how should we understand the notion of government? A close reading of Foucault's various remarks on government, or governmentality, indicates his rather equivocal uses of the terms (Burchell 1993). The neologism 'governmentality' is meant to evoke themes around 'conducting conduct' by structuring individual 'mentalities' (Foucault 1979). It is, however, a clumsy term that Foucault seems (for the most part) to replace with the term 'government'. Even so, the new choice of term does not rescind Foucault's equivocal uses of the underlying concept. Let us take two examples, indicating perhaps the value of reflexively working through an interpretation. First, in some places he speaks of government(ality) as a concept that operates at the same level as discipline and sovereignty. So he tells us, against the view that government yields successively to sovereignty, 'in reality we have a triangle: sovereignty, discipline and government, which has as its primary target the population and as its essential mechanism apparatuses of security' (1979: 19). In this use, discipline and government are rendered as similar, and analytically comparable, concepts. However, this conception is contradicted elsewhere when he speaks of discipline as 'only one aspect of the art of governing people in our societies' (Foucault 1981c: 5). Here, clearly, discipline is subsumed as an element of government, which is now construed as a wider umbrella term. Second, we are told, against his previous separation of sovereignty and government, that government be regarded as 'a manner of directing a group of individuals which was more and more typified by the exercise of sovereign power' (1981b: 219–220). The significance of this statement might be questioned in view of its status as a course outline, and perhaps even as a product of translation, but it does little to rectify the confusing levels of abstraction at which Foucault simultaneously mobilises the term government.

In an attempt to clarify these contradictory uses, I propose that the term government be considered at a level of abstraction that takes account of why Foucault evoked it in the first place. That is, he uses the concept 'government' to conceptualise power outside the state, and as such it would seem analytically comparable with sovereignty. On this reading, sovereignty, with its characteristic law and sovereign model of power exercised over legal citizens, should be counterposed with government. Here, discipline is considered on a different conceptual plane, in that it is one of various techniques of power that characterise governmental power, much like the judiciary is to sovereignty. Of course, government, through its disciplinary techniques, is associated with live individuals rather than abstract judicial citizens and so operates according to a model of power that is different from that of the state's law and sovereign model. In some texts, Foucault (1981b, 1981d) might be seen to suggest a pastoral model of power as appropriate for government (see next section). Nevertheless, and here we reach the nub of the issue, Foucault argues that government is 'an activity of attempting to guide individuals throughout their lives, and placing them under an authority of one who is responsible for what they do, and what happens to them' (1981a: 239). It refers to an ensemble of techniques and procedures that are directed at people's 'conduct' and produce particular kinds of subjectivities at given moments in history. In this respect, government is not only concerned with the creation of disciplined individuals, but also deploys various technologies of self to help shape the self-identities of the disciplined individuals. Reports of a lecture that Foucault delivered provide a concise definition of government as 'the points where technologies of domination of individuals over one another have recourse to the processes by which the individual acts upon himself. And conversely, [one] has to take into account the point where technologies of self are integrated into structures of coercion or domination' (cited in Keenan 1982: 38).

In short, my reading of Foucault on government indicates both that techniques of discipline and self are deeply implicated in the formation of the (neo-)liberal subject, and that government is the synoptic ensemble of the ways in which the two techniques operate and interact (Table 1 provides a summary of my interpretation). But government is not only directed at individual subjects; its pastoral model also operates through – and regulates these subjects in – particular totalities (e.g. the population, society, community). That is, over and above shaping individual subjects, the art of government has created discursive spaces for such political totalities as: populations for the biological regulation of groups through bio-power (Foucault 1978); the 'social' for regulation through social welfarism (Donzelot 1979, 1991); and the 'community' for the neo-liberal control of postmodern subjectivities. Consequently, community mediation might be understood as a governmental form that is directed at individual disputing selves as members of assumed communities, and which mobilises techniques of discipline and self with the aim of reconciling disputants in order to 'restore' peace to communities. In this conceptualisation lies a pastoral model of power to which I now turn.

Table 1 A proposed framework for Foucault on government

	Model of power	Local object of power	General objects of power	Political technologies
Sovereignty	Law and sovereign	Abstract judicial subject – the 'citizen'	Territory, principality, jurisdiction	Spectacles, highly visible symbols of law
Government	Pastoral	Live individuals and selves	Population, the social, community	Discipline, techniques of self

Pastoral power

Foucault offers a third precaution, which advises the enquirer not to presume that power emerges from a single societal source, because there are diverse forms of power that emanate from different loci. For instance, in liberal societies, the law and sovereign model associated with state forms has increasingly been articulated to the pastoral model of government. Each model deploys a different political rationality and employs different technologies of power. I have already alluded to the bases of the law and sovereign model, but let me here make some brief remarks on how to approach the pastoral model in question. Although Foucault may not have aligned government and pastoral power as explicitly or closely as I have proposed, various references to pastorship indicate its significance to his thinking (1988, 1982, 1981a, 1981b, 1981d, 1978). This model of power is concerned with simultaneously regulating singular entities and wider totalities. That is, pastorship achieves a totalised order by addressing the needs of each individual life. Evoking the metaphor of a shepherd attending a flock, Foucault (1981d) depicts pastoral power as deploying techniques of control that focus on the details of each individual member's life, on the assumption that the well-being of each sheep is ultimately related to the well-being of the entire herd. There is a recursive and almost paradoxical relationship between the one and the many.

So, a central problem for a pastoral model of power is to seek order by attempting to reconcile each with all (hence Foucault's title, *Omnes et Singulatim* – 1981d). Although initially directed at congregants of a congregation, pastorship has expanded well beyond its ecclesiastical roots to provide a basic model for various forms of government, from the regulation of live individuals in a population, or society, to the disputing selves of postmodern communities, which will be considered in more detail in the next chapter. In any case, if community mediation is to be considered as a contemporary instance of this pastoral model, then clearly the precaution indicates the importance of exploring how this power operates at a totalising and individual level, and grasping the relationship between these in context. No doubt, too, one would have to understand how this pastoral model relates to contemporary forms of the law and sovereign model, and point to the emerging effects of their associations.

Power-knowledge

The fourth precaution proposes that we do not lose sight of the constitutive relations between techniques of power and associated knowledges. For Foucault, power is always present in the formation of any knowledge or calculation, just as knowledge produces a facilitative facade for the exercise of particular power relations. That is, 'there is no power relation without the correlative constitution of a field of knowledge, nor any knowledge that does not presuppose and constitute at the same time power relations' (Foucault 1977b: 27). Thus truth is inextricably articulated to power and, as such, every society has a 'régime of truth', a 'general politics' related to the production of veracity (1980: 131). At the omnifarious points where power and knowledge converge, one finds intricate webs of discourse that are scattered throughout the social network. But this does not mean that discourse is always subservient to power, or vice versa; instead, altered discourses imply altered power formations, just as shifts in power are facilitated by the introduction of different knowledges. Of particular interest to the ensuing analysis is the notion that the calculations of community justice through which mediation is deployed, and through which its political techniques are legitimated, imply directly the formation of alternative power-knowledge-subjectivity regimes into the dispute resolution complex of western societies. Perhaps, as indicated in chapter 2, the auspices of a modern ethos have given way to a postmodern ethos with its fragmented calculations of justice, and these have licensed the pastoral power of government that operates in community mediation settings.

Individuals and selves

Finally, Foucault warns against viewing power as something that emanates from natural, *a priori* individuals or selves. 'Individuals,' he tells us, 'are the vehicles of power, not its points of application' (1980: 98). This suggests that there is no absolute, 'natural' form of the subject and so power cannot be contingent upon its presumed existence. Instead power 'circulates' through 'a net-like organization' whereby individuals (or collections of these) are simultaneously created as subjects as well as constitute 'objects' for specific power relations.[15] That is, '[o]ne has to dispense with the constituent subject, to get rid of the subject itself, that's to say, to arrive at an analysis which can account for the constitution of the subject within a historical framework' (1980: 117). This can be taken to indicate that governed subjects are produced by processes of governance, and thus they will assume different forms depending upon the governmental rationalities involved. That is, for one form of government there are members of a congregation to be led; for another, living individual species whose lives must be carefully nurtured. Perhaps too, there are free, individual disputing selves of a community who must be given an 'opportunity' to create their own settlements 'voluntarily'. Thus, the individual selves of community mediation are not natural, pre-given entities that exist independently of power relations; nor is the community a fixed manifestation with an inherent nature. As Fitzpatrick puts it, 'neither the community, nor the individual has an intrinsic, holistic content. Theirs is a constrained, attenuated content, created and bound within the operation of a specific type of power' (Fitzpatrick 1992b: 205).

Now, as I have suggested, community mediation may be seen as a type of government that deploys a pastoral model and mobilises various political technologies to help forge particular kinds of individual selves within wider communities. In particular, community mediation deploys techniques of discipline *and* techniques of self in a quest to change individual conduct and self-identities in such a way that disputants settle their conflict in order to restore peaceful relations between them. Discipline is involved, as Fitzpatrick notes, with the creation of normal individuals and structuring their comportment in particular ways. And, as Foucault adds, '[d]iscipline "makes" individuals; it is the specific technique of a power that regards individuals both as objects and as instruments of its exercise' (1977b: 170). These created individuals also acquire self-identities through techniques of self. Such techniques of self have to do with

> the way in which the subject constitutes himself [*sic*] in an active fashion, by practices of self; these practices are nevertheless not something that the individual invents by himself. They are patterns that he finds in his culture and which are proposed, suggested and imposed on him by his culture, his society and his social group.
>
> (Foucault 1988c: 11)

They are the ways in which individuals 'affect their own bodies, souls, thoughts and conduct so as to form and transform themselves' (B. Smart 1985: 108). Community mediation can be considered as a regulatory space that applies social pressure to the individuals that it helps to create by promulgating an interdiction that requires disputants to confess, or discursively articulate, particular kinds of knowledge about their 'selves' for the watchful gaze of the mediator.

The interaction between techniques of discipline and self can be considered as part of the ensemble of techniques through which community mediation governs. It also indicates the rising tide of a regulatory environment that seems to be moving further away from the modern ethos in which disciplinary techniques have flourished. Indeed, one might suggest – picking up on a previously introduced theme – that the (re-)emergence of techniques of self indicates shifting political rationalities and modes of regulation under postmodern conditions. There are various indications to support this view. For instance, under post-Fordist regimes of accumulation, consumerism is deemed to be as essential as production is to the circulation of capital (Liepitz 1988, Aglietta 1979). Here the individual as consumer, and not merely producer, relies on the production of subjective motivations for the expansion of 'enterprise culture' with its consumer-orientated lifestyles (Bonner and du Guy 1992, B. Smart 1992, Weinstein 1991, Baskin 1988). Second, discipline may have been central to the creation and preservation of the social domains of the modern welfare state. The rise of such disciplines as sociology was part of the deployment of a social domain that was to provide liberalism with a modern elaboration of civil society (Donzelot 1991, Burchell 1991). Threats to the integrity of the social order tend to be contained in isolated disciplinary institutions designed to normalise individuals (prisons, hospitals, etc.). Under postmodern conditions, with a significant attack on social welfare through deregulation, privatisation, and so on, the integrity of the social domain has also come under attack. As noted in chapter 1, an effect of such attacks has been the rise, and perhaps re-emergence, of the 'community' as a more effective means of providing voluntary regulation than could be obtained from the social. Community justice, then, is but one example of the segmented social domain and the movement towards community-based (rather than social) control. Such communities tend to be regulated through actuarially based calculations of risk, and individuals given the responsibility to secure (insure) their own futures (Castel 1991, Ewald 1991, Simon 1988, 1987). This regulatory shift implies the formation of different subjectivities as parts of the complicated risk calculations, and this implies different techniques of self. Finally, taking heed of the previous precaution, it seems that, whereas the disciplines might once have been aligned with the deployment of early modern liberal political rationalities, under postmodern conditions neo-liberal discourses align themselves with a somewhat different set of political rationalities.

In tandem, these indications suggest that, under postmodern conditions, both individuals and selves are vehicles for the power of community mediation that governs through techniques of discipline and self. As a contemporary instance of pastorship, community mediation aims to reconstitute the individual comportments and self-identities of disputants in ways that settle conflict. The emerging forms of discipline and techniques of self offered through the mediation process indicate a certain change in the 'social pressures' that are brought to bear upon people as they shape their bodily comportments and actively constitute themselves as selves. In this sense, community mediation provides one of the ways in which the pastoral model of government is in the process of reorientating itself to the altered worlds of postmodern and/or neo-liberal regulatory environments.

A REDRAWN MAP: FOUCAULT, CRITICISM AND COMMUNITY MEDIATION

The interpretation offered above indicates a possible way of orientating attempts to extend the critical discourse around community mediation. In particular, it suggests the value of working within the discursive spaces cleared by new informalists, but extending them to consider in more detail the political rationality of community mediation under postmodern conditions. This dovetails with chapter 2's recognition of an altered ethos where justice is fragmented, and where calculations and the enforcement of justice no longer aspire to the singular unity extracted from a modern ethos. Reinterpreting Foucault's conception of government around the five methodological precautions provides a way of redrawing certain parts of a critical map through which to diagnose the perils of community justice.

Consonant with the new informalist vision, the above interpretation suggests that the power of community mediation be considered not simply as a feature of the power-knowledge relations termed the 'state'. Instead, it calls for us to view community mediation as an instance of a political rationality that operates outside of, but is intimately associated with, state power. The interpretation leads one to conceive of the political rationality of community mediation as a type of government. The latter is understood as an ensemble of political technologies directed at forming, and regulating the comportment of, living individual selves situated in the totality of a community. The local techniques of government are heuristically bifurcated into techniques of discipline creating individual bodies, and techniques of self implicated in the formation of particular self-identities. But there are also more totalising techniques that seek to integrate these individual selves within the wider locales of community. The integration between techniques of discipline and self, and the linking of individual selves with wider community aims, point to the operation of what may be termed (following an admittedly partial version of Foucault) a pastoral model of power. This model is adapting itself to the vicissitudes of postmodern conditions where the profile of techniques of self has been raised and the regulated totality in question has shifted from a unified social domain of the welfare state to the dispersed communities of altered regulatory environments. All such changes in power directly imply an alternation in knowledge and vice versa. With these bases for a redrawn critical chart, an altered grid of intelligibility, I can return to an analysis of my case study. Community mediation in British Columbia might then be analysed around three nodal questions.

First, given the calculations and practices of justice outlined in chapter 3, it seems appropriate to ask, by what logic of government does community mediation seek to regulate action? As we have seen in British Columbia, the purported failure of the lower courts to provide effective justice to individual community members locked in disputes has opened up the space for advocates to claim a purported need for community justice. In response to this 'need' one sees the deployment of different fields of action within which calculations and practices of community justice become both possible and acceptable. Analysing the rationality of governance within such fields can be seen as part of a wider quest to understand 'through the operation of what practices of government and by what kind of political reasoning have we been led to recognise our self-identity as members of those somewhat indefinite global entities we call community, society, nation or state?' (Burchell 1991: 120). The deployment of power-knowledge-subjectivity relations that claim the rubric of community mediation in British Columbia implies a political rationality that uses political technologies of both discipline and self. Neither the rationality nor the technologies have attracted sustained analytic attention. In an attempt at redress, one might here see the possibility of exploring the governmental form that the British Columbia case implies. Stated differently, one might conceive of community mediation as a 'practice of government (who can govern; what governing is; what or who is governed) capable of making some form of activity thinkable and practicable both to its practitioners and to those upon whom it was practised' (Gordon 1991: 3). Conceived thus, I have argued, one might well explore community mediation as an instance of pastoral government under postmodern conditions.

Secondly, in view of the first precaution discussed above, and the clear warning not to underestimate the continued significance of power in the name of state law (to which advocates contrast community mediation), it seems important to consider the following question: how is the government of community mediation related to the courts' state-legal models of power? More particularly, this question seems to require an analysis of the means by which the different political rationalities of the courts and of community mediation, respectively, are articulated within dispute resolution arenas under postmodern conditions. Hence, by drawing on the previous questions' attempt to elaborate upon the 'pastoral model' of power in community mediation, and locating this in relation to the 'law and sovereign' model of the courts, it becomes possible to offer a more precise analysis of their links in the context of British Columbia. In other words, the auspices of the articulations between the formal state legality and community mediation can help to develop a strategic map of the emerging dispute resolution complex that operates in the name of justice.

Finally, with the developing charts of the political rationality in a contemporary dispute resolution complex, one can begin to ask this question: what are the possible dangers contained in the current articulation between community and formal calculations and practices of justice? The question resonates with a perplexing paradox in the early critics' discourse, which harboured a recurring hope that informalism might lead to a progressive social transformation (Matthews 1988). The underlying assumption is the hope that community justice can provide a more hospitable, fair and socially just means of resolving disputes than might be expected from court adjudication. This echoes the eternal promise of justice, the mystical idea of paradoxical attempts to calculate the incalculable, to render finite what is infinite. And it is this promise that drives new informalist critical explorations into past calculations and practices, with the hope of opening a different discourse that would imply different calculations and practices.[16] Deconstruction, let us recall Derrida, 'is justice'. Our text's deconstructions must cease at the point where it locates certain dangers implied by the articulated political rationalities of courts and community mediation, and consider what this might mean for future calculations and practices of community justice.

Of course, orientating the process of redrawing critical maps in the ways suggested above raises a number of issues and many critics will object to its formulation in ways that I may not anticipate. Yet there are a number of issues and problems, particularly relating to Foucault's approach, that I have worked through in arriving at some of the above proposals. It may be of some use to readers to examine these briefly, before proceeding to the elaborations of the final two chapters.

CAN FOUCAULT TAKE COMMUNITY MEDIATION SERIOUSLY?

One issue that many will raise concerns whether the suggested Foucauldian approach will permit useful strategic engagement with community mediation under postmodern conditions. In particular, various criticisms have been directed at Foucault's work, attacking its supposed inability to produce an emancipatory form of politics.[17] A uniting theme amongst these various criticisms is that Foucault's anti-essentialism, his propensity to historicise everything, goes too far, leading to a problematic strand of relativism and/or nihilism (Levin 1989). Many critics of his work argue (appealing implicitly to a modern auspice) that, without an Archimedean point of reference outside of given historical contexts, there is no basis from which to ground one's critique (Habermas 1986, Walzer 1986, Taylor 1986), nor any reason to accept that a future society will be any better than the present (Soper 1986; 1990, Dews 1987, Taylor 1986). Moreover, against Foucault's anti-humanist stance, some critics contend that, without a conception of concrete agency, an absolute 'subject' whose real form is somehow repressed by historical conditions, the very idea of freedom has limited content.[18] A variation on this theme is that if power is so ubiquitous, inescapable even, then why bother to resist? (Soper 1986).

In many ways, the critiques indicate an irresolvable confrontation between modern and postmodern auspices, with critics appealing to a modern ethos to mount an attack on Foucault's approach, which explicitly places itself in a subversive relation to modern conditions, as a 'counter-modernity' orientation (1984: 39). The confrontation, therefore, may be seen to place us squarely within a wider debate between conceptions of political change under modern versus postmodern conditions.[19] With specific reference to the political aspects of these debates, Foucault's critics tend to believe that, although the project of modernity has wandered somewhat off course, it is ultimately a valid one that can be salvaged and rejuvenated by repositioning it on its founding (liberal or Marxist) tracks (see Bauman 1992, B. Smart 1992, Agger 1991, Lash 1990, Habermas 1987).[20] By contrast, the preceding analysis has attempted to place its analyses in a political world without grand theories or grand emancipatory projects.[21] Despite his reluctance to be associated as a protagonist of either

101

modern or postmodern conditions, Foucault's conception of politics is sympathetic to the postmodern condition with its rejection of grand-scale emancipatory projects (1984: 39; see also Pavlich 1995 and Hoy 1988). He too is entirely suspicious of any universal 'metanarratives' that could purportedly ground our critiques of society and denies that human reason can escape the contingent effects of historical context.[22]

In any case, Foucault's basic response to his critics is that they have incorrectly characterised modernity as an epoch, or some features of an epoch, that has produced universal doctrines grounded in unshakeable human reason. By contrast, Foucault wants to recover from modernity an 'attitude' that is to be permanently reactivated, and that adopts a critical posture towards the limits of the present. In this sense, what connects us to the Enlightenment's modernity 'is not faithfulness to doctrinal elements, but rather the permanent reactivation of an attitude – that is, of a philosophical ethos that could be described as a permanent critique of our historical era' (Foucault 1984: 42). As such, Foucault recognises no absolute point to ground critique or ensure the emergence of a better society of the future,[23] although he does provide the rudiments of a non-absolute ethical theory in his later texts.[24] Unlike his critics, Foucault is not troubled that his rejection of universal, moral precepts will lead to the end of politics (Walzer 1986). On the contrary, he simply understands politics in a different way. For him, politics involves an ongoing critique of the present limits of our society. We must continuously ask ourselves, 'How can we exist as rational beings, fortunately committed to practising a rationality that is unfortunately crisscrossed by intrinsic dangers?' (1984: 249). However, under postmodern conditions this critique cannot be guided by absolute principles; rather it entails an unending diagnosis of the 'dangers' that accrue from present limits in specific contexts. It entails a series of critiques directed at social limits, on an ongoing basis, seeking out the perils imminent in power relations; such as those that have constituted community mediation in British Columbia. There is in this no 'final resting point' to history, but a series of power formations whose dangers need to be continually exposed.

Yet, on what basis are we to declare danger? As Foucault's critics note, he does not provide a universal basis from which to diagnose social dangers. Indeed, to do so would be to return to modern auspices that chapter 2 has indicated no longer command the respect they once might have. But this does not preclude the possibility of developing contextually relevant means of assessing social perils and oppression. Indeed, as Wapner proposes, our contextually located 'experiential insight' provides an immediate means of doing this: for those who must endure the torment of ongoing conflict, whose resolution is only ever partial and unsatisfactory, there is little need to speak of justice in any abstract sense (1989: 108). These are the private 'troubles' of which Mills (1959) speaks, and their histories point to dangers in existing social relations, the resolutions of which appeal to the promise underlying our relentless and various calculations and practices of justice. In this sense, as Wickham argues, echoing my chapter 2, '[w]hat are to count as justice in different temporal and spatial locations and what are to count as democracy can only be the outcomes of politics in those locations' (n.d.: 23). The fragmentation of justice emerges alongside the quest to accentuate, rather than silence, the different rationalities across contexts (Douzinas and Warrington 1994). As such, the diagnoses of perils and calculations of justice may well be various, but there may also be resonating homologies across contexts. In any cases, the aim is not to isolate one essential, universal means of declaring danger for *all* contexts, but rather to approach specific contexts with the more modest, less certain and honest attempt to 'problematise' the 'subordinations' so that these may become the 'oppressions' that fuel political struggle (Laclau and Mouffe 1985).

It may also be objected that Foucault's anti-humanist stance does not allow him to rely upon an absolute subject as a means of grounding a social critique. Foucault's critics argue that this prevents him from locating a basis from which to enunciate a definitive concept of freedom from the existing oppression (Soper 1986, Taylor 1986). In response Foucault espouses a vision of freedom that is quite unlike modern formulations. He says: 'Liberty is a *practice* ... The liberty of [people] is never assured by the institutions and laws that are intended to guarantee [it] ... I think that it can never be inherent in the structure of things to guarantee the exercise of freedom. The guarantee of freedom is freedom' (1984: 245). And he responds to those critics who allege that if power is everywhere then there can be no liberty (e.g. Soper 1986) by arguing that freedom is, by definition, endemic to any power relation. That is, without the recalcitrance of freedom to provide some resistance, there can be no attempts to structure social fields of action, and hence no power relations. In other words, 'if there are relations of power throughout every social field it is because there is freedom everywhere' (Foucault 1988c: 12).

Foucault's position in these debates offers one way in which we can begin to conceptualise a 'counter-modern' politics under postmodern conditions.[25] In particular, it suggests a 'politics of difference' that is characterised by a number of factors (Sawicki 1991, I. Young 1990). First, it emphasises 'moving away from the fixation with authoring new principles and towards procedures attuned to recognising the "boundaries" of a heterogeneous world' (White 1987/88: 309; see also Hekman 1991 and I. Young 1990). This entails a certain 'listening', a receptivity, to delineations between social identities – and the subordinations they may endure – that emerge out of the power formations of particular social contexts (Laclau and Mouffe 1985, Nicholson 1990). Second, this politics of difference can potentially avoid problems of either dogmatism or liberal pluralism by suggesting that social differences be regarded as resources for struggle, not as threats to be overcome. Such differences allow us to multiply the sites at which power can be resisted, a point that is particularly significant when one considers that power is not centrally located. In addition, as Sawicki states, 'if we redefine our differences, discover new ways of understanding ourselves and each other, then our differences are less likely to be used against us' (1991: 45). In all cases though, the critic must diagnose dangers – there are no assurances that might obviate the need to do so. Third, this politics of difference ties in with the politics of identity formation that has characterised the growth of new social movements (see Hutchinson 1992, Calavita and Carroll 1992, McCann 1992, Kauffman 1990, White 1987/88, etc.). Taking this alternative politics of difference as a point of departure, my analysis of community mediation in British Columbia could try to formulate a strategy of resistance to the universalising procedures and principles of professionalised justice (Calavita and Carroll 1992, White 1987/88, Wickham n.d.). The quest here might be to search for contextually relevant idioms of justice that listen and are sensitive to the heterogeneity of the contexts in which they operate. On the basis of rarefied categorisations of different social identities such calculations of justice might – following from chapter 2 – seek new moves in just games to develop the promise of justice in the contexts of particular struggles (Lyotard and Thebaud 1985).

With these responses in mind, one might return to the task of substantively redrawing critical maps of community justice along the lines proposed in this chapter. Yet before responding to the three questions raised at the end of the previous section, let me reiterate the central themes of this chapter. I have proposed that one commence the difficult task of redrawing critical charts of community mediation by developing the strengths of the critics' discourse. In particular, drawing on the new informalists, the community justice 'problem' has been recast to elucidate the current deployment of community mediation, not simply an expansion of state control, but rather a more contingent governmentalisation of the law-sovereign model of the state. Under this conception, community mediation deploys a mode of regulation that embraces a logic of government and operates according to a pastoral model of power. Community mediation creates, and integrates, particular regulatory objects (e.g. the 'community' and 'disputing individual selves') and uses techniques of discipline and self to 'restore' its vision of peace to communities. Finally, the analysis has suggested how the effects of current forms of mediation in British Columbia might be assessed for their potential to become part of an alternative politics in the dispute resolution domain. Using the suggested orientating precepts, as indicated by its three proposed questions, the remaining text will endeavour to chart features of the social landscape under analysis in greater detail. The ensuing 'map' seeks to problematise the 'obvious', to note the contingency in assertions of necessity, and to dispel the notion that community justice is a 'natural' outcome of a given social complex; rather, the analysis is in many ways an act of refusal that deliberately defies some insidious aspects of conventional wisdom and the oppressive power relations which such common sense fosters.

6

GOVERNING DISPUTES
Mediating between individuals, selves and communities

This chapter has been summoned to venture into a discursive space that elaborates upon the rationality of government embraced by community mediation. It is, let us recall, a means by which to understand how community mediation is implicated in the governmentalisation of sovereign state justice under postmodern conditions. As such, the following text focuses on the emerging governmental logic of community mediation as a variant of a pastoral model of power that may be traced to Hebraic societies. Of course, the particular manifestation of the pastoral model in the British Columbian context is probably quite different from other instances of pastorship, but it is still concerned with an age-old political problem: how to reconcile the being of singular regulatory objects with the formation of a wider totality. The underlying and paradoxical quest of pastoral power is to achieve a coherent whole by nurturing particular single forms, and reconciling the latter with the former. It aims, that is, to find ways of integrating all with each, to bolster the integrity of the (neo-) liberal state.[1] Community mediation echoes a version of this pastoral theme in its attempt to reconcile the vicissitudes of live, disputing individual disputants with a vision of quiet, peaceful and harmonious communities. Such stable, conflict-free communities, committed to the quest for a particular kind of liberal democracy, may be seen to align rather well with professionalised calculations of justice. Returning to the case of British Columbia, the pastoral logic contained within the deployment of community mediation can be seen as an instance of the pastoral model as it occurs within the shifting political theatre of postmodern conditions. In the following analysis, I shall examine the totalising (community) and singular (individual, disputing selves) regulatory objects of community mediation as well as the ways in which these are reconciled in context. However, the initial task is to conceptualise in more detail the pastoral model of power in a bid to demonstrate its direct relevance to community mediation.

Pastoral power

If postmodern conditions thrive on haphazard and unlicensed uses of pastiche in architectural design, artistic creations, social events and so on, one could then also point to the (re-)use of political models from erstwhile patterns of association. Traces of a pastoral model of power, to wit, are related to the Hebraic image of a single God with kings as mortal deputies (Foucault 1981d). Such traces become more definable presences in early Christian societies that organise associative patterns around the church and pass local leadership to pastors. Unlike magistrates, these pastors are enjoined to take an active interest in the individual lives of all congregants, much as shepherds – to reinvoke Foucault's metaphor – are required to take care of a flock.[2] Pastoral leadership, that is, requires detailed knowledge of each individual life, so that it can be conditioned and nurtured in various ways, thereby securing the well-being of all within the group. Not content with gross assessments of the congregation's condition, this form of power-knowledge is directly concerned with the welfare of each singular being. Like a shepherd, the pastor must attend to the needs of the entire 'flock' by counselling each seeker, calming the disquieted, resolving conflicts between antagonists, admonishing the wayward, caring for the sick, helping the poor and so on. It is only through nurturing and being responsible for the constitution of particular forms of individual being that a composite totality can be created. As such, pastoral power 'involves a power which individualises by attributing, in an essential paradox, as much value to a single lamb as to an entire flock' (Foucault 1981d: 239). Such leadership is clearly different from the leadership required of the sovereign in the law and sovereign model. The pastor, for one thing, is not granted an absolute power over life, and does not simply apply universal laws as a means of securing the well-being of the congregation. Instead, the effective pastor must actively attend to singular, individual needs on a continuous and extensive basis. In this sense, as one commentator puts it, pastoral power 'accords an absolute priority to the exhaustive and individualized guidance of singular existences' (Gordon 1987: 297).

Analysing the notion of pastoral power in past ecclesiastical settings, Foucault identifies four characteristic components of pastoral power (1982: 214–215). First, its purported aim is to procure the salvation of individual congregants in the hereafter. By directing each congregant to accept a particular (Christian) form of mortal being on earth, the pastor cares for souls by holding out the ultimate reward of eternal salvation. Second, the pastor exercises power as an oblate who, in contrast to the all-imposing sovereign, accepts personal responsibility for the well-being of a congregation. As such, the pastor may be required to make sacrifices for the benefit of the whole. Indeed, this ablative aspect of pastorship is a self-effacing one that requires an element of altruism from the leader. Third, pastoral power is an individualising power in the sense that it is directed at the whole congregation through an ongoing focus on the salvation of individual lives. A crucial aspect of pastorship is to encourage individuals to value obedience as a virtuous activity, and so to allow the continuous exercise of power in their personal lives. Finally, such power requires an intimate knowledge of each person and his or her soul. As Foucault puts it, 'this form of power cannot be exercised without knowing the inside of people's minds, without exploring their souls, without making them reveal their innermost secrets. It implies a knowledge of the conscience and an ability to direct it' (1982: 214). Through confessional practices, pastorship is able to extract the detailed types of knowledge from congregants that it requires to operate effectively. Moreover, through this technology, the pastor is able to exert pressure on people (guide them?) to embrace particular sorts of subjective identities.

If the pastoral model is rooted in ecclesiastical settings, over the course of several centuries it has spread to numerous secular regulatory environments, finding support from a range of different institutions. For instance, as Foucault observes, the sixteenth century saw a revival of Stoicism, which promulgated the pastoral model as a plausible response to the 'problem of government' in a discourse on 'reason of state'.[3] This theme was further extended in seventeenth- and eighteenth-century Cameralist thinking in its quest for a 'science of police' that was to inform the project of developing a 'police state' (Pasquino 1979).[4] In both discourses, the formulation of the state as an independent entity *sui generis* facilitated the task of determining what would be required to enhance its strength. As a result, the aim of government and its pastoral model is 'not to reinforce the power of the prince. Its aim is to reinforce the state itself' (Foucault 1988b: 150). In these early traces, there is an emerging governmentalisation of the state, but at the time the quest to strengthen the state was viewed as a means of resisting the havoc that unknown contingencies wreaked on states (e.g. famine, epidemics, accidents).[5] As the art of government increasingly colonises the pastoral model in secular regulatory environments, it unmoors pastorship from its ecclesiastical dock and transforms pastorship in several ways.[6]

To begin with, pastoral power no longer aims at attaining eschatological salvation for its regulatory objects; rather, its promise is to offer security, well-being, peace, freedom, wealth and so on in the here and now. Salvation, therefore, is reconceived away from the eternal and located in the more immediate lives of individuals. In addition, as the model spreads throughout the social network, the local pastors who assumed responsibility for small totalities are replaced by a host of new local authorities. These new leaders derive legitimacy not from religious (or even natural) laws but from the policy frameworks of the diverse institutional contexts to which they are attached (psychiatrists from psychiatric hospitals, social workers from social welfare agencies, and now volunteer mediators from the 'community', etc.). If these shifts indicate various changes to the initial aims and authority structures of Christian pastorship, the rise of government also altered the objects of pastoral regulation. No longer is it directed at the religious lives of individual congregants and their effects on the whole congregation, but now the lives of its objects become framed in terms other than those found in religious decree.

In particular, with the rise of modern societies and their disciplinary knowledges, the biological individual is placed as a singular entity of a collective population (Foucault 1978, 1979, Pasquino 1979). These objects brought with them different discourses which proffered different conceptions of life (both individual and collective) and opened up different fields of knowledge within which the pastoral model could operate. The accumulation of demographic knowledge around notions of population, for instance, promoted political technologies associated with governing the health, wealth, longevity, geography, climate, military might, etc., of given populations. In this version of pastoral power, the production of disciplinary knowledges serves to define both singular and collective regulatory objects that facilitate the efficient administration to strengthen the state.[7] But the enunciation of population as an entity was significant because it produced a totalising object to rival (and yet support) that of sovereignty and to challenge the previous importance of the family (Foucault 1979: 17). Thus, the emergence of the population signalled a discursive event through which 'the problem of government finally came to be thought, reflected and calculated outside of the juridical framework of sovereignty' (1979: 16). At the same time, however, the way in which this population was formulated also identified *individuals* as objects of government, thus introducing notions of both 'population and individuals, where previously, in the old social structure, there were only groups, *stande*, orders and estates inviolable – at least by right – in their eternal hierarchy' (Pasquino 1979: 50).

In the process, techniques of pastoral power became focused on vital, living beings, in all their complexity (not least of all their sexuality), and hence Foucault's term 'bio-power' (1978). The problematisation of individuals and populations as objects for the exercise of power reappropriated the Christian image of sheep in a flock, where live individuals replace the sheep and images of a population the flock. Furthermore, with the emergence of bio-power, the Aristotelian conception of people as beings capable of political action was turned upside down – now it is politics that places human lives in question.[8] In other words, the deployment of bio-power occurs in a discursive field where the preservation, or destruction, of populations becomes a matter of political choice. As such, the strength of the population is determined by the degree to which a government is capable of providing the 'salvation', the well-being, of its composite 'individuals'.[9] In this context, the aim of government is to secure the welfare of the population, its health, wealth, longevity, by knowing and dealing with individual lives.[10]

More recent forms of governmentality might be said to have elaborated upon these regulatory objects and altered patterns of governance accordingly. With the formation of social welfare states, for example, the notion of population, although still clearly evident (e.g. consider the emphasis placed on census data), appears to be supplemented with another totalising object, namely the *social* domain. The rise of the social, and its close articulations with family and population, have been well canvassed by Donzelot (1979, 1991). Indeed, Foucault puts it in these terms: 'What was discovered at the time – and this was one of the great discoveries of political thought at the end of the eighteenth century – was the idea of *society*' (1989: 261). The disciplined individual postulated and produced by the knowledges of modern human sciences is located within a totality, the 'social', and it is to this domain that welfare is directed (Dean 1994, 1991). Advocates of social welfarism viewed the social arena as a means of securing spontaneous associative patterns between individuals, and aimed to achieve a certain 'collective voluntarism' outside the coercive controls of state legal apparatuses (Janowitz 1975). As such, the social is deemed to have its own particular reasonable nature (e.g. Durkheim 1982), which if properly understood could offer a mode of regulation (solidarity) that would depend on the spontaneous voluntarism of individuals and provide them with the possibility of regulating themselves (Cohen 1985). Here the pastoral paradox of encapsulating the well-being of the social as directly related to the well-being of each individual entity is preserved.

However, under neo-liberalism the integrity of a universal social entity is questioned. Indeed, with the inroads carved into the very substance of the welfare state, under the banners of such processes as privatisation, deregulation and decentralisation, the very core of the social is challenged. If Donzelot has written a history of the rising social, a chart of its fragmentation has yet to be fully analysed. No doubt, such an analysis would also include an in-depth analysis of the associated rise of (or return to?) concomitant notions of community (Cohen 1985). As noted previously, this return to images of community (as opposed to society) to connote spontaneous associative patterns is evident in various shifts away from the older social institutions to community control; for instance, community (as opposed to social) work, community policing, community correction, community justice, and so on. In the rising influence of the community icon in neo-liberal discourses lies a tale of the reorganisation of the social, which more and more becomes better known as a 'community of communities'. One of the products of such reorganising trends is the altered form that the pastoral model of power assumes in neo-liberal (as opposed to liberal) patterns of governance (Foucault, 1982, Gordon 1991, Burchell, 1991, 1993). Most notably, its regulatory objects have changed.

On the one hand, there are processes establishing visions of community in addition to continued processes that sustain population and society. On the other hand, as noted, over and above the techniques of discipline that have fashioned modern individuals, one finds a proliferation of techniques of self by which the aims of neo-liberal states are incorporated into the emerging selves that sustain the lifestyles of a globalised, postmodern ethos (Turner 1994). Yet, even if such changes are important under postmodern conditions, the aim of neo-liberal government and its version of pastoral power remains curiously (and paradoxically) consistent: 'to develop those elements constitutive of individuals' lives in such a way that their development also fosters that of the strength of state' (1981d: 252).[11] And it is with this in mind that I can now turn to a more explicit analysis of the form of pastoral governmental rationality that is emerging through the deployment of community mediation in such contexts as British Columbia.

COMMUNITY MEDIATION AND PASTORAL POWER

Quite aside from the notable links between many community mediation programmes and the church in British Columbia (e.g. the Mennonite Church's VORP programmes), the deployment of community justice seems to evince a pastoral political rationality in several ways. First, like pastoral instances before, it promises a kind of salvation. But its secular aims are not eschatological because they are focused on the well-being of empowered individuals in peacefully ordered communities. Thus, as we have seen, advocates see community mediation as helping 'parties to come to a realistic, mutually satisfactory agreement'.[12] Behind this lies an assumption that community mediation can help individuals to 'maintain control over the outcome of their disputes' by empowering them to help restore peace to communities. Emulating the pastoral model, the goal here is to secure the welfare of the whole (the community) by attending to the well-being of singular lives (empowered individual disputants). And this well-being, this peace, is not incompatible with the wider aims of the neo-liberal state (Pavlich 1992a).

Secondly, community mediation sanctions a type of leadership that bears more than a passing resemblance to the oblate of Christian pastorship. Like the altruistic, care-giving pastor, mediators are described as people who 'really feel the need to help people' (interview, 11/01/1990). In many cases, they are volunteers and must make the personal 'sacrifices' of undergoing training (sometimes at their own expense) and conducting mediations with little or no remuneration (Callahan and McNiven 1988). Such sacrifices are seen as partial ways in which local authorities can claim to be altruistic helpers working for the good of the 'community'. Also, through

111

the use of numerous mediators, the ramified local authority structures of pastoral practices are preserved in the deployment of community mediation. Thirdly, as with other versions of the pastoral model, community mediation is an individualising power. Chapter 3 indicates that the disputants of community mediation in British Columbia are overwhelmingly conceptualised as individuals within a community. Conflict is mostly attributed to a breakdown in the relationships between individuals in the first instance, and this is seen to have negative effects on the communities from which these individuals purportedly emerge. To restore peace, the mediator must listen to disputants, recognise their claims, acknowledge their emotions, and provide a safe environment within which disputants can tell the truth about themselves in relation to a specific dispute. The mediator must provide 'verbal reward' and should recognise that 'what was just said must have been really, really difficult to say and we recognise how difficult it was and appreciate that they were able to share that with other people present' (interview with a mediator, 11/01/1990). If church-based pastorship pays constant attention to the spiritual 'needs' of congregants, mediation explicitly attends to the emotions and feelings of disputants. Indeed, a commonly enunciated feature of the process is articulated as follows: 'Mediation allows parties to be heard, acknowledged and have their concerns addressed' (advertising pamphlet of Westcoast Mediation Services).

Also, in attending to the well-being of individuals, advocates of community mediation argue that they are thereby attending to the welfare of the community (Pavlich 1992a, Shonholtz 1993). But as the final precaution of the previous chapter indicates, the community and the individual are not fixed, *a priori* entities; the very processes by which mediation targets and selects its regulatory objects are directly involved in their constitution. This takes seriously the view that the objects of a given mode of regulation do not exist in any primordial sense: their identities are inextricably tied to the political logic of the regulatory modes that 'identify' (read: create) them as discrete entities of control. For example, by (implicitly) defining a 'community' as an entity with specific features, community mediation advocates help to produce and sustain a vision of that to which their regulatory mechanisms are directed. In many cases, the object may exist as a moment in surrounding discourses (e.g. community development and planning), but specific modes of regulation are likely to colonise such moments as elements in their own discourses and may support, oppose or simply ignore others. Similarly, the individual, though a well-entrenched identity in liberal democratic polities, is selectively recast as a somewhat different type of subject (i.e. disputant) in the postmodern conditions under which community mediation is deployed. So, when a case is screened by case workers during the initiating call to assess its suitability for mediation, individual subjects are measured against intake criteria (e.g. is this person

112

sufficiently motivated to settle the dispute?). This commences a process that adds an identity of minor disputant and reasonable, malleable self capable of transformation to that of the more widely created identities of (neo-)liberal individuals. In this sense, Baskin correctly points out community mediation is 'a critical arena in which a particular kind of individual can be produced' (Baskin 1988: 110). At the same time, however, mediation deploys political technologies that help to direct the subjective aspirations of the disputing selves. As such, both *individual disputing selves* and *community* can be located as integral components of the pastoral forms that community mediation reflects.

Finally, techniques of community mediation require the formation of very specific kinds of knowledge about the objects that are regulated. Like previous forms of pastorship, the very processes of mediation are predicated upon the assumption that individual disputants will expose, declare through discourse, intimate aspects of themselves and their subjectivities. This partially explains why advocates promise confidentiality and focus on the informal, warm and safe dimensions to mediation. Without the active participation of individual disputants, the techniques of mediation cannot succeed; participant silence destroys the mediator's capacity to guide the processes by which identities are created around a particular dispute. In turn, this implies the importance of confessional techniques through which authorities or trained experts guide the self-identities of individuals in conflict.

In sum then, the version of pastoral power evident in the deployment of community mediation indicates a goal of securing the stability of communities by attending to individual selves who are involved in minor disputes. By attending to the different emotional needs, interests and perceptions of each individual disputant, community justice seeks to restore harmony and peace to a community. This paradoxical link between the one and the many, in practice, entails the deployment of political technologies that on the one hand create the totalising space of community, and, on the other, help to produce (or reinforce) particular kinds of individuals and selves who are amenable to resolving conflicts. The degree to which people's subjective aspirations come to be aligned with wider (neo-liberal) aims is very much part of contemporary regulatory mechanisms devolved into communities (N. Rose 1992). But let me here explore, drawing on my case study as appropriate, the technologies involved in the pastoral model of government embraced by community mediation practices.

VISIONS OF COMMUNITY

We have seen that the community is never a 'settled resultant'; it is mobilised in various ways for different purposes (Fitzpatrick 1992b). In British Columbia, its recent incarnations are related to neo-liberal destructuring impetuses and the rise of community control under postmodern conditions (Pavlich forthcoming). By constructing 'disputants' as members of a community, informal justice attempts to carve out a general space, a congregation as it were, within which it seeks to regulate particular forms of action (i.e. minor community disputes). The popularity of what Cohen describes as a widespread 'rhetorical quest for community' is captured in his apt observation that '[i]t would be difficult to exaggerate how this ideology – or, more accurately, this single word – has come to dominate Western crime-control discourse in the last few decades' (1985: 116). In British Columbia, the rise of the 'community' as a discrete, discursive entity of importance to the resolution of disputes has opened up a 'space' within which conflict between individuals may be settled outside of the courts (Butcher 1985, Becker 1975). There are a number of ways in which the truths of this 'community' (what it is, what it ought to be, etc.), and the importance of mediation in it, are declared. For instance, local 'experts' often appeal to a growing academic discourse on mediation in Canada and the United States in a bid to lend credence to their enunciations.[13] Such enunciations find voice in social fields where specific people are implicitly cast as 'experts' of community mediation, and who can thus speak the truth about how to resolve conflict in the community.[14] However, it is important to emphasise that advocates are still in the process of delineating the community as a regulatory object in the informal dispute resolution arena.[15] The most visible evidence for this can be found in two previously noted features of community justice in the province: the lack of demand from the community for mediation services; and the relentless public relations exercises that programme representatives engage in. Both issues betray the early deployment of this mode of control, which has yet to institutionalise its *modus operandi* and has still to entrench the identity of its regulatory objects.

Nevertheless, advocates of community mediation have enlisted the community as an object of control within the informal justice domain, and implicitly harbour various truths about its purported nature. But what attributes have they ascribed to this 'community'? In chapter 3 we saw that advocates in British Columbia seldom explicitly define it, even though they assume that it has certain core features.[16] For instance, it is seen to be a hospitable, familiar and 'informal' arena in which individual disputants are empowered to be free. The notion of voluntary choice is crucial to the advocates' attempts to mark the community off from the tutelage of state impositions (i.e. being free from state control). Similarly, the heightened differentiation between court adjudication and mediation is symbolic of the attempt to ascribe to a community the quality of being a non-imposing domain of freedom, of being a 'total comfort zone' for participants. This image credits the community with a spontaneity that advocates portray as the basis of specifically democratic states. Many mediators see themselves as agents for social change, and see mediation as a 'life skill' that is crucial for revitalising democratic coexistence in the community (interviews, 12/09/1991, 15/01/1990). So, the narrative goes, if democracies are to take heed of the 'people', they must return to the community to listen to its needs. Notwithstanding the imputation of *a priori* needs, this exemplar is an important one because it situates the community in an interstice between the democratic state and the individuals whom this purportedly represents. As such, the community is seen as a viable point of intersection for the mutual gathering of information: the state from individuals and vice versa (Butcher 1985). This logic was clearly behind the initial formation of Justice Councils in British Columbia, even if it proved to be susceptible to reversal in the hands of the Social Credit government in the sense that Justice Councils were used to 'educate' the community (Cossom and Turner 1985). In any case, the community is heralded as an object of governance independent of the state, and yet capable of providing useful political information and of effectively disseminating central decisions.

In addition, the advocates' discourse reveals much by its perception of a 'normal' community; that is, an organised domain of consensus that is conflict-free and that develops spontaneously when individuals interact in the absence of state intervention.[17] Conflict is viewed as abnormal, unhealthy and destructive – as something that must be healed because it threatens the very stability and solidarity of spontaneous community cohesion. It creates distances, so the reasoning goes, and destroys the harmonious communality that secures lasting community order. As such, the restorative aspects of community justice are emphasised so as to help disputants 'better understand each other (i.e. developing communication skills) and work towards healing some of the damage done (e.g. mostly things said or done)'.[18] This focus on healing the 'damage done' is explicable when one considers that the integrity of a community is considered dependent upon its ability to deal effectively with conflict and to expunge tensions quickly and efficiently (Burdine 1990, Sander 1980). Therefore, an important part of governing a community entails neutralising minor disputes as soon as they arise. Because mediation is inexpensive (especially where volunteer mediators are used), informal (not slowed down by 'red tape') and able to secure lasting settlements, it is promulgated as a viable alternative to the courts.[19] It is offered as a solution that maximises voluntary individual participation in the community without dwelling on questions of cause, blame, guilt or innocence (Harrington 1985, Abel 1982b).

This implicit discourse on the nature of the community presents a field of knowledge that licenses particular political (governmental) practices. It sanctions a managerial, administrative functionalism that equates techniques to remove conflict from communities with the constitution of a viable community. Here, the notion of dispute resolution is separated from discourses of justice in philosophy or jurisprudence, and is linked to administrative discourses that seek the most efficient technical responses to the 'problem' of 'community conflict'.[20] As such, the overriding aim is merely to settle individual cases quickly, inexpensively and with minimum recurrence. This emphasis on administrative efficiency is reinforced by the position of funders who determine the 'success' of particular programmes purely on the basis of a head-count of the cases resolved.

So, we see how community mediation advocates attempt to (re-)create the community as a distinct regulatory object. In the process, the community remains an amorphous discursive construct, a trace, which advocates mobilise in different ways in their calculations of community justice and their practices of community mediation. It is interesting to note that their emphasis on this object is congruent with the previously referred to trend where the (Fordist) Keynesian welfare state, and its social domain, is being transformed (Burchell 1991, Baskin 1988). In the more splintered social environments of postmodern conditions, solidarity amongst people is sought by removing conflict from specific communities and by linking these peaceful communities into an interlocking 'social order': a community of communities. In short, as previously noted, these developments have fractured the social domain into smaller units of community that try to integrate the aims of a localised totality (the community) with the subjective aims of its constituent entities. Of course, however, the latter observation takes us away from the totalising dimensions of the pastoral model and focuses attention on the particular, differentiated entities that are said to comprise the community. In its individualising dimension, the pastoral model of community justice is chiefly directed at individual selves within the community (or neighbourhood) who are involved in 'minor' disputes.[21]

INDIVIDUAL, DISPUTING SELVES

The disparate processes of community mediation that aim to regulate minor disputes are implicated in the very formation of the identities of individual disputing selves. The advocates' discourse presumes that people are innately free agents whose voluntarism should be respected and preserved in the community. Thus, so the reasoning goes, when community conflict does arise it is important to have in place procedures that empower individuals to exercise their voluntary capacities to find acceptable settlements. And yet it is precisely in this process that community mediation individualises conflict by channelling it into calculated fields of mediation expertise whose aim is to transform disputing selves into subjects who have reached a mutually agreed upon strategy for peace.[22] In these fields, disputants are obliged to accept the rules of mediation, to agree with its compulsion to act as reasonable, free, individual subjects who creatively try to reach settlement. They are, that is, required to be the 'voluntary participants' who 'negotiate an informed settlement to issues in a dispute' if they are to continue with the mediation process (Mediation Development Association of British Columbia 1990: 3). Indeed, as noted, the first stage of mediation requires a (usually signed) commitment to abide by specified rules, a condition that must be met to continue. In my observations of mediator training role plays, mediators were told to be 'firm' and even 'aggressive', in encouraging and soliciting the active involvement of disputants. Exposed disputants are then subjected to the mediator's guidance (through reframing, probing, positive or negative reinforcement, etc.), which helps to fashion particular identities in relation to a given dispute. In the process, disputants are rendered both objects and subjects of a mediation process that pressures them to behave in particular ways, and to accept specific self-identities, in relation to a dispute.

The individualisation of so-called community disputes takes place under the auspices of a wider discourse on mediation (Burdine 1990, Kressel and Pruitt 1989, Goldberg *et al.* 1985, Fisher and Ury 1983, etc.). The discourse specifies criteria to determine when mediation is an appropriate dispute resolution response, and to provide guidelines on how mediators can achieve effective settlement. It also isolates diverse, and often subtle, methods by which mediators are advised to structure a field of action within which disputants can be obliged – if they are to continue the process – to negotiate mutually agreeable settlements (Burdine 1990). From the orientations of the previous chapter, we have identified two main processes by which community mediation individualises disputes in its quest for settlement. First, the bodies of people involved in so-called minor community conflicts are placed in regulatory spaces where various, and often subtle, disciplinary techniques are deployed. Drawing on Foucault (1977b) and Fitzpatrick (1988), one might note that community mediation deals with people as individuals who share the common ground of communality. Mediation, from this point of view, is an 'examination' in which bodies are spatially organised to extract a specific individuality by rendering them highly visible to hierarchical observation and normalising judgement (Foucault 1977b: 170–194).

Secondly, mediation employs various practices that seek to control the limits within which the disciplined individual is encouraged to turn 'him- or herself into a subject' (Foucault 1982: 208). Community mediation offers a forum in which normal individuals are encouraged by the mediation process to articulate a version of self in relation to a dispute and to reflect on how that self might be expected to change if it is to avoid protracted conflict in the future. This is 'ethical' work done of the self by the self, with the active guidance of a mediator, who encourages disputants to re-create themselves, not as selves in conflict but as peaceful subjects (Foucault 1985). The basis of mediator guidance here is the imparting of 'life skills', or putting on offer a range of non-disputing lifestyles for selves to choose. At issue here are the very means by which aspects of subjective selves are transformed through so-called 'technologies of the self' (Foucault 1988b). In the context of mediation, the primary technique of self is that of confession, in which disputants are enjoined to speak the truth about themselves and their conflicts, to reveal their true selves in relation to a dispute and to submit these to the guiding, caring concern of a delegated authority figure – the mediator.

With this in mind, one can explore community mediation through its main techniques of discipline, which seeks to produce particular kinds of (neo-liberal?) individuals, and techniques of self, such as confession, which aim at erecting self-identities that restore peace to communities. Although these are here separated for heuristic purposes, they are inextricably intertwined in the context of any given mediation session.

Techniques of discipline

The modern individual is a product of a disciplinary legacy whose imprints are lodged firmly within the mediation process (Fitzpatrick 1988). With the marked demographic shifts of the eighteenth century, the rise of capitalism and the political ascendancy of the bourgeoisie came disciplinary techniques that spread well beyond the limits of their founding institutions (e.g. the army). Such discipline, as Foucault (1977b) observes, is a technique for training bodies to perform in specified ways that focuses on minute acts and precise movements. Implicit in the exercise of such power is the knowledge that the human body is docile, that its capacities may be improved or transformed (through training), used, subjected and controlled (Foucault 1977b: 136). Discipline moulds and shapes particular forms of individuality; 'it is a specific technique of power that regards individuals both as objects and as instruments of its exercise' (Foucault, 1977b: 170). So, from docile bodies, discipline fashions (liberal) individuals who are then the vehicles through which it operates. Behind the liberal enunciations of a natural, or essential, individual subject lies an array of disciplinary techniques that operate continuously to forge this particular form of being. They mark the body out in naked singularity, train it to be a normal, free signifier, and inscribe reason into its very core.

Foucault argues that the rise of disciplinary techniques involves at least two political rationales. First, through discipline, the logic of economics – how to produce something with maximum efficiency – is imported into the political realm (hence 'political economy'). This entails not only reducing associated fiscal costs, but also exercising power as discreetly as possible in order to minimise direct resistance and maximise regulatory efficiency. Thus discipline operates as a continuous, unobtrusive, far-reaching and intense means of structuring action that colonises existing political forms. Second, discipline is directed at the ephemeral and indefinite domain of non-conformity through which it structures potential forms of resistance.

Conversely, this is to say, discipline operates through a logic of normalisation where non-conformity is created, defined, scaled and classified. This
allows individuals in a social body to be placed in and around a normal
distribution. Here, norms operate not as universal, formal principles (e.g.
as a law), but rather as more supple, informal averages that are able to
change with modifications to the scaling, classification and distribution out
of which they emerge.

Foucault (1977b: 170–194) isolates three main sorts of practices or techniques associated with discipline: hierarchical observation (surveillance);
normalising judgement; and a combination of these in the form of the
'examination' (the medical, psychiatric, judicial, etc.). The first of these
practices seeks to organise physical fields of action in such a way as to
orientate bodies through space as individuals who are highly visible
to observation practices that are hierarchically ordered. Such practices place
bodies in fields of action that maximise their potential to come under the
scrutinising and watchful gaze of a delegated authority figure, such as
the expert, the guard, etc. Bentham's 'panopticon', an architectural plan for
a prison, provides an exemplar for the kind of techniques that operate
here.[23] The efficiency of this mode of power lies in its invisibility to those
that fall within its gaze, because its objects never quite know when they
are being watched. This nurtures a perception of continual surveillance and,
in turn, encourages self-surveillance within individuals. That is, because the
expert's gaze is invisible to subjected individuals, they do not know when
(or how) it will alight on their actions, when it will pass its normalising
judgement. Community mediation adds to existing hierarchical observation
sites by situating disputants in fields of action that render them visible to
the hierarchical gaze of sanctioned mediators. In so doing, the overall
quantum of such sites is complemented, with the result that specific actions
are now targets of control that might previously have escaped governmental
attention. How loudly one snores, how ferociously one's dog barks, how
teenagers relate to their parents, or how friends interact with one another
are all now potential threats to an assumed community order, and hence
appropriate cases for community mediation. As such, community
mediation extends panoptic practices to local communities, with the possible effect of increasing self-surveillance therein.[24]

By focusing the disciplinary gaze precisely, it is possible to render minute
aspects of the body highly visible and to regulate these through the second
practice of normalising judgement. Community mediation employs various
techniques to evaluate the actions of its participants according to a somewhat flexible normative framework. These techniques concentrate on the
details of actions, encouraging normality by rewarding conformity and
punishing non-conformity. Mediators offer a variety of rewards in
mediation sessions, ranging from verbal affirmations, encouragement and
praise to discreet body language signals. Indeed, for some participants,

there is reward enough in having one's point of view acknowledged and listened to. This is clearly reflected in one client's response to what he regarded as the most favourable aspect of mediation: 'I got to say what was on my mind . . . I got to air my views to the mediators' (interview, 30/05/1990). Similarly, mediators are able to use verbal cues and body language to punish non-conformity. A non-conforming disputant may be interrupted with this statement: 'This is now the third time you have violated the rules we set up at the beginning of the process – I'm afraid we cannot continue if you persist in doing so!' A trainer at one role-play suggested that the effect of the statement could be enhanced by making stern eye contact with the offender and by speaking in a deep voice. As this trainer suggested 'When you get direct, the sugar coating falls away and this is your power as a mediator.'[25]

The aim of this micro system of punishments and rewards is not to repress actions on the basis of universal codes, but rather to evaluate behaviour against floating averages that constitute norms at given times and places. At root then, mediation entails a dual process here: one that seeks to negotiate norms pertinent to the case at hand; and another that evaluates specific actions in relation to these. With respect to the former, mediators try to establish common ground between disputants through actively intervening with techniques such as probing questions, reframing, 'brainstorming' sessions, refocusing discussions, redirecting issues, specifying general assertions, private meetings with disputants, and so on. In effect, this emphasis on the common ground between disputants aims to establish agreed-upon norms around a given dispute. At a role-play session, the training mediator noted that 'as a mediator you have tremendous power', which could be used to some effect to elicit 'norms' (observation, 15/04/1991). At all times, however, mediators are required to solicit agreement from disputants, thereby preserving the appearance of voluntary consensus in the process.[26] As such, mediation sessions require disputants to transpose their previous actions into a spoken format with the active intervention of mediators who ensure that a normative negotiation can occur within definite limits to avoid the possibility of developing iconoclastic norms, or norms that destroy the image of a cohesive, consensual community.

For example, in one custody and separation mediation session, a woman suggested that she have a 'break' from her children for a few weeks – the head mediator simply ignored the suggestion and continued the discussion as though it had not been said. In informal conversations after the session, the mediator noted that the 'mother' was in a 'bad way emotionally' and that she could not have meant what she had said. Without speculating on the apparent operation of gender stereotypes here, or conceptions of motherhood, what is clear is the degree to which the normative framework of a mediation session is controlled by the mediators to ensure that it does not depart from perceptions of wider community norms. Or, to be more precise, the process of mediation performs the specific task of selecting, from a diverse array of what are perceived to be wider community norms, those supposedly most salient to the cases at hand. Here, mediators play a crucial role in the process of selecting such norms by shaping the agenda that sets the stage for the resolution of disputes: disputants' respective transpositions are clarified, summarised and reframed by the mediator(s) into statements pertaining to the dispute (Burdine 1990: 21–22).[27] This reframing, or transposition, of what the dispute is 'actually' about also isolates which of the disputants' actions must be modified if the parties are to settle their differences, normalise their relationship and return as normal individuals of the community. Having established the norms for the session, mediators then evaluate – using a micro system of rewards and punishments – the actions of the respective disputants against the emerging normative framework. This is particularly evident in the final stage of the mediation process, where participants are encouraged to resolve their disputes. In deciding which criteria are suitable for a fair agreement, and what specific action each disputant needs to perform in order to achieve this, the mediator in effect helps to classify actions around norms that the session has generated. Here, the disputants' reconstructions of the dispute are implicitly evaluated against norms of a purportedly consensual, harmonious and peaceful community, with the aim of *normalising* those behaviours that have strayed beyond the realms of acceptable deviation in context.

The third mechanism Foucault isolates as crucial to the functioning of discipline, the 'examination', combines the two previous techniques through a 'normalising gaze' that collects information about specific individuals and ranks them in relation to a norm. For instance, in the medical examination or the psychiatric interview or the mediation session, bodies are isolated in a field of visibility where they become the objects (patients, cases, clients, etc.) through procedures of objectification (creating files, dossiers or tape recordings, or detailing agreements). In mediation sessions, such bodies are individualised through procedures that define them as disputants (or clients) involved in a case. Such procedures include bringing bodies into a field of action where they are marked as individuals involved in a dispute and subjected to the normalising gaze of trained mediators. With the initial contact, the case-screening procedures determine which cases and clients are suitable for mediation. Someone who is non-compliant, who resists the rules of mediation from the outset, is simply not accepted into the regulatory field. For acceptable clients, a case file is opened that situates them in a 'network of writing', which documents the date of initial contact with the Centre, who initiated the case, the nature of their dispute, its outcome, etc. (Foucault 1977b: 189). This documentation is then further transformed into statistical averages, which serve as measures for the 'success' of particular programmes for funders.

At the mediation session itself, bodies are spatially located in fields of action that require them to comport themselves as individuals. They are seated in convivial patterns, usually around round tables, to underscore the informal, non-hierarchical nature of mediation. Many mediators adhere to the advice of the manual:

> The setting should be as peaceful and private as possible and chairs should all be similar in height. If a table is used, it should avoid setting up power positions, such as one party having the head of the table or being placed in an adversarial position to the other. Round tables obviously avoid this problem.
>
> (Burdine 1990: 15)

Although the setting varies from session to session, those that I observed focused on minute details to create settings that were conducive to fostering dialogue between disputants. In all instances, for example, great care was taken to ensure that I was seated in such a way as to underline my observer status (e.g. in the corner of the room or on a raised platform at the rear of a room). In addition, most mediators seated themselves with their backs to the entrance to the room. When questioned on this, several mediators suggested that it was an intentional attempt to limit perceptions of 'escape' and to keep parties 'focused' on matters *in* the room.

This is not insignificant, for it reinforces the closure that defines the physical and symbolic limits of the field of action that mediation seeks to regulate: those actions pertaining to a specific dispute. There are rules for entry and participation in this field, as articulated by mediators at the introduction to the session and referred to throughout the session. These rules, together with the organisation of physical space at mediation sessions, serve to render disputants highly visible to the mediator's normalising gaze. This gaze – especially in the absence of its 'sugar coat' – is used to encourage conformity to 'normal' behaviour and to defuse, or neutralise, acrimonious exchanges. The disciplinary gaze finds expression in a number of ways in the process of mediation, but, in general, is closely articulated to an intricate system of rewards (acknowledgement, praise, support, positive gestures, etc.) and punishments (e.g. eye contact, the use of brief, specific commands). Many of these are extremely subtle. For example, one of the means of normalising relationships between disputants is to ensure that they communicate directly with one another, rather than through the mediator. To achieve this interaction, mediators may simply instruct disputants to direct their discourse to one another, and insist that the parties address each other by name. Where disputants fail to do so, mediators may prompt them, or point to the other party through hand gestures and eye motions. However, should this prove unsuccessful, mediators may break eye contact altogether with the speaker and simply look at the listening disputant, offering no supportive gestures until the speaker conforms to 'normal' interaction with the other disputant. Failing this, the mediator may interrupt the speaker to translate third-party references ('he' or 'she') into the first person ('Lara', 'Pete'). Such normalising gestures are remarkably effective at prompting (even hostile) disputants to re-create the appearance of a 'normal' interaction between them.

Another example of the mediator's normalising gaze in the mediation sessions is particularly evident from cases where there are heated and angry exchanges between disputants. Here, the mediator's gaze is often sufficient for neutralisation if directed in a particular way. Burdine suggests that, when people become angry, one way to avoid dealing with them is to '[n]ormalise the feeling if not the behaviour' (1990: 40). This may be accomplished, for example, by statements such as: 'I understand that you are angry about the whole issue, with good cause, but if we are to resolve this dispute we have to avoid screaming at each other.' Such interventions serve to defuse the 'disruption' and, if successful, allow the mediator to maintain normalising control over the situation.

In tandem, these disciplinary practices identify people as individual disputants and attempt to restructure their relations through procedures of normalisation. The aim is to restore peaceful relations between individuals by neutralising their disputes – to further the crusade of expunging conflict from the community. Community mediation sessions extend the points at which individual lives become accessible to authority figures and could – if successful – expand 'normality' to greater numbers in the population, thereby helping to preserve a given associative pattern. But, as I have noted above, if discipline operates on the body, there are also a variety of techniques that help individuals to create themselves as particular subjects in the confines of mediation sessions. That is, there are also various processes whereby people help to fashion particular self-identities, subjectivities, through such techniques as confession. Discipline and confession interact in mediation sessions to enjoin highly visible individuals to speak out and to present a definition of self in relation to a dispute for public assessment.

Techniques of self: Confession

The subjective self is a core element in contemporary liberal democracies. Yet, as N. Rose succinctly notes: 'The regulatory apparatus of the modern state is not something imposed from outside upon individuals who have remained essentially untouched by it. Incorporating, shaping, channelling, and enhancing subjectivity have been intrinsic to the operations of government' (1990: 213). Subjective moulding of this kind is not simply accomplished through the tentacles of an *external* but omniscient (Orwellian) state apparatus; rather, it is achieved through a complex deployment of heterogeneous technologies of self. As noted previously, these technologies take the form of various social and cultural pressures that influence the 'ethical work' that individuals perform when they construct themselves as selves. The techniques are dispersed throughout a given social network, including in such regulatory domains as community mediation, which employs several techniques in order to produce particular self-identities. That is, mediation provides a forum in which 'disputants' are encouraged to enunciate specific conceptions of themselves in relation to a given conflict.

To be sure, performing ethical work is not an entirely voluntary quest: it is a precondition for participation in the mediation process. Disputants are obliged to exercise a freedom to be actively 'committed to working together to resolve the conflict' (Burdine 1990: 6). They are required to enunciate various definitions of themselves in relation to a dispute: their needs, their perceptions of fairness and their conceptions of an acceptable resolution. They are, that is, required to confess, to become the authors of a dispute-settling process. Mediators, for their part, are encouraged to 'dig for more information' when it is not forthcoming, and to sift through it for 'relevance' when it is (observation, 04/04/1991). In addition, the mediator scrutinises the disputants' interests, fears, emotions and hidden assumptions, and either tries to neutralise those that appear obstructive to achieving settlement or reinforces self-identities that are likely to increase the chances of resolution. In this way, disputants expose their motivations, needs and perceptions of a dispute to the guiding influence of a mediator in confidential (private) settings that have (public) consequences for the wider community.

In particular, as noted, the norms established in the mediation sessions typically reflect wider 'community norms' and one of the mediator's tasks is to try to align disputants' motivations with the overarching norm of peace. The most significant technique of self within the context of mediation, underscoring its pastoral political logic, is its use of confessional practices. The presence of confession in mediation becomes especially clear when one considers the salience of three criteria that Hepworth and Turner propose for defining confession: there is a confessor who confides fully about his or her transgressions to an authority; one can locate a discourse that details the reasons for its practices; and it entails a private act of speaking out that has public consequences (1982: 6–7). Community mediation satisfies all these criteria rather nicely, because it provides a confidential field that, 'lies at the sensitive intersection between the interior freedom of individual conscience and the exterior requirements of public order' (Hepworth and Turner 1982: 15). As such, a core technology of self in mediation is genealogically related to pastoral practices of confession that sought – through an act of charity – to reconcile sinful individuals with a sinless community. To return to the pastoral metaphor, this was an act of grace that guided the passage of wayward sheep back into the wholesome flock. Confession, unlike excommunication, is an ameliorative or restorative set of practices that provides a passage for the faithful, with their momentary lapses of faith, to return to the congregation. Analytically, the architecture of the confessional in community mediation sessions is similar to other contexts in so far as it deploys a setting in which,

> Each person has a duty to know who he [*sic*] is, that is, to try to know what is happening inside him, to acknowledge faults, to recognise temptations, to locate desires and everyone is obliged to disclose these things either to God or others in the community.
>
> (Foucault 1988b: 40)

The confession of disputants to mediators would thus seem to be genealogically related to those of congregants to pastors. Looking back to 1215, the year when the Lateran Council codified the Sacrament of Penance, it is possible to indicate a long history of confessional practices in European societies. This code in effect restricted the practice of compurgation (by which acquittals of a charge were secured through the positive testimony of credible witnesses[28]), by requiring individuals to vouch for themselves in annual confessions. They were required to confess truths about themselves and in the process hold up aspects of their subjectivities for scrutiny by authorities (N. Rose 1990: 219). With the rise of the modern 'individual' (and its constituting disciplinary practices), confessional practices were colonised by secular governmental practices, and particularly by those concerned with the inscription of 'freedom' and 'subjectivity' into the very heart of individuality.[29] Consequently, as Foucault notes, '[t]he truthful confession was inscribed in the heart of procedures of individualisation by power' (1978: 58–59). By the nineteenth century, confession could be identified as a core technique of diverse institutions: the medical examination, the psychiatric interview, the juridical inquisition. This trend has continued and, indeed, '[t]he obligation to confess is now relayed through so many different points, is so deeply ingrained in us, that we no longer perceive it as a power that constrains us; on the contrary it seems to us that truth, lodged in our most secret nature, "demands" only to surface' (Foucault 1978: 60). Of course, the technique has undergone modifications and adaptations: the identities of the confessors are multiple; the knowledges surrounding confession are markedly different; and the social identities of those to whom confessions are made have changed (physicians, psychiatrists, social scientists, mediators). But the effect of exposing one's self for public scrutiny, judgement and guidance, to restore the order that is disturbed by lapses in conforming to community norms, remains fundamentally intact.

As one of many contemporary confessional sites, community mediation carves out a regulatory space that pressures individuals to adopt subjective aspirations and conceptions of self that rid them of conflict with others. There are three features of this site that seem particularly pertinent. First, the process of self formation occurs through an overt obedience to the rules of mediation. The requirement that disputants sign an agreement to abide by the rules of mediation at the outset indicates rather graphically the sort of obedience in question. However, obedience to the process is not simply solicited through signed declarations; it also is won through attempts to legitimate mediation as a useful (voluntary, empowering, cost-effective, etc.) alternative to the courts. In addition, the obedient subject is cast as a free self who must voluntarily choose to participate in the process, and whose free participation is demanded by a comfortable and informal mediation setting. The less intrusive the setting, the more likely disputants are to embrace its normality (Rose 1990: 220). Obeying the demands of mediation includes the fundamental duty to speak out about, and resolve, disputes. Burdine notes that one of the central tenets of the process is that 'all pertinent information will be shared', and so offers various criteria (norms) that are designed to establish which clients are likely to submit themselves to the rules of the process (1990: 17 and 5–6). She suggests that the most likely candidates are individuals involved in ongoing relations (i.e. they come into more or less frequent contact even if they do not want to), who have explored other alternatives, who are voluntary participants and who are motivated to reach an agreement. Each of these criteria increases the likelihood that disputants will be motivated to speak out, to enunciate concepts of self in relation to a dispute, and to subject these concepts to the scrutiny of a confidential mediation session.

In parenthesis, without obedience and active participation, mediation is rendered ineffective. For example, in one of my comparative observations in the Chicago area, a poor woman of colour had come into conflict with her landlord. Clearly intimidated by the process of mediation, her only response was loudly to castigate her landlord for a purported breach of contract. When told by the mediator that her outbursts contravened the spirit of mediation, she retreated into almost complete silence, offering little more than dismissive gestures. Hers was a surly act of refusal, of resistance, and the awkward silences she introduced certainly highlighted the degree to which the entire process of mediation requires the *active* confessions of its participants. Without such participation, the mediation – to use the words of the mediator involved – 'was flat' and hampered by uncomfortable silences. The obligation to confess is therefore crucial to the operation of effective mediation.

Secondly, the pressures that are brought to bear upon individuals in community mediation, to guide the ethical work performed on themselves, are controlled by the mediator to a significant degree. The mediator, the purportedly 'neutral' facilitator, exercises control by claiming a unique relation to disputes. That is, disputes are credited with a certain latency in which their 'real nature' cannot be ascertained without comprehensive information, without all sides of the dispute being told and interpreted. They are, that is, multifaceted and more complex than any one presentation. As such, a third party is required accurately to interpret, summarise or reframe the dispute with an eye to establishing a 'common ground' that is acceptable to all disputants, and from which a settlement plan can be constructed. Hence the facilitating mediator is rendered crucial to the process of mediation. This is significant, because, as Foucault notes, confession cannot occur without the presence of someone 'who is not simply the interlocutor but the authority who requires the confession, prescribes and appreciates it, and intervenes in order to judge, punish, forgive, console and reconcile' (1978: 61–62). The mediator assumes the authority to empower people by managing a process that extracts intimate knowledge of the self in relation to a dispute, and tries to structure the ways in which individual disputants reconstruct aspects of their self-identities with the aim of expunging conflict from their relationships.

The mediator is thus directly involved in mobilising particular cultural and social pressures to guide the formation of self in the process of mediation. To list some of the ways in which mediators guide the process, we might point to the methods of continuous probing, reframing issues and soliciting possible identities by requiring individuals to 'brainstorm' solutions. In addition, Burdine advises mediators that '[y]ou may also have to interject in order to keep a speaker from wandering too far afield, such as the detailing of a lengthy past history, or lengthy anecdotes. Remind the speaker of the purposes of the opening statement and refocus them on the last relevant statement they made' (1990: 20). This underscores the notion that mediators must remain in control of sessions, a point that was reiterated by a trainer in a role-play session who advised trainee mediators not to use 'blaming language' but always to remember that '[y]ou are driving the car – take them [the disputants] where you want to go' (observation, 04/04/1991). Burdine offers numerous other techniques for 'guiding the process' (1990: 24), but in each case the mediator directs the format of the confession and thereby guides the ensuing enunciation of self-identities.[30] In light of this, the mediator is surely less 'neutral' than might appear at first blush. This is not to say that s/he necessarily sides with one of the disputants (although this does, no doubt, happen[31]), but rather that the mediator has already taken the side of 'consensual community order' in facilitating a process that is designed to 'restore' peace and harmony to the community. All of these practices encourage disputants to be more flexible and to experiment with altered self-identities with which they can identify and are less likely to provoke future conflict.

Finally, one could analyse what is involved when disputants reconstitute aspects of themselves. Foucault suggests that 'ethical' work of this kind has four important dimensions, all of which seem to operate within the confines of the mediation process (1984: 352–357). To begin with, the process of self-reconstruction involves 'ethical substance' or the area of the self's identity that is isolated for ethical work (i.e. what areas of the self need to be bracketed off for sustained scrutiny?). The third stage of Burdine's model is particularly significant in identifying areas of self that need to be altered to settle a dispute. This relates to the point at which, to return to the type provided in chapter 2, Lara and Pete recognise what aspects of their current self-identities need to change to settle the dispute between them (e.g. the self as being less considerate of others than it should be). Then there is the 'mode of subjection', or the ways in which selves position themselves in relation to moral or normative codes and see it as an obligation to obey their dictates. In mediation, the mode of subjection is entertained and articulated through the very processes of identifying and selecting norms that (with the help of the mediator) are deemed appropriate to a given dispute. So in Lara and Pete's dispute, both might recognise the relevance of a norm that requires individuals to be considerate of their neighbours, and begin to establish what it would mean for each self to obey its dictates in context (e.g. Lara should avoid disturbing Pete's afternoon nap, while Pete might see his angry outbursts as a symptom of a more fundamental problem).

Thirdly, there is the actual 'ethical work', which involves active processes by which the self reforms itself. This dimension entails all the various activities that Lara and Pete must invoke to transform themselves from being locked in conflict to assuming subjective identities that settle the dispute between them. In other words, how does each self change in response to the diverse pressures directed at it through processes of mediation? Finally, Foucault refers to the 'telos' or the vision of self that is held as a goal for ethical self-transformation. In the final stages of community mediation, such visions of self are inscribed in a written, signed agreement that demands particular sorts of self-conduct from individuals. Thus Lara and Pete are required to be, say, more considerate of each other, which implies a telos of self-formation. But, in less specific terms, mediation also tries to perform the educative function of imparting a life skill to individuals by showing them how to resolve future conflicts by embracing the notion of a flexible self, and to recognise the partiality of any telos that might need to be renegotiated to avoid conflict in the future.

In all its various dimensions, the above discussion provides a glimpse of the sorts of processes by which disputants are shown, and tempted to accept, specific subjective identities through confessional techniques of the mediation process. Considered as a form of pastoral power, confession in the diverse local contexts of mediation equips approved agents with a regulatory technique that not only helps to guide the intimate process of an individual defining him or herself as a subject, but also provides detailed information about the kinds of conflicts that transpire at a local level. One might add that such information is no doubt useful to the technocratic, administrative language through which community mediation has been deployed.[32]

INTEGRATING COMMUNITY, INDIVIDUALS AND SELVES

Through the previous analysis, the governmental rationality of community mediation in British Columbia becomes somewhat more transparent. One sees how its deployment, its discourse and its practices reflect a pastoral logic that is both totalising and individualising.[33] I have examined the various kinds of practices involved in the creation of its regulatory objects – the community and individual, free, subjective disputants. This is a logic that seeks to restore collective peace by individualising and neutralising conflict through a process of mediation (Peachey 1989b). Yet it also betrays the profoundly pastoral nature of its political rationality as it seeks to integrate the concerns of the many (the community) with those of each subject (the individual): *omnes et singulatim*. This coincides rather precisely with Foucault's observation:

> I think the main characteristic of our political rationality is the fact that this integration of the individuals in a community or in a totality results from a constant correlation between an increasing individualiz-ation and the reinforcement of this totality.
>
> (1988b: 161–162)

It also isolates the nub of a governmental logic that attempts to integrate the personal, subjective aspirations of each individual member with the goals of local community totalities. In British Columbia, one can point to community mediation as one of the ways in which the state tries to secure its order, its community of communities, by establishing in each individual the personal goal of consensually 'getting along' with all others and learning appropriate conflict resolution skills. But how is the logical integration of the one and the many accomplished practically? The key is processes of normalisation: by defining the normal disputant as one who has a range of choices open to her or him, it becomes possible to construe the domain in which that person operates as a domain of freedom (e.g. the community) outside of the state. Mediation integrates its objects around a common theme of normality by enunciating the normal community as a harmonious one, and construing the 'normal' relationship between indi-vidual selves as a 'non-disputing', peaceful one.[34]

In more general terms, community mediation programmes are encour-aged to adopt this vision of normality in several ways. There are several techniques of inclusion and exclusion that operate here. For instance, state agencies grant or withhold funding, networks open or close their doors, and organisations seek alliances or confrontations. Through such procedures, community mediation programmes are encouraged to endorse a conservative view of dispute resolution as a simple matter of settling disputes between individual subjects. Community mediation becomes a means of forging homologies between normal (non-disputing) subjects and normal (peaceful) communities. The governmental logic here is one of creating a politically docile realm of normality that perpetuates, rather than undermines, the existing *status quo* (Fitzpatrick 1988: 190). It sees strength in ordered, harmonious, consensual communities that are integrated with free individual selves who are able to resolve their disputes within the community and without recourse to the state's court system. In this logic, community mediation emerges as a means by which pastoral power is exercised to integrate communities, individuals and selves by expunging 'minor conflict' and aligning the personal aspirations of subjects (i.e. not to be disputants) with the wider goal of a non-rebellious community of communities. It creates its objects and integrates them through processes of normalisation, through establishing the norm of agreement, harmony and consensus.[35] In both cases, it defines normality as a state in which there are resolvable 'minor disputes' – the clear implication being that, although there may be resolvable minor disputes in contemporary society, there are no irresolvable major disputes. The existing normative order is thus left fundamentally intact. And it is through the latter that we can best understand, to pre-empt the discussion of the next chapter, how community mediation furthers a wider governmentalisation of the state.

To reiterate the themes of my narrative so far, this chapter has identified the governmental logic of community mediation as a pastoral one directed at governing individual selves as disputants in communities. As noted, the process of mediation creates the 'objects' of its regulation in various ways and with different effects. The discussion has paid particular attention to the ways in which mediation operates on individual disputing selves through the techniques of discipline and confession. It has also looked at how normalising processes aim at integrating these regulatory objects through images of the 'normal' community (i.e. one free of conflict) and the 'normal' (i.e. non-disputing) subject. Moreover, I noted the manner in which advocates of community mediation view the integrity of communities as being dependent upon the well-being of the individual selves who constitute it. In this one sees a decidedly pastoral political logic that articulates each with all.

Having thus detailed the governmental rationality of community mediation, a further question arises: how does this rationality relate to other political rationalities (e.g. the state's courts), and what are its effects? I have noted one effect, namely that community mediation helps to fragment the social domain by locating informal justice within the community. Moreover, by reconciling individual subjectivity with local community norms, which themselves form part of a community of communities (a social order?), one begins to see an emerging picture: the reconciliation of disputants and communities has the potential to help – as with previous forms of governmentality – further the strength of the state. In particular, when the pastorship of community mediation is deployed as a 'system-based', complementary alternative to the legal system (e.g. in British Columbia), it often serves to reinforce the strength and integrity of the state. This is by no means a necessary or inevitable effect, and for that reason it is necessary to detail – in a specific historical context – the relationship between the pastoral power of community mediation and the sovereign-law model of power associated with the court system of the modern liberal state. Charting the auspices of this relationship is crucial for apprehending certain perils in current community mediation practices.

7

GOVERNMENTALISING THE STATE
Intersecting political rationalities

If it be deemed apposite to ascribe rationales to social practices, then it is surely also appropriate to speak of political logics associated with the deployment of different modes of regulation. We have already indicated the pastoral logic of community mediation, but its practices are very much part of a wider political theatre. To the extent that different forms of power within that theatre are articulated at given times and places, their internal logics intersect (or not) to produce wider, synoptic power formations. The aim of this chapter is to explore, drawing once again on the case at hand, the intersection of regulatory logics in a wider dispute resolution arena where practices of community justice are deployed as 'complementary alternatives' to courtroom adjudication. It is a venture that deconstructs elements of existing debate, reorganising its own moments in a preface to an alternative politics of dispute resolution that could develop a recalculated justice.

Even so, the following recognises the heuristic value of separating two models of power in the dispute resolution arena: on the one hand, a visible, centralised political form of a sovereign (liberal, democratic) Parliament exercising control over citizens through the laws of courtrooms; on the other, more ramified, diffuse, capillary-like pastoral practices of community justice that employ 'norms' directed at live individual selves in a community.[1] The adjudicative practices of the courtroom deploy a contemporary version of what one may call a 'sovereign-law' model of power,[2] which is quite different from the pastoral logic of community mediation. However, even if it is useful to distinguish these for analytical purposes, it is important not to lose sight of the fundamental links between them in a governmentalised liberal state. Here, the pastoral model of community mediation is involved in the preservation of the sovereign-law model's presence in (neo-)liberal political environments. Conversely, the state's formal processes of law are directly involved with the deployment of community mediation in British Columbia. So, to return to Fitzpatrick (1988) for a moment, one might agree that state, law and community justice are *constitutively* related.

132

One way to explore the apparently paradoxical links and separations between law and community mediation – their mutual constitution in a governmentalised state – is to examine the contextual articulations between underlying models of power. If successful, this can indicate a composite political rationality within a governmentalised state, and allow one to point to dangers that bear on the formation of an alternative politics around dispute resolution. However, such an endeavour must come with an early caveat: amalgamations between community mediation and law are never fixed, determined or static. To hypostatise this tenuous amalgam as a completed, or necessary, state expansion is to exaggerate, if not obfuscate, the relations at hand. No doubt, when the political forms are successfully articulated, they can increase the quantum of control sites and potentially enhance the state's *capacity* to regulate people's action. But this is not a case of simple state expansion, because the nature of articulations, as well as the outcomes of pastoral power and government, are not always predictable. This indeterminacy must surely rescind the pessimism embedded in early critics' fears of monolithic state expansion, for it suggests that the spread of professionalised state justice throughout the dispute resolution arena is never a *fait accompli*.[3] There is always room for rupture and dislocation, making it possible to alter synoptic practices that link the models.[4]

In British Columbia, the alternative dispute resolution arena is constituted through synoptic practices that articulate the sovereign-law and pastoral models of power, which connect the court system with a range of alternative dispute resolution techniques (arbitration, conciliation, minitrials, mediation, etc.). Because community mediation has been calculated and deployed as a 'system-based, complementary alternative' to litigation in British Columbia, it is *ipso facto* linked to the legal system. This link in a governmentalised state is, moreover, a constitutive one that articulates the sovereign-law model of power within formal legality to the pastoral model of informal justice. The ensuing association has the effect not only of maintaining *law* but also of preserving *order* in a postulated community. To comprehend the political importance of the nexus between the courts and community mediation, or law and community order, in the dispute resolution arena, it may be useful to say more about the sovereign-law model of the courtroom before exploring its constitutive alliances with the pastoral model.

THE SOVEREIGN-LAW MODEL

The roots of the sovereign-law model lie, *inter alia*, in: the ancient Greek *polis*; Roman society's notion of the *patria potestas*, which gave a father absolute power over the lives of slaves and children; religious regimes where power was formally ensconced in the church hierarchy; the various forms of monarchical consolidation; and the modern state with its parliamentary and professional officials.[5] In each case, there is some conception of sovereignty, of an entity that claims a legitimate right to exercise power over a specified domain (be it geographical, social or political). The political logic of modern versions of this model, which are still prominent in the British Columbian context, refer to Hobbes's (1968) conception of *The Leviathan*, where power is thought to be concentrated in the hands of a centralised authority, a sovereign, who stands at the pinnacle of a hierarchical formation and wields power over citizens below through law (Held 1987). Power, in this model, is presented as an instrument of constraint, of repression, which demands – or forbids – legally specified actions (rights and duties) of those who are governed. Although coercion is fundamental to this model, it is not exclusively coercive (any more than, say, the pastoral model is one entirely based on consent). Rather, there are various degrees and combinations of coercion and consent in all models of power;[6] indeed, as Weber (1980) suggests, the authority of a sovereign requires at least an element of legitimacy if it is to survive, and this suggests a degree of consent on the part of those who are governed.[7]

In the context of western liberal democracies, the sovereign (Parliament) claims legitimacy by pointing to the democratic procedures through which it was elected.[8] The underlying assumption here is that individuals are natural beings who are free and rational, and thus capable of electing representatives to govern them. When this logic is transposed to the dispute resolution domain, it takes the following form: in view of the freedom of individuals in liberal (and neo-liberal) democracies, disputes are bound to arise (between citizens, citizens and the state, etc.) and these may ultimately require resolution in formal courtroom settings where appointed judges impartially apply laws enacted by a democratic Parliament, or inferred from previous decisions, to given situations. Of course, this echoes the auspices of modern justice, which were noted in chapter 2: formal, liberal law claims to be *universal* in the sense of appealing to rational laws equally applicable to all citizens, yet it relies on historically located courtroom procedures to interpret and evaluate *particular* sets of circumstances. But, as noted, the pure type of modern legal reasoning faces severe challenges under postmodern conditions, promoting a surge in the governmentalisation of judicial procedures. Hence, the rise of law reform agencies (both federal and provincial) as institutionalised features of the dispute resolution domain, and indeed the expansion of informal alternatives to complement the sovereign-law model.

In any case, one can discern at least four differences between the sovereign-law and pastoral models of power as manifested in British Columbia's dispute resolution domain, and others like it. To begin with, the objects they seek to regulate are different: the pastoral model is directed at live, individual, disputing selves, whereas law continues to target abstractly defined legal persons. Second, the sovereign-law model still evokes classical criminological visions of judicially constraining free and rational citizens. By contrast, the pastoral model is more closely aligned with the positivist, medical model of the therapeutic state in that it seeks to preserve, nourish and create life within peaceful communities.[9] This difference centres around regulation achieved through the legal organisation of judicial subjects versus a calculated management and administration of individual selves in communities.[10] Third, and related to the previous point, the form of sanctions in each case is different: one measures behaviour against what judges accept as hierarchically ordered statutes and case precedents, whereas the other places behaviour within a scaled distribution of contextually enunciated norms. Whereas the former punishes illegal acts to prevent future offences, the latter tries to rehabilitate 'abnormal' individuals to bring them back into the realm of the 'normal' (Pfohl 1985). Finally, although the sovereign's hierarchies seek to concentrate power, they also make its exercise visible in the symbolic displays of the courtroom. Overt, ritualist spectacles are basic to this model's ability to secure its authority and exercise power. By contrast, the pastoral model exercises power in confidence, as silently and invisibly as possible, recognising that its invasive form is 'tolerable only on condition that it mask a substantial part of itself. Its success is proportional to its ability to hide its own mechanisms' (Foucault 1978: 86).

If these differences alert us to certain discontinuities in the respective models, they also provide a framework from which to understand articulations between them, to grasp how community mediation in British Columbia is deployed as a 'system-based', 'complementary alternative' to litigation, designed to resolve 'minor' disputes. This connotes many different features of its proposed and actual deployment. In particular, it suggests: subservience and deference to the state's formal justice 'system'; a different form of dispute resolution that is both useful and acceptable to the court system ('complementary'); and an alternative form of dispute resolution that is limited by its attachments to the legal domain. In each case, however, the legal system is integrally involved in constituting the very identity of community mediation, both limiting its expansion and promoting specific knowledges and practices. Equally, however, community mediation, by its very presence in the dispute resolution arena, transforms – even if in a more limited manner – the nature of the legal field in various ways. So the respective identities of law and community mediation seem intimately associated; let us therefore turn to an analysis of community justice by examining 'the mutual constitution of law and the informal' (Fitzpatrick 1988: 190).

LAW AND THE IDENTITY OF COMMUNITY MEDIATION

In British Columbia, although formal processes of law have directly shaped the identity of community mediation through such statutes as the Divorce Act of 1985, there are various other less direct – and probably more profound – ways in which it constitutes elements of community mediation. The pressures to constitute a community justice domain are no doubt related to contradictions that liberal forms of legality seem to be facing under postmodern conditions. As Fitzpatrick (1988) cogently argues, in order to maintain its hegemonic dominance in the legal field, and thus to perpetuate a stable 'liberal social ordering', the legal system must secure *both* 'law' and 'order'. But in an ethos of prevailing liberal democratic values, this cannot be achieved through continued naked force without undermining the very discourse through which liberal legality seeks legitimacy (Dean 1994). Consequently, the legal system has come to rely on other forms of control to secure 'order' because '[l]iberal legality would prove too delicate for a society founded on coercive authority, were not this authority embedded indistinguishably through discipline in the domain of the normal, of the unremarkable' (Fitzpatrick 1988: 190). To rephrase this somewhat, one might say that the sovereign-law model of liberal legality is increasingly sustained by its close articulations with pastoral models of power, which embed its authority in the taken-for-grantedness of everyday life, in the 'normality' of the private lives of individual selves, in the freedom of the community. What is at stake here is an articulation that strikes at the very heart of liberal political thought; namely, between security and liberty (Burchell 1991, Gordon 1991). And this implies at least two areas in which the law's constitutive relations with community mediation are apparent.[11]

First, formal law is not simply a negative mechanism of restraint on the natural, 'unbounded freedom' of the individual subject, as liberal conceptions may insist. Liberal legality presumes the primordial existence of free, rational, individuals – the bearers of its rights, duties and freedoms. This implies that such individuals exist naturally, and merely require political structures to vindicate that natural form.[12] In other words, the liberal version of the sovereign-law model is predicated upon the existence of free individuals and operates to constrain their unlimited freedom either in the interests of community rights, or as a means of enforcing rights, duties, obligations, etc. (J. Turner 1971). But the problem is, as I have noted, such individuals and selves are not naturally occurring entities: they are the historical products of particular power formations. The individual, to return to Marx, is not 'the starting point of history' but rather something that is 'socially determined' (1973: 83–85). Thus law relies upon the formation of a particular conception of individuals and selves (liberal, neo-liberal, etc.) in fields that are related to, but operate at a suitable distance from, its own institutions (Foucault 1977b). The deployment of a particular vision of community justice, with its pastoral model of power, helps to create the individual, responsible, rational and free selves that are the substance of legal reasoning.[13] And to secure such entities, the legal establishment plays an important role in creating the spaces for these to emerge. Thus, the 'dark side' of liberal legality lies in its capacity to help create and sustain a complementary domain of freedom in which the individual bearers of its rights can exist independently of state regulation.

Already in the late eighteenth century, liberal economists had developed an opposition between 'civil society' and the state (the private and the public) to limit the state's sphere and to declare an autonomous realm of individual economic action.[14] The creation of a realm of private individual freedom, beyond the jurisdiction of the state, may have sought to limit the influence of the contemporaneous states, but it certainly did not limit the sphere of governmental regulation. On the contrary, as Gordon astutely observes,

> Adam Ferguson's notion of civil society can be read ... as being concerned with the task of inventing a wider political framework than that of the juridical society of contract, capable of encompassing individual economic agency within a governable order.
>
> (1991: 37)

As such, developing a private domain of individual freedom was deemed to be an important aspect of an emerging governmental mode of regulation. In this instance, the sovereign-law model of power limits its own exercise, and defers to a less predictable but less visible (and more efficient) pastoral power the task of creating individuals and norms upon which its law depends.

In more recent times, the impetus to create a domain of freedom – the 'community' – where individuals (disputants) are 'free' to select informal mediation to settle their disputes seems to be an attempt to secure a normative order alongside the formal apparatuses of law.[15] The integrity of the province's liberal sovereign-law model is related to its success in developing and sustaining a 'complementary' pastoral domain of freedom. Indeed, the emerging dispute resolution domain has been created in large measure by the space that the legal establishment has allowed for the operation of community justice. This may explain why even some advocates bemoan the fact that community mediation 'is not growing from the bottom-up at this stage' (interview, 26/09/1990). In British Columbia, the expansion of the community as a postulated domain of freedom was initially pushed by the socialist New Democratic Party government in a postulated attempt to democratise society (Clague *et al.* 1984). In the hands of the neo-liberal Social Credit Party, which held office from the mid-1970s to early 1990s, the community became a residual category for its quest to 'decentralise', 'privatise', 'deregulate', 'corporatise' social services (Pavlich forthcoming, Callahan and McNiven 1988, Magnussen *et al.* 1984). In the dispute resolution arena, as noted in chapter 3, this neo-liberal quest to recover notions of community initially took the form of 'taking justice back to the community', and later was translated into using the community as a means of 'increasing access to justice' (Hughes 1988, Smith 1989). Here, community mediation is touted as one of various effective, informal means of conflict resolution that is able to increase the number of points where individuals can vindicate their 'natural' rights. Community justice is thus viewed as more accessible to ordinary individuals than the courts in a number of important ways (e.g. linguistic, geographic, procedural, administrative, financial and temporal). This trend has yet to be reversed.

As a mechanism to increase access to justice, the shape of the community justice domain was structured, through very early experiments, as very much part of the legal establishment's ongoing legal reform initiatives (Becker 1975, Hogarth 1974). Hence, state legal structures have from the outset been instrumental in defining the shape of community justice. This explains, perhaps, why courtroom law is bestowed a particular respect by those advocates of community mediation who have located themselves within the dispute resolution spaces granted by the legal establishment. Thus, in all the interviews conducted for this research, and in much of the advocates' literature,[16] there is little disagreement that mediation should address only 'minor' disputes, and that the final means of appeal on any of these disputes must be the formal legal system. Indeed, as with programmes elsewhere, mediators tend to use the possibility of court appearances as a thinly veiled threat for recalcitrant disputants (Tomasic 1982). Thus the courts provide a carefully erected boundary around the voluntary domain of community justice.

Secondly and closely related to the previous point, the identity of the community justice domain has been significantly shaped by specific impetuses within the legal establishment. Most notably, to contend with perceived crises that courts face as result of increasing case-loads, administrative failures and so on, there is a pressure to manage so-called minor cases outside courtroom settings (Hughes 1988). One result has been the search for alternatives, but within definite limits that do not fundamentally challenge the precepts of liberal legality; hence the clear involvement of the legal establishment in attempts to shape the identity of community justice in the province. Most notably, it has attempted to colonise aspects of community mediation through: funding practices; legal experts who enunciate the form of community mediation (Pitsula 1987, Pirie 1987, CBA, Task Force Report 1989); the formation of joint associations (e.g. Mediation Development Association of British Columbia); statutory provisions; its mediation training schemes (Chalke 1988, Pirie 1987); and judicial encouragement in certain areas (e.g. family mediation) versus prohibition in others (e.g. more 'serious' criminal offences). Moreover, early experiments that established the auspices of community justice (focused on individual needs, success determined by case throughput, etc.) were funded and evaluated on the basis of criteria that are entirely congruent with particular managerial aims (see Justice Development Commission, Courts Division, 1976, Smith 1989, Dolan 1989). In so doing, the formal legal apparatuses were directly involved in defining the nature of community mediation programmes within a dispute resolution arena bounded by courtrooms. Even if the law's effect on community mediation has been profound in British Columbia, there are some, perhaps less consummate, ways in which community mediation has affected the identity of the province's (neo-)liberal legality. Let us turn to these.

COMMUNITY MEDIATION AND THE LAW

As we have seen, advocates argue that community justice supports the legal edifice by removing 'minor' cases clogging up the court system and resolving them more effectively than is possible through adjudication. To the extent that community mediation actually does do this, it is involved in a process of re-configuring the lowest rungs of the court system.[17] That is, community justice offers the courts a way of dealing with the multiplicity of 'minor' disputes whose dense presence threatens the administrative and symbolic efficiency of the liberal judiciary. By trivialising such disputes as 'minor', and providing alternative, informal forums that emphasise voluntarism, settlement and individual participation, community justice helps to neutralise conflict while nurturing normative behaviours sanctioned by law (Abel 1982b). It reinforces the structure of law by dispelling conflict in two related ways: first, it helps to disaggregate collective challenges to the legal system by individualising disputes and seeking settlements congruent with the legal system; and, secondly, it employs subtle and flexible procedures that trivialise conflicts that might otherwise threaten the integrity of law.[18] In this dual process, community justice also helps to reconcile contradictions between the increasingly discredited view of law as a universally accessible means of vindicating all individual's 'rights' equally, and the rather different story of its application at local levels.[19] Indeed, as advocates of community mediation point out, such access is especially restricted in local contexts for those without sufficient financial means, technical know-how, time, etc. (Hughes 1988). In so far as community mediation tries to redress this problem of access, it alters the identity of law in a direction of greater 'responsiveness to the community' and increased 'access' to dispute resolution mechanisms. It also underplays, to some extent at least, conventional adversarial techniques and ascribes an openness to the legal system. As indicated in the previous section, this reconstituted identity is closely associated with a neo-liberal quest to deregulate state agencies, to do away with bureaucratic 'red tape' and to deal with legitimacy crises facing the court system. But it also renders aspects of the legal system far more flexible than is possible under the rule of law – something that seems increasingly evident in modes of regulation under postmodern conditions (Harvey 1991).

To some extent, community justice also transforms the identity of law by underscoring an important feature of the modern liberal sovereign-law model; namely, the appearance of judicial independence from the state. The latter is crucial to the preservation of 'legal neutrality' and to uphold claims that law is a fair, impartial, universal and independent mechanism. Under postmodern conditions, this modern appeal is upheld, not through modern auspices, but by creating perceptions of a 'gap' between the state and the law.[20] In counterposing itself to both formal law (i.e. as an 'alternative' form of dispute resolution) and the state (i.e. as operating in 'the community'), community mediation establishes a symbolic distance between these and sets itself apart from both. This supplements the multiple political processes that seek to annul the appearance of an immediate connection between the state and law, by placing the 'community' as a mediating space between these domains. Moreover, by claiming an ability to resolve only minor disputes, informal justice reinforces the authority of the law by relinquishing more serious (important?) disputes to the courts.

THE SYMBIOSES OF MUTUAL CONSTITUTION: 'REMOTE CONTROL'

So far, my analysis has pointed to various significant articulations between the political models of state law and community justice. Their political rationalities and tactics coincide, intersect and also cleave in a number of different ways, producing (through their diverse associations and disjunctions) a governmentalised state. But what precisely is the relationship between the relations that claim the rubric of the *formal state* and community mediation in British Columbia? Fitzpatrick's 'integral pluralism' concept offers an astute means of formulating a response: the state and community mediation, like the state and law, or community mediation and the law, are constitutively related to one another (1983). This is to say, these fields are, to a greater or lesser extent, directly implicated in each other's identities, being constituted in diverse ways by their various inter-relations. This means that a shift in the articulations between any of the fields is likely to have ramifications that affect the identities of those involved. So, for example, if the state were to withdraw all its funding for community mediation programmes (in response, perhaps, to pressures from the economic field), the ensuing character of community mediation in the province is likely to change, because certain political practices sustaining its identity will have shifted. In turn, the state's identity will have been altered to some extent, as would other related fields (e.g. the courtroom).

However, there are two points to bear in mind here. First, the relations between fields are not equally reciprocal; the state's impact on the identity of community mediation has been far greater than the other way around. Second, even though fields may be constitutively related to one another, no field is ever completely 'sutured' (Laclau and Mouffe 1985). On the contrary, there are always (greater or lesser) areas of autonomy in the fields, providing the bases of historical contingency. Thus, although constituted to a large degree by the state and legal fields, community mediation does harbour autonomous and autochthonously deployed elements. There is an 'unembedded' dimension to community justice and therefore at least a potential capacity to offer some resistance to the strictures of formal legality; but, at present, such resistance appears to have been effectively silenced through procedures of state exclusion.

Notwithstanding such considerations, the state, law and community mediation in British Columbia are unilaterally related in a bid to secure associative cohesion and stability. Their relations converge in the dual aims of achieving both *law* and *order* and imply 'the tricky adjustment between political power wielded over legal subjects and pastoral power wielded over live individuals' (Foucault 1981d: 235). This adjustment involves a series of alliances between the state, law and community mediation that seek to achieve mass obedience by aligning the aspirations of conflicting individuals with the state's wider objectives of order (Rose and Miller 1992, N. Rose 1990, Miller and Rose 1990). Such an argument entails a far-reaching integration of: the sovereign-law with the pastoral model of power; laws with norms; the aims of authorities and subjects; and the judicial rights of citizens with the normal individual lives of community members.[21] The alliances between the legal, state and community justice fields are sustained by multiple, unstable, synoptic practices that produce strategic envelopes between fields.[22] Perhaps one of the most important means of exerting control, while preserving a suitable symbolic distance between state, law and community, is through existing funding practices. By encouraging certain kinds of programme applications, setting explicit guidelines for programme proposals, funding very specific kinds of community mediation programmes, and providing model community justice experiments, the state and law have been constitutively related to the formation of community justice while preserving a semblance of distinction from it (Callahan and McNiven 1988).[23]

Through such associations between the political models of state and law on the one hand, and community mediation on the other, one glimpses how the modern liberal state is increasingly governmentalised under postmodern conditions. In its quest for community cohesion, the state no longer relies only on the legalisation of citizen's rights/duties and a disciplinary (social) order, but has also incorporated techniques of self to produce the selves who choose and aspire to the regulatory aims of postmodern political environments (Edge 1994, T. Miller 1993). Community mediation is an example of a site where laws, disciplinary norms and techniques of self intersect in complex combinations, sometimes through the legalisation of normal subjects but also in a normalisation and subjectification of laws.[24] The links between laws and norms, between judicial litigants and normal disputants, seek to (re)constitute a harmonious relational complex devoid of conflict, called the community. And what, one might well ask, are the regulatory effects, the dangers, of this governmentalised state in the dispute resolution arena under postmodern conditions? As noted, the conjunctural links across particular political rationalities and practices could be viewed as producing a wider, synoptic rationality that is constituted by, but transcends, local rationalities. In other words, the governmentalising articulations between the sovereign-law and pastoral models in the dispute resolution arena yield a further political rationality comprising, but yet beyond, both models. This more general political rationality of the governmentalised state in British Columbia's dispute resolution arena has produced what one may call *remote control*.[25] Such a mode of regulation is the effect of the conjunction between the sovereign-law and pastoral models of power in the dispute resolution arena. Although there are numerous aspects to this type of regulation, let us here focus on four of its most important consequences.

First, the governmentalisation of the state alters the objects of regulation, the sites in which regulation occurs, the ways in which actions are governed and the political techniques employed. As such, the conjunction of the sovereign-law and pastoral models under postmodern conditions has produced a collection of practices, over and above the judiciary, that have fragmented the social domain into disparate local communities (see chapter 1 above). Although the fragmented communities are constitutively related to legal structures, they do contain much more than the legal relations. As N. Rose succinctly observes,

> Rather than being rigidly tied into publicly espoused forms of conduct imposed through legislation or coercive intervention into personal conduct, a range of possible standards of conduct, forms of life, type of 'lifestyle' are on offer, bounded by law only at the margins.
>
> (1990: 226–227)[26]

Through pastoral techniques that shape 'lifestyles' and subjective aspiration, remote control can potentially intrude into areas of regulation involved with the constitution of free subjects. For example, in the very process of assuming the self-identity of a mediation 'client', participants in community mediation are said to have freely chosen how to resolve their disputes. But

142

there is an extreme irony in freely choosing one's mode of regulation, of being granted the dubious freedom to choose one's own chains. Accepting this freedom, and participating in the institutions that bear its name, comes at the considerable cost of imposing a regulatory enclosure whose normative decrees are enunciated in the shadows of a ubiquitous disciplinary gaze and an obligation to confess. In short, this amounts to no less than a conjunction of a particular vision of liberty and security, in order to preserve the integrity of the neo-liberal state. It has little to do with another sort of liberty, a liberty whose effect is not necessarily community order and security.

Second, and related to the above point, remote control involves regulatory forms that are less visible than public judicial decrees. In its pastoral moments, it aims at creating fields in which actions are subject to rational calculation and regulation, and which eliminate the unpredictable through planned, continuous management. This ideal lends itself to a technocratic, managerial, administrative, human science discourse that seeks to engineer the 'consent' of those that it governs (Harrington 1982, 1985, Hofrichter 1982, Gramsci 1980). Central to this is the notion of planning, which works from the premise that there is an intrinsic logic to the community and that probable actions within specific fields of this domain can be calculated. For instance, community mediation is deployed as a way of securing consensus, harmony and peace by focusing on the common ground that is assumed to be intrinsic to communal being. Programmes are *planned*, and later evaluated, on the basis of calculations designed to measure its effectiveness at resolving 'minor' disputes. Here the aim is to develop a field of action that can neutralise potentially disruptive community conflicts quickly, cost-efficiently and permanently – there is little place for the grassroots input of those to whom programmes are directed. In this sense, remote control governs its objects by creating and structuring fields of action on the basis of prior calculation or planning and of continued evaluation, wherein specified community problems (e.g. conflict) – problems that threaten to undermine community solidarity – are designated for administrative solution. No doubt, this effect is entirely congruent with Lyotard's important insight that under postmodern conditions it is the technocratic legitimation of knowledge that 'is gaining new vigour' (1984: 35). It is also entirely congruent with the expanding body of literature that notes current regulatory trends towards calculations of risk and insurance technologies, rather than definitions and institutional containment of 'dangerousness' (Ewald 1991, Castel 1991, Simon 1988).

Third, as the concept 'remote control' implies, calculations and decisions taken in one context are not immediately translated into actions in other contexts through hierarchical bureaucracies. For example, there is no formally constituted bureaucracy to convey central cabinet decisions to actions in particular mediation sessions. Rather, under postmodern conditions, there is a complex assemblage of networks – state authorities, funders, associations, programme coordinators, volunteers, mediators and experts – through which this is (or is not) achieved. Such networks do not reflect a clear, hierarchical chain of command that links decisions in one place to action at another. Rather, as Miller and Rose put it, such networks involve

> alliances formed not only because one agent is dependent upon another for funds, legitimacy, or some other resource which can be used for persuasion or compulsion, but also because one actor comes to convince another that their problems or goals are intrinsically linked, that their interests are consonant, that each can solve their difficulties or achieve their ends by joining forces or working along the same lines.

(1990: 10)

In other words, the articulation of the two models of power results in a more intricate set of relays than found in the codified, hierarchical account-ability of state bureaucracies. This is not to deny the considerable discretion of certain bureaucrats, but only to highlight that the pastorship of com-munity mediation indicates a different means of relaying political calcu-lations and decisions to local contexts. Here, the process of authorisation is less well defined and appears as an amorphous conjunction of various agents. Critical amongst these are the volunteers who, if persuaded that they share interests with the state, are likely to translate decisions to local contexts with some efficiency. After all, volunteers who carry out political decisions often make these decisions appear as freely elected courses of action or as caring, altruistic gestures adopted by concerned community members. In remote control then, the efficiency of power is directly pro-portional to a certain capacity to mask and even deny, its own format.

Fourth, remote control does not operate as an Orwellian totalitarianism that stifles the true individual self, a nightmare that is often close to modern, liberal critiques of the state. The latter has not become an expand-ing leviathan controlling our every move, but has instead taken a different and in some ways more dangerous form. Remote control colonises the body, invades the individual's self-identity and subjective aspirations, and becomes an internal voice that regulates conduct with minimal extraneous intervention. A significant danger here is its operation by stealth in the shadows of appealing claims to empowerment, voluntary control over disputes, liberty from a therapeutic state, etc. The very processes of com-munity mediation that try to align individual notions of self with peaceful communities, regardless of the inequities that might be required to sustain these so-called communities, are examples of political technologies that seek to bring 'the varied ambitions of political, scientific, philanthropic, and professional authorities into alignment with the models and aspirations of individuals, with the selves that each of us want to be' (N. Rose 1990:

144

213). In other words, the conjunction of the sovereign-law and pastoral models of power does not produce a totalitarian state that controls our every move; instead, the governmentalised state produces a power that is endogenous to the very constitution of the 'us' as individual selves. As such, the governmental rationality of our age does not so much constrain individual, subjective beings as it constitutes them. This would suggest that we problematise our historically produced subjectivity not as a necessary basis of liberation but as a possible source of profound constraint.

COMMUNITY MEDIATION AND THE FUTURE: DANGERS, RESISTANCE AND STRATEGIC ENGAGEMENT

By conceptualising the growth of community mediation in British Columbia as part of an emerging 'remote control', one is better poised to grasp some immanent dangers of community justice. For within its deployment lie the perils of a dubious conjunction of liberty and security, a technocratic legitimation of its calculations of community justice, an invisible political force that moves stealthily in the shadows of the present, and a set of techniques that seek to colonise individual selfhood and aspirations. In tandem, these refer to a further danger of claiming to secure a popular, community justice as an alternative to professionalised calculations of justice. The constitutive relations between professional and community justice, and indeed the previously noted lack of grassroots participation in the deployment of community mediation in British Columbia, militate against such claims. Yet in the advocates' claims lies the immediate danger of community justice enlisting the unwitting support of disputants under dubious pretences. Indeed, as argued above, and as Fitzpatrick (1992b, 1993) notes, popular justice is impossible so long as its models of power are designed to complement those of professional justice, and so long as popular and professional calculations share common mythological auspices. The practical attempt to divorce community justice from professionalised justice, to develop an alternative politics of dispute resolution, would involve no less than the radical disarticulation of the pastoral and sovereign-law models of power, especially at those moments where their conjunction fortifies (complements) professional calculations of the just. The calculation of a popular, community justice would thus involve – to return to Derrida for the moment – an experience of the impossible, of the silences beyond current enunciations licensed by the governmentalised state.

Such is the monumental scale of reconstitution involved in altering the auspices of postmodern practices of justice fortified by remote control. No doubt, the uncoupling of the political rationalities requires a form of resistance that is unlikely to be completed by staying within, and is made considerably more difficult by the subtle techniques of, regulatory forms under postmodern conditions. Even so, beginning such a task implies at least two forms of knowledge. First, it requires us to conceptualise resistance in the realm of community justice; because the exercise of power here is not always visible, conceptions of resistance should be sufficiently assiduous to take account of the seemingly invisible. Although the idea of resistance is somewhat obscure in Foucault's work, other theorists provide some bases from which to develop a 'game opening' (e.g. Fitzpatrick 1988, Sawicki 1991). Secondly, to avoid the implicit political apathy of the early critics, it is important to address the practical question: what strategically can be done? The emphasis here must be on the word 'can', to emphasise the speculative nature of my remarks here; I claim no special right to tell others what prescriptively what *must* be done. In any case, to develop aspects of both these knowledges, I shall start by considering notions of resistance and then focus on each of the four effects outlined above. The aim of the latter is to contemplate issues of importance to strategies that seek to reverse those aspects of community justice's current deployment that help to sustain professionalised calculations of the just.

Conceptualising resistance: The case of community justice

For Foucault, resistance is simultaneously inside and outside of power (1978, 1982, 1988c). That is, for a power relation to exist, there must be resistance (1982: 219–222). As he puts it, '[w]here there is power, there is resistance and yet, or rather consequently, this resistance is never in a position of exteriority in relation to power' (Foucault 1978: 95). As we have seen, he repudiates his critics (e.g. Soper 1986, Taylor 1986) who suggest that if power is endemic to all forms of social being then there can be no escape from its clutches. For him, society, or community, is an indeterminate domain structured by power relations, but that harbours various possibilities of both domination and resistance. To suggest that there is no escape from power relations, as though it were possible to reach outside of Weber's 'iron cage', is for Foucault to misunderstand the 'strictly relational character of power relationships' (1978: 95). Since power is endemic to all associative patterns, there is no powerless void beyond the limits of the present; there is only the possibility of different power relations that may not entail the subjugations and oppressions of the present (Hiley 1984). His is a Hegelian view in which power exists only where there is resistance: without the intransigence of freedom where people are faced with different possible modes of action, the tactics and strategies that characterise power relations become redundant (Sawicki 1991: 25). In short, power does not obliterate resistance, but rather depends on antagonism for its very being (Foucault 1982). In those situations where opposing forces seek to eradicate one another completely, there may be relations of confrontation or violence, but not power (Foucault 1981d: 253).

146

A number of theorists, especially feminist writers, have developed Foucault's fragmentary observations on resistance into a more useful framework for concrete struggles that are of value to the present question (e.g. Sawicki 1991, Diamond and Quinby 1988, McNay, 1994, 1992 and also Rajchman 1986, Flynn 1989). As noted, Fitzpatrick (1988) also provides such an analysis, and, given his specific concern with informal justice, it may be just as well to concentrate on his account. In view of his more recent pronouncements on the impossibility of popular justice, one can say that the aim of such resistance is not to capture an eternal popular justice, but rather for a more modest recalculation of justice that itself may alleviate some contemporary forms of oppression, but which itself is unlikely to be exempted from danger. Thus the calculation and recalculation of justice has no end: it involves the relentless pursuit of the impossible beyond the limits that define presence in context (Derrida 1992). In any case, Fitzpatrick outlines various issues that are important to consider when developing a 'counter power' out of community justice. To begin with, in successfully engaging with power, at the very point of opposition, a counter power simultaneously modifies the power relation it opposes and is itself altered by that relation. That is, resistance is not simply a residual, or negative, aspect of power, but rather the very process of engagement transforms both power and counter power. In this sense, as Fitzpatrick puts it, '[a]n act of resistance entails, even if sometimes implicitly, some positive project of power which engages with and seeks, at least in part, to reverse or modify the power it opposes' (1988: 185). One implication is that, if resistance were to be planned and organised around a precise strategy, it need not simply comprise fragmentary, or isolated, acts of recalcitrance. It could, that is, emerge as a positive counter power to contest the dominant power effectively. An organised, synoptic opposing power might, if successful, transform the process of engagement with a dominant power in such a way as to alter intersecting patterns of domination.

However, there are a number of problems that confront those who prepare to engage with dominant powers. The first concern sceptics of this tactic are likely to raise is that of co-optation: what is to prevent agents from being co-opted through engagement? This is an especially pertinent problem when one is dealing with a flexible (neo-)liberal legality and with a dispute resolution arena dominated by that legality. In response, Fitzpatrick reinterprets Foucault's insight that resistance is simultaneously inside and outside power to provide more content to power-counter power engagements. When engaging with dominant powers, resistance strategies are both *included* and *excluded* by the dominant power. As one astute interviewee put it, the liberal state's typical response to an 'experiment' (such as diversion or mediation) in the legal field is to 'absorb and neutralise it. And that's the effective liberal way of dealing with innovation . . . you adopt it, you take it under your bosom, you adapt it and neutralise it' (interview, 21/01/1991). In British Columbia, although the legal establishment may have adopted the idea of community mediation, it has adapted some of its basic tenets. For instance, from informal justice's emphasis on individual empowerment it has recovered notions of 'increasing access to justice', thereby neutralising the potentially disruptive features of the experiment. At the same time, however, a dominant power may exclude a counter power by denying the latter's existence, or significance, or both. In the community mediation arena, such exclusion is evident from the manner in which everyday, common conflicts are trivialised and treated as 'minor' disputes. In so excluding legitimate conflict from its midst and transposing it to the informal justice arena, the legal establishment denies the source of a possible counter power. By both including and excluding potential counter powers surrounding the community mediation movement in British Columbia, the legal system is able to split, reappropriate, deny and contain resistance in manageable units (the community, the disputing family, the individual, etc.).

On the basis of these observations, Fitzpatrick offers two cautionary notes for a possible resistance strategy. On the one hand, one cannot assess the importance of a counter power empirically, because its very existence may be systematically denied. Thus, one ought not to reject too quickly various alternatives to professionalised justice, even if – and maybe especially if – they are ridiculed and dismissed by the existing dispute resolution domain. This suggests that a sustainable task for an alternative politics of dispute resolution under postmodern conditions is to seek subjugated knowledges, those trapped in the shackles of silence, and to provide forums in which these might be articulated as multiple claims to justice. That is, resistance might involve a politics of difference that resurrects implicit knowledges that belie many disputes; the knowledges that articulate, say, what it is to live in a society that can place one in the fetters of a miserably poor existence in which paying the rent is the least of one's concerns. Justice in such instances might be calculated as an attempt to convey subordinated knowledges, multiply the games of the just and voice the silences beyond the limits that enunciate what is (Lyotard and Thebaud 1985).

On the other hand, Fitzpatrick is pessimistic about the possibility of attaining significant transformation through political technologies sanctioned by dominant powers. More concretely, he has serious doubts about the efficacy of adopting current legal definitions of community justice, because this implies a tacit acceptance of the authority of law.[27] He warns a counter power to law cannot be surrounded by law; rather its 'terms of engagement' must be 'set and supported from outside law' (1988: 195). In this sense, an effective counter power, an alternative politics of dispute resolution, may well seek to operate from within the shadows cast by community and formal justice (Gregory 1987, C. Smart 1989, Pavlich 1995). Such a politics would, to return to the previous paragraph, likely sit most comfortably with those unvoiced settings that dominant patterns of power have pillaged or banished to silence. It is here, he tells us, that we must seek to recover a domain in which 'the vitality of alternative traditions' remains (Fitzpatrick 1988: 196). This conceptualisation of resistance provides a knowledge from whence to begin the difficult task of developing an alternative politics of dispute resolution and of redefining the identity of the community mediation movement of British Columbia. It calls for a type of engagement that resists articulations between the two models of power, and the consequent remote control, that enlists a specific vision of community to complement professionalised justice. Knowledge of such engagement takes us to the next issue of examining each of the four ways in which community mediation governs at a distance in British Columbia. This knowledge could inspire, or directly imply, concrete practices that aim to resist the hegemony of neo-liberal, professionalised calculations and practices of justice that haunt our time.

THE PROMISE: AN ALTERNATIVE POLITICS OF DISPUTE RESOLUTION

Liberty and security

At the heart of remote control, as we have seen, is the conjunction of liberty and security where 'domains of freedom' are closely associated with the security of the state. This has important consequences for political technologies, such as community mediation, that purport to operate in a spontaneous, free sphere (e.g. the community). In its current form, community mediation does not resist the state's sovereign-law model, as its voluntaristic rhetoric might imply; on the contrary, there is a complementary, continuous and mutually constitutive relation between the courts and community justice and their underlying political models. The paradox of simultaneously claiming to be an 'alternative' that is yet 'system-based' reflects the close articulation between the 'freedom' created by pastoral power and the hegemony of the sovereign-law forms of power. A closer look at this paradox reveals some important dimensions to community justice. For instance, community mediation is 'system-based' not only because its margins are bounded by formal legality (e.g. through the courts, statutes, traditions and funding patterns), but also because it is internally colonised by system-orientated practitioners. It is also 'system-based' in that its goal is to preserve the *status quo* by expunging conflict from the community, thereby preserving an 'order' within which law may function. With this in mind, mediation may be an 'alternative', but not because it is empowering or especially voluntary; rather, it is different because it employs an alternative model of power. This is to say, the purported voluntarism and empowerment that informalism affords to its participants cannot be divorced from the security requirements of the governmental state under postmodern conditions. The freedom ascribed to community mediation by its advocates, although possibly appealing to those who face the daunting prospect of litigation, is itself an invidious form of subjugation. The very process of creating the limited freedoms of individual selves through mediation is certainly not a means of resisting professionalised justice in British Columbia. An authentic alternative to such a pluralised, postmodern, dispute resolution environment is surely not to be found between state law and community mediation, but rather between the professionalised justice of (neo-)liberal dispute resolution fields and the calculations of a justice yet to emerge.[28]

Although an alternative politics of dispute resolution might develop from here, it need not replicate the confrontation between postmodern legal theory's quest for local, small-scale resistance (e.g. Handler 1992, O'Hagan, 1988, Unger 1983) and the traditional left's quest for large-scale political change (Hunt 1990a: 533, Dews 1987). On the contrary, given the articulations between pastoral and sovereign-law models, a politics of resistance might, depending upon context, include aspects of both micro and synoptic forms of resistance. As Gramsci suggests (1980: 235), struggles against contemporary social forms must occur in the outer 'trenches' as well as against centralised state apparatuses. In any case, resistance to remote control implies that we place in question the freedom that mediation offers to its clients and the consensus-orientated community it holds as an ideal. It also suggests, for example, that the prevailing tendencies within the community justice movement towards the implementation of 'standards' or mediator certification require revision. Such tendencies amount to a dangerous professionalism of community justice that inscribes the concerns of professional justice into the very heart of the community justice movement, allowing the sovereign-law model to include, co-opt and reorganise fragments of pastorship to suit very particular purposes.

The difficult task for those pursuing an alternative calculation of justice in a different political theatre is to uncouple community justice from its extreme dependence on state law, to separate liberty from security. What is required here is the formulation of strategies to thwart practices in particular programmes that weld abstracted notions of individual freedom to a community order. At the same time, it seems important to reconstitute the present forms of engagement between community mediation programmes and the state/law in terms that are not dictated by the latter. Of course, this no simple matter and is unlikely to be completely achievable. But it would nevertheless involve such fundamental reversals as: rearranging present funding practices that encourage programmes to follow the dictates of state agencies or legal foundations rather than to nurture multiple calculations of justice; developing ways to assess the value of specific programmes that de-emphasise administrative or technocratic criteria and emphasise contributions to the recovery of subjugated knowledges; revoking the exclusive use of lawyers or social experts as mediators and loosening their grip on local networks; and resisting practices that portray lawyers and social experts mediators as a unified body (i.e. fragmenting this constructed unity may be important to oppose the hegemony of a 'system-based' informal justice).

Calculated social fields

As noted, community mediation is part of a wider attempt to structure fields of action designed to expunge conflicts from the community. Deploying such mediation programmes involves planning and calculation to set up relational fields in which agents can educate consent and neutralise potentially disruptive disputes. This process provides support for the *status quo*, without due regard for wider inequities and oppressions that might have generated conflict in the first place. Impeding this aspect of community mediation requires directing counter powers at the rhetorical justifications for the current deployment of mediation, and the specific procedures that neutralise legitimate conflict. Turning to the first – the rhetorical justifications – one could refer to the various insights of the ideology critics discussed in chapter 4. In British Columbia, as noted, one of the main rationalisations for the deployment of community mediation centres around its capacity to redress the administrative failures of the court system. A counter power might well seek to resist the technocratic legitimations of knowledge under postmodern conditions and refuse to accept the advocates' discourse on administrative, technical planning by refocusing attention on the kind of justice that community mediation imparts. This is to say, a counter power in such an ethos might jettison technocratic justifications along the lines of community mediation being implemented to streamline the court system, or increase 'access to justice', turning to a more fundamental recalculation of community justice from altered auspices. In practical terms, this also requires a reversal of the growing concerns about standards, certification, as well as the flood of experts into the field. Moreover, it demands that the criteria used to evaluate the 'success' of specific mediation programmes do not take the administrative, technocratic form of calculating case-loads and resolution rates.

Secondly, procedures of community mediation that neutralise conflict by individualising disputes require attention. The individualisation process not only obfuscates structural conflicts but inhibits the possible formation of coalitions amongst people involved in structurally generated conflict (e.g. conflicts pertaining to race, class or gender). By fragmenting conflict, community mediation, in its current form, does not encourage a search for structural lines of dissent that given disputes may indicate.[29] A counter power could reinvoke a search for idioms that afford local participants the opportunity of diagnosing the nature, scope and dimensions of given conflicts before developing effective responses to them. Here, conflict need not be seen as intrinsically destructive; it could also be an important way of locating and communicating contradictions, inequities and injustices that affect particular people in given power-knowledge-subjectivity formations. In other words, community mediation might, instead of trying to extinguish conflict in its proximate manifestation between individuals, seek to uncover wider dangers of given associative patterns. It could attend to these in forums designed to bring conflicts to the forefront of the political theatre in a manner quite unlike the artificial, expert-controlled environments of present mediation sessions.

Government through relay

Another important issue to consider when developing counter powers concerns the realisation that remote control is most effective when it is not visible. Community mediation is relayed through almost inscrutable networks, assemblies of coalitions and opposing forces, where, as one interviewee put it, the importance of 'reputation' is central.[30] Although beyond the scope of the present study, a knowledge of the relays, the collusion and the cleavages that characterise the paths of governance is crucial to the formulation of effective counter strategies. I have, however, pointed to a cleavage between lawyers and social 'experts' as mediators, which may profitably serve as a means of fragmenting the hegemony of a relay pattern that subordinates community justice to formal legality. But there is also the more positive task of recovering subjugated knowledges, vital alternative practices, through which to constitute an alternative set of power relays. This would likely involve recovering the autonomous dimensions of resistance hidden in the shadows of associative patterns that dominant powers have created.

In practice, a counter power would surely oppose the advocates' fascination with 'marketing' community mediation, with educating the 'community' about their vision of informalism. Indeed, an alternative calculation of justice may well suggest the exact opposite: community mediation might become part of a range of democratic practices through which people are able to formulate social identities that best capture the particular oppressions they must face on a daily basis (Laclau and Mouffe 1985). That is, it may learn from the postmodern quest for a 'politics of difference' that permits nuances between oppressed groups to emerge (Sawicki 1991, Di Stefano 1990, Yeatman 1990, I. Young 1990, Flynn 1989). At the same time, this need not preclude associations between groups; on the contrary,

152

to be effective, an alternative community justice movement could form synoptic alliances with new social movements that are congruent with its aims (Hutchinson 1992, Kauffman 1990, Plotke 1990). A broadly based coalition of counter-forces that coalesces not on the specific contents of their various forms of subordination but on a common aim of recasting oppressive power formations is likely to be far more effective at shaking hegemonies than solitary groups working in isolation. In the difficult processes of developing alliances between these social movements, in the multiple procedures by which synoptic practices are formed, the silences of subjugated knowledges can provide a possible base for an alternative calculation of justice. In the combination of local practices that would comprise a politics of difference and synoptic alliances between relevant new social movements, an alternative dispute resolution arena could emerge. It would entail a politics whose terms of engagement with state law are set outside of this, in the vital alternative traditions of new social movements (Ratner and Pavlich 1993, McCann 1992, Calavita and Carroll 1992, Epstein 1990).

Subjective aspiration

If remote control colonises subjective aspiration, a counter power would surely seek to subvert the means of colonisation. For instance, it could target acts of refusal at the regulatory objects of community mediation – communities and their purportedly constituent individual, disputing selves. In such acts of refusal, it is important to be extremely cautious of the 'quest for community', in both its nostalgic conservative form (Cohen 1985) or its more liberal guise of 'halting' state totalitarianism (O'Hagan 1988). Notions of community – whatever their formats – situate people in regulatory environments, and therefore the establishment of 'community' releases us neither from power nor from dangerous effects (as the suggestion that they are domains of freedom might imply). To the extent that appeals to community encourage political complacency and limit the critiques directed at finding oppressive structures in power relations that sustain them, specific modes of governance are able to avoid direct scrutiny. Moreover, as I. Young points out,

> The ideal of community presumes subjects can understand one another as they understand themselves. It thus denies the difference between subjects. The desire for community relies on the same desire for social wholeness and identification that underlies racism and ethnic chauvinism on the one hand and political sectarianism on the other.
>
> (1990: 302)

Even if one were to allege that Young overstates her case here, she does make the central point that notions of community are susceptible to the extreme danger of forging unchecked unities that can have disastrous consequences (e.g. race).

In tandem, refusing the objects of governance attacks also its complex panoptic processes that encourage political docility. The efficiency of such governance lies in its capacity not only to conquer the observable, but to do so invisibly, to dictate from the shadows of the discursive facades it erects. Its success lies in an ability to produce obedient subjects – individual selves whose cognition is geared towards particular forms of production, lifestyles that reproduce the social order and human aspirations that reinforce the political aims of the dominant (N. Rose 1990, Miller and Rose 1990). A counter power cannot therefore direct itself exclusively to the centralised, sovereign-law model of power. On the contrary, remote control requires us to takes seriously the political significance of acts that refuse dominant subjective patterns, and the techniques that produce these.

Since pastoral power attempts to integrate subjective aspiration with wider political aims, an alternative calculation of justice is unlikely to be furthered by a search for the essential subjectivity ascribed (imparted?) to normal disputants. Perhaps what is more significant here is a refusal of the subjective identities produced by pastoral power. As Foucault succinctly argues, '[m]aybe the target nowadays is not to discover what we are, but to refuse what we are. We have to get rid of this kind of political "double bind", which is the simultaneous individualisation and totalisation of modern power structures' (1982: 216). At stake here is a refusal of the techniques of self by which community mediation encourages disputants to adopt non-disputing self-identities. Understood as a practice, liberty entails the transgression of limits, practices and techniques that rigidly locate individual selves as subjects of a professional justice that circumscribes our present being. Here again we encounter Foucault's notion of ethics, which, *inter alia*, calls for a politics of ourselves to reverse the Kantian strategies by which a particular conception of the subject is designated as the universal condition of morality (Foucault 1984; see also Bernauer 1990, Rajchman 1991, B. Smart 1985). More positively, this ethics calls for us to conduct an 'historical ontology of ourselves' and to develop other kinds of subjectivities than those nurtured by the spread of professionalised calculations of the just (Foucault 1984: 46).

Refusals of this kind problematise consensual lifestyles that entice disputing selves to adopt new self-identities, as well as the enervated 'freedom' associated with the 'choices' these provide. Such acts of refusal occur at the level of personal life, questioning the very spaces and ways in which we constitute ourselves as selves. In community mediation, one might question the disciplinary constitution of individuality, rescind the dubious confessions that disputants are obliged to make, and will often be required to reject the calculated normalising judgements of the mediator. Indeed, here one ought to be wary of the techniques that promise fulfilling self-identities, that try to steer conflicts into quick individual settlements at the expense of more far-reaching resolutions. This requires specific analyses of the means by which mediation creates subjectivities that perpetuate wider inequities. Of particular significance here is the need to explore the ways in which gender, race, class, age, sexual orientation, and so on, are perpetuated in the kinds of normal subjects that mediation produces.[31] It is important to examine the ways in which such issues affect, and are affected by, the mediation process.[32]

Opposing the normalisation processes that integrate subjective aspirations with wider objects of the state involves deconstructing the 'consensus politics' of community mediation. Is there necessarily 'common ground' between 'disputants' who share a 'community'? Instead of assuming normative consensus and unity, and thereby ignoring structural incongruities, a counter power might seek out contradictions that bear directly on given conflicts. There is far less common ground between, say, a wealthy, white, male landlord and a single mother of colour on welfare than current forms of mediation would have the observer believe. It is important to grasp the qualitative social distances between actors, and not simply to refuse them by assuming the presence of a fundamental, underlying consensus.

IN LIEU OF A CONCLUSION

By way of synoptic review, to parody what is customary in conclusions, this book commenced its narration with an analysis of the auspices of professionalised justice. The latter were considered through modern, liberal legitimating metanarratives that allow justice to be calculated through neo-Kantian eyes as universal principles grounded in the dictates of a reason deemed intrinsic to all human subjects. Such calculations support practices of justice that apply the same codified procedures to specific cases, and that claim to decide between cases on the basis of reasoned deductions from a wider law, be it statutorily formulated or based on case precedent. The auspices of these calculations and practices have encountered fundamental challenges that have left them in veritable crisis. Despite much debate around the formulation, I spoke of attacks on modern metanarratives that seem to have occasioned a move towards a discursive ethos conditioned by altered auspices. The idea of a postmodern condition was alighted upon to indicate the effects that such altered auspices have had on contemporary calculations and practices of justice. In general, we saw that justice has been fragmented, that images of a singular entity have been replaced by plural images of justice occupying different spheres and harbouring different rationalities. In such an environment, there is a quest for dispute resolution idioms sensitive to local nuances that do not eliminate differences by striving to apply one set of procedures to all cases. It is in the ruptures of the emerging ethos that community justice calculations and community mediation practices offer their 'justice without law'.

Community mediation in British Columbia was selected as an example of practices licensed by calculations of community justice. In my case study, and with obvious parallels elsewhere, community justice is calculated by its advocates as an informal alternative to law, an individually empowering means of resolving disputes, a means of strengthening communities and a way of restoring peace to communities. But critics challenge this rather sanguine view, arguing – in their diverse ways – that community justice as currently conceived actually expands state control. Continuing the critical dialogue in the directions opened by the new informalists, the preceding analysis reinterprets both Fitzpatrick and Foucault to approach community mediation as a form of government under postmodern conditions. A closer look at the ways in which mediation employs techniques of discipline and self to achieve peaceful relations between individual disputing selves, in order to restore community order indicates a contemporary version of pastoral power. This provides some background to the concerns of the present chapter, where community mediation is shown to help governmentalise the state by merging its pastoral logic with that of the sovereign-law model. The conjunction between these types of power has shaped the present form of the British Columbian dispute resolution arena, and has introduced a different mode of regulation, namely remote control. Such control couples the aspirations of individual, disputing selves with the requirements of a normal community order that aligns with the aims of a (neo-)liberal state and its legality. The relational alliances that now constitute dispute resolution domains, and that regulate actions through remote control, are shown to harbour four core features. These features could, so the argument goes, serve as a means of diagnosing important dangers in the current deployment of community justice in the province (and others like it). They may be used to help conceptualise resistance to an elusive alliance that has the effect of subordinating alternative calculations to professional calculations of justice. The narrative invites considerations of strategic engagement that resists the subtle political rationalities that do not allow, or disqualify, the formation of an alternative politics of dispute resolution.

So much for the theoretical ambitions of the preceding pages; what of the substantive contributions? Clearly, the narrative takes issue with the advocates' calculations and practices of community justice in British Columbia, and indeed with similar sorts of cases in other contexts (e.g. Shonholtz 1993, Sander 1990, Marshall 1988, Blair 1988). Deployed in British Columbia as a complementary, system-based form of dispute resolution, community justice is shown to be – despite, or perhaps even because of, the claims of its defenders – neither voluntary nor individually empowering, nor even an alternative in any profound sense of the word. At best, it is a compromised attempt to redress what are certainly legitimate criticisms of the formal justice system; at worst, it comprises a manipulated field that promises to resolve disputes justly, but that is radically constrained by its acquiescence with, and subservience to, the dictates of an emerging remote control.

In short, community mediation's promise to liberate litigants from the inhospitable procedures of the courtroom has so far turned out to be an empty one. Community disputes are still individualised and trivialised by processes hellbent on neutralising conflict as efficiently as possible. Furthermore, it is but a pyrrhic victory to have reached agreement on a given set of circumstances in the knowledge that wider patterns of association – which have probably nurtured those conditions in the first place – remain fundamentally intact.[33] One can speculate on possible calculations and practices of a more effective community justice, but it is unlikely to be one that emulates the individualising format of professional justice practices. It would probably be involved in a concerted attempt to dislocate the mutual constitution of law and community mediation. To encourage liberty as an ongoing practice, to divorce liberty from a technocratically conceived community order, would require a dispute resolution process that does not: individualise disputes; ignore social distances between people in their associative environments; reframe silent voices on a bias towards consensus or an elimination of difference; professionalise mediation proceedings or train mediators as technical experts; and emphasise technocratic measures of success. It would, that is, experiment with the impossible, calculate and envision practices of justice yet to come – a justice that strikes at the heart of processes that expunge rather than promote difference, and that seek idioms for subjugated voices to be inscribed onto the hierarchical tapestries of our discourses on justice. But this, no doubt, requires its own elaboration, a task that extends beyond the aims of the present narration but that might take what has preceded as clearing a space for its departure.

There comes a point in any narrative when the writing must end, allowing a text to settle between its opening title, a final period and the interpretations of its readers. But implications of finality are entirely spurious, and it would be arrogant, even contradictory, to suggest that absolute conclusions have been reached. If at all successful, what has been sketched in the preceding pages is no more than a conversational bridge between the discourses I have sought to engage and those that are yet to come, negotiating but one small bend in the ongoing flow of narratives about 'our condition'. And it is here that I turn my spade, peering into the abyss of alternative calculations and practices of justice that have yet to take form. To venture further into the mists of silence, the abandoned caverns of subjugated knowledge, would be to stray too far from the discourses I have sifted through. There is little chance that an alternative politics of dispute resolution will extricate itself entirely from dangerous effects; but there is always the promise of escaping present limits, including those by which a rigid professionalism continues, despite all, to pose as the only possible source of justice.

NOTES

1 IN SEARCH OF A BEGINNING...

1 For example, see Balkin (1994), Douzinas and Warrington (1994), Cornell (1992), Derrida (1992), Murphy (1991), I. Young (1990), MacIntyre (1988), Walzer (1983).

2 See the Alberta Law Reform Institute (1990), Canadian Bar Association, Task Force Report (1989), Emond (1988), Pirie (1987) and Pavlich (forthcoming).

3 See, for example, Abel (1982a), Hofrichter (1987), Baskin (1988), Santos (1982), Harrington (1985) and Matthews (1988).

4 This standpoint does not deny existence *per se*, but merely rejects that the enunciated identity of a thing at a specific moment in history is essential or absolute. Thus, different societal contexts may well have different modes of talking about things, for the coherence of such discourse is constituted not by the 'things' themselves but from the 'rules of formation' that specify how statements are to be dispersed within a theoretical space (Foucault 1973).

5 This is remarkably similar to Wittgenstein's (1983) notion that the meaning of a word lies in its use. If he spoke of language-games as the indissoluble combination of sign, social practice and referent, then I am here using discourse in a rather similar way. However, I shall not be content with Wittgenstein's turned spade of conventional practice, but will seek to show how such practice is unrelentingly antagonistic and forged through relations of struggle.

6 That is, articulation is 'any practice establishing a relation among elements such that their identity is modified as a result of the articulatory practice' (Laclau and Mouffe 1985: 105).

7 Some might object that if elements are floating, if the transition to moments is never complete, then how is it that identity appears to be 'fixed'? Laclau and Mouffe (1985: 112) respond by suggesting that practices of articulation construct certain privileged 'nodal points' that appear to have fixed meaning. But this fixed quality is illusory, not only because signifiers are intrinsically 'floating', but also because the social domain in which articulations are forged is open. As such, the appearance of determinism, or absoluteness, in truth statements is wrested out of complex struggles and antagonisms that forge articulations and produce the form of identity.

8 For instance, Pavlich (1995), B. Smart (1992, 1993), McGowan (1991), Hebdidge (1989), Featherstone (1991).

2 THE FRAGMENTED AUSPICES OF COMMUNITY JUSTICE

1 See also Bauman (1992: xi–xiv).
2 I have selected this text rather than Kant's more explicit analysis of justice – *The Metaphysics of Justice* – because it provides an explicit analysis of the discursive strategy underlying his analysis of morals. For an analysis of Kant's analysis of justice and its relation to Rawls and Lyotard, see May (1990).
3 A caveat: the selection of two texts indicates a certain arbitrariness, which would not (could not) be overcome were one to select five, or even five hundred. The point is not to suggest that these texts are representative of any other texts, as if to say that they offer similar views of justice. Indeed, there are diverse visions and interpretations of justice under modern conditions, which Miller (1974) summarises around three nodal points: 'to each according to his rights; to each according to his deserts; to each according to his needs' (*sic*; 1974: 27). Be that as it may, my purpose here is merely to indicate that influential modernist interpretations of justice continue to make extensive use of the three discursive strategies that Kant (1990) explicitly forges. This allegiance is by no means limited to the texts selected and indeed is likely to be present in one form or another in all texts that continue to draw upon the grand narratives of modernity for their sources of legitimacy.
4 As one commentator notes, certainly without exaggeration, Rawls' book, 'has dominated the philosophical discussion of justice since it was first published in 1971' (Cullen 1994: 17). See also Wellbank *et al.* (1982) for a glimpse of the sheer volume of texts commenting on Rawls' theory a decade after its publication.
5 Rawls' general conception of justice is this: 'All social values – liberty and opportunity, income and wealth and the bases of self respect – are to be distributed equally unless an unequal distribution of any, or all, of these values is to everyone's advantage' (1973: 302).
6 See Rawls (1973: 302) for a final statement of the two principles.
7 Indeed, as if to underscore this insight, MacIntyre entitles his book, *Whose Justice? Which Rationality?*
8 Here Young clearly takes her cues from various postmodern feminist texts (see Nicholson 1990).
9 Refer to Vattimo (1992), B. Smart (1992), Hebdidge (1989), Featherstone (1988) and Lyotard (1984).
10 See Bauman (1992) for an extended, and insightful, diagnosis of this condition referred to here.
11 See, for instance, Foucault (1973), Derrida (1976), Feyerabend (1975) and Heidegger (1962).
12 For example, see Walzer (1983), S. White (1987/88), Lyotard and Thebaud (1985), I. Young (1990), Wickham (1990), Flynn (1989), Derrida (1992), and Douzinas and Warrington (1994).
13 Douzinas and Warrington put this in slightly different terms, but concur with the basic issue: 'Justice is thus caught in an unceasing movement between knowledge and passion, reason and action, this world and the next, rationalism and metaphysics' (1994: 408).
14 What is at stake for Lyotard is as follows: 'Justice here does not consist merely in the observance of the rules; as in all games, it consists in working at the limits of what the rules permit, in order to invent new moves, perhaps new rules and therefore new games' (Lyotard and Thebaud 1985: 100). Instead of silencing difference in universalising frameworks, his call seems to be to work at the limits of all disputes, to focus on the rules (the grammar) of language-

games which bring participants to the point of conflict. The practical task is not to silence, or enforce a settlement, but to seek idioms that recover the rationalities of all parties to a dispute. Then, from Lyotard's point of view at least, the task is to seek novel rules within the various language-games of the disputants, to seek new moves that might help to renegotiate the auspices of the participant's being. As a critical language-game, Lyotard proposes that justice be directed at the rules that set the limits of discourse in different contexts. Such a language-game is to be concerned with the 'grammar' of language-games – by working with existing rules, it must seek 'new moves' to render the finite infinite and escape the limits of a given game. The overtones of Derrida's 'deconstruction is justice' reappear.

15 For an overview of community mediation in the United States see Wahrhaftig (1982), Adler *et al.* (1988), Alper and Nichols (1981), Cook *et al.* (1980); in Canada, see Hogarth (1974), Becker (1975), Blair (1988), Canadian Bar Association, Task Force Report (1989), Pavlich (1992a), and in Western Europe see Garth (1982).

16 For a detailed account of the rise of community mediation in British Columbia, Canada, see Pavlich (forthcoming).

3 CALCULATING COMMUNITY JUSTICE

1 In attempting to tap into the discourses of local community mediation advocates, to provide the substance of my case study, I have used various forms of discourse analysis. These included an analysis of written texts, participant observations of events organised and attended by advocates (e.g. conferences, training sessions, numerous role plays, community events, regional network meetings, etc.), and nineteen in-depth interviews with most (if not all) the advocates who – in the estimation of their peers – played key roles in deploying community mediation in the province. Access to mediation sessions proved to be more difficult (given the confidentiality espoused), but I was nevertheless able to observe seven sessions (three in Chicago as points of comparison) and solicited responses from clients via an open-ended questionnaire (I had no control over the distribution of these, and received a 23 per cent response rate with n = 23). In addition, and most crucial for the work of chapter 5, I observed a series of coaching sessions for prospective mediators where techniques of mediation were discussed and practised in great detail. In one of these sessions, an absent member of the class occasioned my having to 'fill in' as a role-playing disputant, and afforded an opportunity to 'test' some of the questions I had about the process of mediation.

2 For example, Bohannan (1957, 1967), Gluckman (1965), Schapera (1955), Nader (1979), Nader and Todd (1978), Gulliver (1977), Hamnett (1977), Bossy (1983), Comaroff and Roberts (1977, 1981), Merry (1984), Starr and Collier (1989) and Roberts (1979).

3 Galanter (1981), Fuller (1971), and Frank (1970).

4 Matthews (1988).

5 See Danzig (1973), Alfini (1986), Ford Foundation (1978), Auerbach (1983), Buckle and Thomas-Buckle (1982), Cook *et al.* (1980), Ray (1989, 1990), Walker (1980), Tomasic and Feeley (1982), Conner and Surette (1977), Eliff (1971), Fisher (1975), Nader (1979, 1984, 1988), Nader and Singer (1976), McGillis (1986), McGillis and Mullen (1977), Goldberg *et al.* (1985), Abel (1982b), Hofrichter (1987), Harrington (1985), Sander (1990, 1977, 1976) and Rifkin (1982).

6 See, for instance, Emond (1988), Pirie (1987), Pitsula (1987), Peachey *et al.*

(1988), Estey (1981), Benoit *et al.* (1984), Kennedy (1985), Peachey (1989a, 1989b), Alberta Law Reform Institute (1990), Horrocks (1982), Perry *et al.* (1987) and Pavlich (forthcoming).

7 This project ran from 15 May to 30 August and signalled the rise of community-based mediation in the province. There were related experiments prior to this – such as the 1974 Victoria Diversion-Mediation Project, which diverted 'minor' criminal offenders out of the court system (see Solicitor General, Canada 1977) – but these were not explicitly touted as community-based projects.

8 The formation of such networks reflects an intense desire for unity amongst mediators to entrench and protect common interests in society; as one advocate put it, borrowing heavily from a famous United States' statesman, 'If we don't hang together, we'll hang separately' (Moir 1987).

9 See *The Mediator* (37), 1993.

10 The universities of Victoria and British Columbia (particularly through institutes or units of their Law Faculties) offer a range of conflict resolution courses, including mediation.

11 For instance, in 1985, the Justice Institute of British Columbia developed a formal Conflict Resolution Certificate Programme out of earlier, less structured courses. In addition, the Continuing Legal Education Society of British Columbia offers short courses on various facets of ADR.

12 For example, a programme located in the Surrey/White Rock area holds various programmes for the volunteer mediators that it relies upon.

13 For example, Folberg and Taylor (1984), Peachey *et al.* (1983), Fisher and Ury (1983), Kressel and Pruitt (1989), Kolb (1983). See also Sloan (1992) for an overview of local thinking on the power of mediation as a process.

14 For a series of case studies on how different mediators approach disputes, see Kolb *et al.* (1993).

15 Fees are often calculated on a sliding scale in accordance with participants' income levels.

16 As an indication of this government's official policy, one might cite the then Minister of Human Resources: 'In the past, centralised decision-making has led to great frustration in the communities and has encouraged professional groups to dominate the field of services to people. We must give that function back to the communities ... It is the policy of the government that all defined services to people should be operated at the community level by citizens who are volunteers and professionals, and the government will assist in financing these and providing field staff to advise them' (Normal Levi, in Clague *et al.* 1984: 38).

17 Indeed, a Federal Government Task Force was established in 1977 to, as its title indicates, assess *Community Involvement in Criminal Justice* (Sauvé *et al.*, 1977).

18 Dolan (1989: 77) too notes the low participation rates in his analysis of a particular programme in the province. See also, Pavlich (1992a: 48).

19 See Connor (1988) and *The Mediator* (21), 1989: 3.

20 This point was echoed by most interviewees.

21 See also CBA, Task Force Report (1989: 77).

22 Although referring to another context, the following echoes this sentiment and indicates a more general discourse: 'Comunity is built when people are empowered to pursue justice through direct participation' (Lederach and Kraybill 1993: 327).

23 Interviews, 12/09/1991 and 11/01/1990.

24 Similarly, Rifkin (1984) and Harrington and Rifkin (1989) examine this line of thinking in the context of the United States.

25 Personal correspondence with a programme organizer, 19/06/1990.

26 For example, one interviewee, a 'social expert' mediator, relayed an anecdote of being invited to speak at a function alongside a lawyer who stated – in a most discourteous and inconsiderate fashion – that she did not think non-lawyers should be permitted to practise mediation (12/09/1991).

27 For insight into the kinds of standards (which are to be decided by the 'mediation community') this discourse has in mind, see *The Mediator* (37), 1993, insert, *The Mediator* (3), 1990: 3–4 and *The Mediator* (18), 1988: 5. By contrast, advocates of VORP (mediators associated with the church) are rather more cautious of the quest for mediation standards and the possible effects this might have on the community focus of mediation (e.g. Worth 1989: 12). Similar concerns have been raised in the United States by such authors as Pipkin and Rifkin (1984), Shonholtz (1988/89) and Wahrhaftig (1982, 1984).

4 THE CRITICS RESPOND

1 This is not, of course, to suggest that critics fall clearly into one of these three camps. Rather, the categorisation according to their central concerns should be seen as a heuristic device to commence a discussion of the discourse, recognising that – as should become apparent – there is considerable continuity and overlap between writers.

2 For instance, Tomasic (1982), Harrington (1982, 1985), Harrington and Merry (1988), Nader (1988), Abel (1981, 1982a, 1982b) and Adler *et al.* (1988).

3 For example, Hofrichter (1982, 1987), Selva and Bohm (1987), Spitzer (1982) and Baskin (1988, 1989).

4 Here, I am specifically referring to the work of Santos (1982) and Fitzpatrick (1988).

5 See especially Abel (1982a) and Tomasic (1982), but also Abel (1982b), Harrington (1982, 1985, 1988), Merry (1982), and Auerbach (1983).

6 The early mediation experiments out of the Small Claims Court in British Columbia highlight this issue.

7 Harrington and Merry point out that, even though there may be divergent philosophies within the informalism movement, most protagonists are committed to the 'consensual justice' of the courts (1988: 717). It is therefore not surprising to find increasing pressure to professionalise the mediation movement and to increase legislation over mediation in the purported interest of standards. From this perspective, it seems likely that mediation will be institutionalised as no more than another tier in the overall justice system. In addition, the pressure to professionalise mediation comes from the legal organisations and mediator umbrella groups, under the guise of keeping 'standards' (see Harrington 1985: 71–72).

8 For instance, Tomasic (1982) and Abel (1981, 1982b).

9 Nader (1988) makes a similar point in reference to the wider alternative dispute resolution movement.

10 See Abel (1981).

11 Indeed, Abel suggests that, because informalism merely responds to surface manifestations of structural conflicts, it will not be able to resolve grievances on a lasting basis (1982b: 309).

12 See also Cohen (1985: 161–196).

13 They clearly follow (via a reference to Cotteral) a Weberian model whereby

ideologies are seen to be both structurally constrained by the limits of past history and yet open to the contingent potential of human agents in social interaction.

14 It was, as one commentator suggests, a conservative resolution that 'stifled discussions of power by means of indirect controls ... by means of harmony ideologies' (Nader 1988: 286).

15 Terms such as 'empowerment', 'informal', 'community' are examples of often-used 'buzzwords' in the advocates' discourse. An example of a 'false comparison' in the discourse is the tendency to compare mediation with adjudication when, as Abel notes, 'most mediated cases would have been handled by negotiation' (1982a: 9), not by court adjudication. This creates the illusion of separation through a deceptive comparison.

16 See Abel (1982a: 8–10) and Wahrhaftig (1982: 83).

17 See, for example, Cohen (1985, 1988), Abel (1982a), Harrington (1982, 1985), Tomasic and Feeley (1982) and Auerbach (1983).

18 Some even suggest, as does Abel, that, in this ideology, '[p]olitical choice is portrayed as blind necessity, the interests of dominant groups are dressed up in the wishes of the dominated, and informal processes appear as their mirror images' (1982a: 7).

19 See also Cohen (1985, 1988).

20 Moreover, the objects of such control are not random; on the contrary, Abel notes, informal justice targets the 'dominated categories of contemporary capitalism; the poor, ethnic minorities and women' (1982a: 9).

21 See, for example, Gramsci (1980, 1985), Boggs (1984), Bocock (1986), Bobbio (1989), Anderson (1976/7), Mouffe (1979).

22 See Carnoy (1984: 128–152) for a more detailed analysis of this conception of the state.

23 Gramsci used the concept ambiguously, in at least three different ways (Anderson 1976/7). In any case, his use of this concept marks a deliberate attempt to redress the 'fatalism' of rigid, economistic interpretations of Marx's work that reduce political struggles to purportedly underlying economic processes (Gramsci 1980: 175–185; see also, Laclau and Mouffe 1985). Through it, he emphasises the importance of political contests, especially those that seek to organise the consent of the governed (as opposed to those that involve coercive force to secure social 'order'). His analysis outlines the means by which a ruling class secures hegemonic control over all other classes in society by making its 'ideology' synonymous with 'common sense' or the 'natural order' (e.g. Gramsci 1980: 257–264).

24 That is, an illegitimate set of institutions is likely to face uncontrolled resistance and instability rather than secure the stability required for capital expansion. As a result, the state must at least appear 'neutral, universal and autonomous' to most people (Hofrichter 1987: 28).

25 Hofrichter includes the family, community, culture, art, and so on in this realm (1987: 35).

26 Hofrichter also suggests that, if hegemonic, this view will be accepted as 'natural', universal, inevitable, neutral, obvious, etc., by members of a society. And when this occurs, the power struggles that have produced such a common-sensical world view fade into the background and become obscured (1987: 34). But this process is never a *fait accompli*, nor is it entirely stable, because it is the outcome of ongoing struggles. But one should note that these struggles are further complicated by the state's ability to resort to coercive force should its hegemony become threatened (1987: 38).

27 See Hofrichter (1987: 131–142).

28 Apropos predictions about its future, Hofrichter feels that, by blurring the distinction between the state and civil society, 'such that the state does not appear to be the state but rather part of the landscape of community social life' (1987: 153), neighbourhood justice is likely to have various unintended effects. For example, he predicts this would increase the state's discretionary powers and, in turn, undermine the 'rule of law' and the importance of state professionals; these would sabotage the state's claims to neutrality and competence. Although this might translate into a legitimacy crisis for the state, it is almost sure to weaken the rights of moderate- or low-income groups and obfuscate underlying conflicts (1987: 157). In his opinion, the movement is sure to fail because of its internal contradictions and inherently exploitative nature (1987: 159). Indeed, because it is an 'alien state institution' incapable of resolving collective problems (1987: 159), using sham rules and an artificial notion of participation, neighbourhood dispute resolution is unlikely to receive widespread support.

29 See Cohen (1988: 206) and Gallagher (1988: 138).

30 See Jessop (1990) for an excellent overview of regulation theory, and Carnoy (1984) for a synopsis of state-derivation theories. The theorists that Baskin seems to use most are Hirsch (1981, 1983) and Aglietta (1979).

31 This movement, so the argument goes, entailed the progressive involvement of the state in social life as more traditional institutions disintegrated. Thus, whereas Taylorism sought to create the most efficient worker through effective training, the Fordist state seized the opportunity to expand such training to the social domain in the form of 'welfare'. Given the escalating cost of this strategy, the state soon faced a 'fiscal crisis' (O'Connor 1973, Offe 1984) and hence the neo-Fordist (sometimes referred to as the 'post-Fordist') state, which attempts to secure the same effects but by using so-called 'private' agents of control.

32 This explains why many of the cases that are mediated would not reach the formal state (courts) anyway (Baskin 1988: 104).

33 Most simply, community mediation expands on the commodity form to social life by requiring a fee (even if on a sliding scale) for service. Ironically, this injects the appearance of voluntarism into the regulatory form, because people are now presented with a 'choice' as to which type of regulation they wish to be subjected to. Perhaps, as Offe notes, this is all part of a trend, from the 1960s onwards, in which the state tries to 'solve the problem of the obsolescence of the commodity form by politically creating conditions under which legal and economic subjects can function as commodities' (1984: 124).

34 These motivational patterns are nurtured through encouraging 'possessive individualism' and by individualising conflicts. It thereby reinforces the 'basic motivational patterns constitutive of the social norms of production and consumption' (Baskin 1988: 109–110). This is not an insignificant contribution, for, '[a]s profits under capitalism have come to depend less on price consumption and cost of production and more on maintaining monopolistic control over markets and elevating levels of demand, the cultivation of consumer habits, the creation of "consumptive communities", and the shaping of consciousness have become the *sine qua non* of capitalist growth' (Spitzer 1979: 199).

35 This occurs at two levels: first, to the extent that people settle their disputes they are less motivated to resist dominant relations; second, payment for mediation service reinforces the idea that everything can potentially be converted into a commodity.

36 In general, he suggests that the state disperses tensions into 'an apparently

chaotic sequence of administrative failures and successes, of honoured and violated political compromises, and acts of repression and facilitation (whether enforced or merely announced)' (Santos 1982: 251). Although that state has some autonomy in its responses, it is limited by structural 'homologies' that link the political and economic spheres, such that 'state action is subordinated to the logic of capital' (1982: 251). To support this claim, he refers to the 'non-capitalist' residues of the past that still exist in contemporary society as well as to the apparent need to disguise the nature of capital's real logic for it to operate effectively (1982: 250). This provides the basis for the state's 'autonomy' from purely economic processes.

37 That is, for Santos (1982) the law's autonomy is severely truncated because the state manages its 'independence' from the economy.

38 Because these are presented as Weberian 'ideal types', they seldom exist in pure forms in concrete contexts and, instead, combine in complex (and often unanticipated) ways. Such is the nature of the legal pluralism in this account. Although there may be many possible articulations between these structures of law, Santos describes three that are commonly present in capitalist societies (1982: 52–55). First, he speaks of 'quantitative co-variation', which suggests that the more dominant structures of bureaucracy and violence are in a particular society, the less significant rhetorical structures will be. Second, 'geo-political combination' refers to the notion that political domination is not uniform across a field, since the state uses different forms of domination. For instance, it may use mechanisms of neutralisation and exclusion to disperse contradictions at the centre of the social network, while resorting to integration and trivialisation (e.g. informal justice) at the periphery. Third, one often finds 'structural inter-penetration' in capitalist societies, which is to say that these structures tend to 'contaminate' one another, thereby assuming hybrid forms. Thus, he argues, rhetoric has been 'qualitatively' contaminated by the more dominant structures of bureaucracy and violence in our society so that even rhetorical appeals make use of threats of violence or are cast in technocratic discursive moulds.

39 Hence the increased use of neutralisation and exclusion evident in modern capitalist societies.

40 Thus, he argues, these forms of power are quite 'complementary – each is made tolerable (and is reproduced) by the other' (Santos 1982: 262).

41 Nevertheless, Santos argues that, even here, 'civil society' served to mask the fundamental continuity between the so-called private and public (state) domains (1982: 262 at note 15). He thus clearly rejects the tendency in liberal theory to separate state (power and violence) from civil society (freedom and equality).

42 However, he predicts that, although this material expansion of the state is likely to be curtailed (because of a wider fiscal crisis), it will continue to expand symbolically (and hence ward off its legitimacy crises).

43 He also sees the joint effects of the fiscal and legitimacy crises as an important impetus for the rise of informalism (see Santos 1982: 260).

44 See, for instance, Abel (1982b: 270), Baskin (1988: 103), Harrington (1985: 170), Hofrichter (1987: 57–58), Selva and Bohm (1987: 53), Spitzer (1982: 187) and Santos (1982: 262).

45 For some indication of the qualitative differences between forms of regulation see, for instance, Auerbach (1983), Baskin (1988), Harrington (1985), Santos (1982).

46 This connection is discussed in more detail in Rose (1990: 5ff) and Foucault (1979, 1981a,b, 1982).

47 For instance, Hofrichter argues that, because hegemony is never determined in

advance, the mediation movement is susceptible to challenge: 'Every moment of domination suggests a space for opposition and liberation, so that we need not be completely bounded in envisioning future directions or the possibility for challenge through extra-legal means' (1987: 159). Baskin argues that if community mediation provides ways in which individual problems can be translated into 'collective action' then it could inspire general insurgency (1988: 112). For Abel, a failure in mediation may prompt general despair with the legal system and thus generate resistance in which people would seek 'unmediated political confrontation with their adversaries' (1982b: 309). Santos notes that resistance is likely to be most effective here if it is 'highly diversified, especially if it is to be a global resistance' (1982: 259). By contrast, Harrington (1985) remains rather more consistent in her scepticism of informal justice's transformative potential.

5 REDRAWING CRITICAL LINES OF ENQUIRY

1 See Cohen (1985: 240, 1988) and Matthews (1988).
2 Fitzpatrick offers his 'new informalism' (see chapter 1) as a response to the 'rise' and 'reduction' of informalism, in which community justice was initially viewed by advocates as a completely 'self-sufficient' entity, and later reduced by its critics to an instrumental feature of formal power. His position acknowledges that the informal has some identity, but that this identity is constitutively formed by framing social fields (1988: 179–182).
3 Fitzpatrick sees merit in both the advocates' perception of informal justice as an autonomous identity, and the critics' conception of it as a residual feature of something else (economy, state, etc.). Indeed, he sees this 'divide' as a reflection of two forms of power in modern societies that are linked together in ways that need to be analysed in more detail (1988: 179).
4 Fitzpatrick acknowledges his reliance on Foucault, but feels his work marks an 'axial shift' within the latter's framework.
5 As Fitzpatrick argues, ' "Law" need not continue to reside definitively with the state . . . Indeed, if we set aside those sociological and jurisprudential arrogations of law as simply emblematic of "society", law is revealed as an object of unresolved contestation between different sites of power and not as located definitively with the state' (1988: 195).
6 See Poulantzas (1978) and more recently Hunt (1993) and Hunt and Wickham (1994).
7 This stance does not entail a rejection of Foucault's (or indeed Fitzpatrick's) previous work, but is rather an 'elaboration of themes that were present in his earlier work but never fully developed' (McNay 1992: 81).
8 I use the term 'approach' here intentionally, for Foucault insists that his is not a general theory of power. Rather, it is a much more modest account, a nominal point of departure, which is more implicit than explicit, and which is guided by certain rules of thumb that he adopts as framing guidelines for his specific historical analyses of power relations. His reluctance to offer a full-blown theory stems from his belief that, 'if one tries to erect a theory of power one will always be obliged to view it as emerging at a given place and time and hence to deduce it, to reconstruct its genesis' (1980: 199). Consequently, the question that we should ask is not 'what is power?' but rather 'how is power exercised in present forms of community mediation?' and 'what are its effects in these contexts?' (Foucault 1982: 217).
9 The Nietzschean overtones of this approach are clear, for it connotes the tension

within opposing lines of force that constitute associational patterns, and whose unpredictable ruptures change the course of history. It is this image, I believe, that grounds much of Foucault's analysis of power.

10 In this respect he feels his portrayal is the 'exact opposite' of Hobbes' Leviathan because it concentrates not on the centralised amalgamation of individual subjects as a form of power (sovereignty bolstered by law), but on the other moments of power in diffuse contexts that may or may not be linked to the former model (Foucault 1980: 97–98).

11 Or, as N. Rose puts it, 'Rather than the state extending its sway throughout society by means of an extension of its control apparatus ... we need to think in terms of a "governmentalization of the state" – a transformation of the rationalities and technologies for the exercise of political rule' (1990: 5).

12 In this sense, power is exercised not directly on individuals but 'upon their actions, on existing actions or on those which may arise in the present or the future' (Foucault 1982: 220).

13 Community mediation seeks to maintain the distinction between 'state' and 'civil society' while ensuring – from a regulatory point of view – that the aims of these domains remain homologous. As such, it is located in what may be called a 'social' domain, so long as we do not see this as an absolute, or fixed, domain with an *a priori* essential existence of its own. On the contrary, it should be seen as a 'space' without definite form, forged out of the ongoing shifts between different power-knowledge relations, which produce a series of political practices and semi-autonomous identities. Laclau and Mouffe suggest that we 'consider the openness of the social as the constitutive ground or "negative essence" of the existing and the diverse "social orders" as precarious and ultimately failed attempts to domesticate the field of differences ... There is no sutured space peculiar to "society", since the social itself has no essence' (1985: 95–96).

14 These struggles can terminate specific relations of force, leaving more unstable situations where opponents (collective or individual) confront each other directly as adversaries in a 'free play of antagonistic reactions' (Foucault 1982: 225). Situations of confrontation are purportedly different from power relations to the extent that advance calculation and manipulation are absent. In these situations, people merely react *ex post facto* to events. But the aim is always to annihilate the other's means of combat so that more stable mechanisms of power can be put in place.

15 Here, Foucault is clearly impressed by the ambiguity of the 'subject': on the one hand it denotes a certain autonomy (i.e. the subject who exercises power); on the other it connotes subjugation (i.e. subject to control; Foucault 1980: 98).

16 See Fitzpatrick (1988), Cain (1988), Matthews (1988) and Cohen (1985, 1988).

17 See, for example, Levin (1989), Soper (1991, 1986), Dews (1987), Taylor (1986), Walzer (1986) and Habermas (1986).

18 For some this would refer to natural, individual subjects (Taylor 1986), or the working class (Poulantzas 1978), or an amalgam of these that comprise given 'agents' (Dews 1984).

19 Ultimately, it is here that one confronts Flynn's 'postmodern dilemma', which requires a choice between 'either the ethos of Enlightenment or its universalist doctrine, either a sceptical Nietzschean laugh or a deadly serious neo-Kantian moralism, either the "privileges" of the poet or the privileging of scientific knowing, either the afternoon of limited, tactical resistance or the twilight of unlimited control' (1989: 197).

20 For example, Habermas (1984, 1987) and Soper (1991). For more detailed discussions of this position see Angus (1990) and Bernstein (1985).

21 See Wapner (1989: 109), Lash (1990), Nicholson (1990), Lyotard (1984), Wellmer (1985), Wickham (1990), and Jameson (1984). In his analysis of the relevance of postmodernity to justice, White (1987/88: 306–308) suggests four dimensions of this postmodern problematic: it rejects metanarratives; it emphasises the importance of new 'information technologies'; it recognises a number of new problems associated with the rationalisation of society; and it favours the appearance of new social movements as contemporary agents of resistance (Epstein 1990, Kauffman 1990, Plotke 1990). The last two of these problems are particularly relevant to Foucault's work.

22 As Foucault puts it:

What reason considers as its necessity or much more what various forms of rationality claim to be their necessary existence, has a history which we can determine completely and recover from the tapestry of contingency. They rest upon a foundation of human practices and human faces, because they are made they can be unmade – of course, assuming we know how they were made. (1989: 252)

23 See Hiley (1984, 1985) for a more detailed analysis of Foucault's specific responses to the second criticism.

24 See Rajchman (1986), Sawicki (1991), Davidson (1986), Hacking (1986) and Foucault (1984).

25 The following discussion draws on Flynn (1989), Wickham (1990), White (1987/88), Sawicki (1991), Nicholson (1990), Wapner (1989), Laclau and Mouffe (1985), B. Smart (1991), Bauman (1992), and Diamond and Quinby (1988).

6 GOVERNING DISPUTES

1 This theme enunciates a mode of governance that is different from the law and sovereign model of power (Foucault 1978, 1980) and that takes as its exemplar the notion of 'pastoral care' (rather than 'sovereign rule'). Here, singular existences (of each) enter into political calculations regarding the collective (of all) by equating the strength of the latter with the well-being (welfare) of the former.

2 Church registers bear witness to the details of individual lives that were deemed of relevance to pastorship (Hepworth and Turner 1982).

3 In pursuit of the 'reason of state', the discourse assumes that the state was 'governed according to rational principles which are intrinsic to it and which cannot be derived solely from natural or divine laws or the principles of wisdom and prudence; the State, like Nature, has its own proper rationality, even if this is of a different sort' (Foucault 1979: 14).

4 Here the term 'police' is used in a far broader sense than is customary in common parlance today, being closer to what we speak of as 'policy'. In any case, these are etymologically related (see Gordon 1991).

5 See Foucault (1979).

6 Indeed, he suggests that the model now operates in numerous institutions, including the family, psychiatry, medicine (Foucault 1982: 214), and perhaps even informal justice (Foucault 1988a: 168).

7 Hence the rise of various discourses, including demography, statistics (i.e. a description of state) and later criminology, psychiatry and sociology. See Foucault (1979: 16) and Hacking (1991).

8 As he puts it, 'modern man is an animal whose politics places his existence as a living being in question' (1978: 143). In this sense, bio-power 'brought life and its mechanisms into the realm of explicit calculations and made power-knowledge an agent of transformation of human life' (1978: 143).This reversal has certain effects, including on the sovereign's unequivocal right to extinguish the lives of subjects. Indeed, the strength of pastorship lies in its capacity to preserve, nourish and sustain life within a population. Yet, there are occasions when the life of a subject is necessary, but this is now rationalised in different terms: 'One might say that the ancient right to *take* a life or *let* live was replaced by a power to *foster* life or *disallow* it to the point of death' (Foucault 1978: 138).

9 The 'social security' of the welfare state is clearly at the back of Foucault's mind here, for he tells us that the government of populations occurs through the 'technical apparatuses of security' (1979: 20). This was a line of thinking he developed in lectures on the liberal appropriations of pastoral power where the theme of individual liberty – as we shall see in the final chapter - is closely tied to notions of security (Gordon 1991, Burchell 1991). In any case, one can identify the rise of the welfare state, with its apparatuses of social security, with a climate where the pastoral theme was expanding beyond populations into the 'social' (with knowledge such as sociology) and where the administration of 'individuals' through 'care' was embraced.

10 See Foucault (1979: 17). Here, the population's strength is valued over, say, a concern for how a sovereign might maintain rule over citizens, as was the case with Machiavelli, or from whence the sovereign's legitimacy could be traced (e.g. Hobbes).

11 As a nineteenth-century example of this, Foucault (1978) points to the dramatic growth of discourses on sex in which the sexualized individual body was integrated with the life of the 'species'. Thus, as Dreyfus and Rabinow put it, '[s]ex became the construction through which power linked the vitality of the body together with that of the species' (1982: 140). Furthermore, the shift from a 'symbolics of blood' to a 'biological' version of sex, with its relation to individuals and the species, gave rise to modern versions of racism. Foucault (1978) sees this connection through sex as an insidious expansion of an administrative network that posed in the form of greater sexual freedom.

12 Westcoast Mediation Services advertisement/pamphlet.

13 For example, Landau et al. (1987), CBA, Task Force Report (1989), ALRI (1990), Shonholtz (1978, 1984, 1987), Wahrhaftig (1982) and Sander (1977).

14 In the course of my research there were two large conferences that focused on aspects of community mediation in Vancouver: one on family mediation and the other a CBA annual meeting whose central theme was alternative dispute resolution (CBA, Task Force Report 1989).

15 No doubt, the federal government's image of Canadian society as a 'community of communities' helped advocates of mediation in their bid to redress minor conflicts within the context of local 'communities'.

16 This absence betrays a realisation that conceptual ambiguity can – in some cases – mean broadened political appeal (Cohen 1985: 116).

17 Here one might point to the importance of Shonholtz's (1978, 1984, 1988/89) thinking on the advocates in British Columbia.

18 Personal correspondence with a programme organiser, 19/06/1990

19 For example, see Burdine (1990), Landau et al. (1987), Peachey et. al. (1983) and Folberg and Taylor (1984).

20 This echoes Harrington's (1985) and Hofrichter's (1982) observations on the

technocratic dimensions of mediation, where politics is reduced to simple 'blind necessity' (Abel 1982b).

21 This realisation, of course, echoes the point made by many of the critics, including Abel (1982b), Harrington (1985), Santos (1982) and Baskin (1988), that informal justice trivialises (hence the disputes are considered 'minor' – see Sander 1977, Danzig 1973 and Tomasic and Feeley 1982: 60–77), neutralises and, most important for our argument here, *individualises* conflict within communities. These should not, however, be seen as different, because very often individualisation involves the trivialisation and neutralisation of such conflict.

22 Abel suggests that this tends to have the effect of informal justice being 'directed toward the economically, socially and politically oppressed ... [and is] ... preoccupied with the poor, members of ethnic minorities and women' (1982b: 274). My own observations in British Columbia, though insufficient to make confident statements to the contrary, at least initially suggest that we treat Abel's assertion with caution. Indeed, what has struck me in the course of research is the extent to which rather less oppressed members of society (e.g. corporate business people) are attracted to mediation. This, however, is not to undermine Abel's more profound point that mediation, in effect, currently serves to perpetuate the stratified and unequable *status quo* of capitalist societies.

23 See Foucault (1977b: 195–228).

24 I say 'potentially' here, because to suggest otherwise in British Columbia would be to over-exaggerate community mediation's current importance as a control mechanism.

25 Observation, 04/04/1991. It is interesting to note here an insightful and related study by Silbey and Merry (1986), which examines four strategies used by mediators to mobilise power in mediation sessions to achieve settlement. In particular, these authors refer to the ways in which mediators present themselves, how they control what is said at a mediation session, how they regulate the process of mediation and, finally, the various means of soliciting norms and commitments from disputing parties.

26 This is mainly achieved verbally through asking questions – derived from my observations – of the following kind: 'Are you comfortable with that?'; 'Do you agree that...?'; 'How does what I have just said sit with both of you?'; 'We've agreed that the main issue is... have we not?'; etc.

27 For example, if the dispute revolves around, say, a neighbour accusing another of stealing his or her garden hose, the mediator would reframe this into a positive and neutral statement. For example, the latter might suggest, 'It seems that you, Gertrude and you, Mike, wish to re-establish trust in your interactions as neighbours' rather than the more direct suggestion that these 'disputants' are here to establish whether one stole the hose or not. This no doubt requires a certain alertness, for the mediator must absorb the information quickly and then reframe it in such a way that it increases the chances of later settlement (for further examples, see Burdine, 1990: 21).

28 See Foucault (1978: 58).

29 See, for instance, Hepworth and Turner (1982: 11) for a more extended analysis of the confession and subjectivity. Foucault (1978, 1982, 1988b), Burchell (1991) and Rose (1990: 220–228), however, make the more explicit link between individual, subjective freedom and the confessional practices within liberalism that produce this. It is both the irony and strength of these practices that they should present their product as a 'natural' or 'essential' one.

30 This is particularly pertinent to the last two stages where the issues set up in the agenda of the second stage are explored and a means of resolution developed.

31 Indeed, there appears to be rather general consensus amongst the mediators interviewed that the most difficult mediations to conduct are those where their sympathies lie with one of the parties. For this reason, many favoured co-mediation so that they could cede the mediation to another mediator in the interests of preserving 'neutrality'.

32 It is important to realise that I have here focused on the *techniques* of mediation rather than on the subject identities that these produce. This is a critical distinction because, even though Foucault's work is extraordinarily insightful on political techniques, his work has been rather less successful in elucidating the ways in which wider patterns of social inequality replicate themselves through these techniques in micro contexts. As indicated, the kinds of subject identities produced through the notion of disputant often reflect the gross inequities between dominant subject identities of capitalist societies (notably gender, race and class). Indeed, the very technique of confession is an important way in which wider (unequal) norms may be perpetuated and people encouraged to assume identities commensurate with these.

33 In community mediation, as the critics have noted, the degree of conflict within a community is seen to depend upon the success in regulating individuals in such a way as to avoid disputes between them. The assumption here is that conflicts in a community can be explained through individual factors (failures in communication, intransigence, etc.) rather than through wider contradictions in capitalism generally (Abel 1982a, 1982b, Baskin 1988, Santos 1982). In this sense, conflict is individualised and this affords the opportunity of describing disputing individuals as problematic or in need of assistance to restore them to a normal, non-disputing condition.

34 This derives from Fitzpatrick's (1988) insightful observation that informal justice is a normalising mode of regulation.

35 Harrington (1985) and Abel (1982b) offer warnings that informal justice comprises an insidious means of promoting 'consensus politics'. The need for such politics is important because, as Abel (1982b: 285) observes, whereas conflict may have served to reinforce social norms in homogeneous societies, it tends to undermine the normative order of heterogeneous societies.

7 GOVERNMENTALISING THE STATE

1 Recall, most explicitly, Santos's (1982: 261) 'cosmic' versus 'chaotic' power distinction. However, a distinction of this kind is implicit in Harrington's unification through decentralisation (1985: 64), Baskin's (1988) post-Fordism (which inculcates aspects of Fordism with more dispersed forms of regulation), and Hofrichter's (1987) distinction between coercive (legal) and hegemonic forms of control. The distinction is also rather well entrenched in Spitzer's (1982) analysis of formal as opposed to informal mechanisms of control. What is absent from these is a systematic way of analysing the informal and the chaotic independently from the more formal, or cosmic, means of control.

2 I have elected to use the term 'sovereign-law' rather than Foucault's (or rather Foucault's translators') more cumbersome 'law and sovereign' phrase, not only for stylistic reasons but also because – unlike some passages in Foucault – I do not wish to underplay its importance in the context of contemporary Canada.

3 For an excellent summary of the 'professionalised' justice embedded in the courts, see Cain (1988).

4 See Laclau and Mouffe (1985) for an extended discussion of the open form of the social domain.

5 For example, the Greek *polis* sought to regulate the lives of citizens through the sovereign rule of an assembly of selected citizens (Held 1987). In the Roman family, the *patria potestas* granted the father of the family an absolute right to take the life of his children and slaves: just as he gave them 'life' so could he remove it (Foucault 1978: 135). By contrast, the rise of Christendom shifted such authority from the wisdom of the father to the 'earthly representatives' of God. As Held puts it, 'The Christian world view transformed the rationale of political action from that of the *polis* to a theological framework' (1987: 37). Interpretations of 'God's will' were articulated with secular systems of power, and were closely entwined with religious dogma until the Reformation (Held 1987: 36–41). Here, Calvin and Luther's teachings were damaging to the sovereign authority of religious dogma because they embraced a conception of people as 'individuals', 'alone' in front of God. They even approved of independent secular political activities in areas that did not infringe upon religious practice. In so doing they had made way for important shifts in the reason of sovereignty, and the rise of the modern state directed at individual citizens.

6 See Hunt (1993) for a view of how consent operates in law, and Tomasic (1982) for an overview of coercion in community mediation.

7 It is important to recall that this is a model, a Weberian 'ideal type' as it were, and as such is an abstraction that may be replicated in specific contexts in different ways (Weber 1978, 1980).

8 No doubt, federal-provincial elaborations of this model are also significant in Canada, and pertinent to alternative dispute resolution trends, but this is a massive topic in and of itself that awaits further elaboration.

9 See Taylor *et al.* (1973) and Pfohl (1985) for extended analyses of these two positions in criminological theory.

10 See Donzelot (1979, 1991), Foucault (1977b), Burchell (1991) and Gordon (1991).

11 In parenthesis, it is important to note, however, that my focus here is on a contemporary liberal version of the sovereign-law model as it exists in British Columbia, realising that this is only one aspect of a far wider formal legal system, which, no doubt, uses numerous pastoral techniques within its very confines. But this issue – how pastoral power operates in the very processes of formal law (e.g. prosecutorial and judicial discretion) – is beyond the scope of the present analysis (see Hunt 1993).

12 This is graphically reflected in Rousseau's adage: 'Man is born free and is everywhere in chains' (1974: 8). See also Cappelletti and Garth (1981).

13 Of course, there are numerous other sites where pastorship operates to create such selves under postmodern conditions (community psychology, community work, etc.), but community mediation is interesting in context because it is positioned as a direct alternative to courtroom justice.

14 This theme is extremely well canvassed in articles by Burchell (1991) and Gordon (1991). Keane (1988a, 1988b) and Bobbio (1989) offer extended descriptions of the rise of the concept of 'civil society'. But it is well to bear in mind that 'civil society' 'was a quasi-political concept, opposed to the administrative power of the states at that time, in order to bring victory to a certain liberalism' (Foucault 1988a: 167).

15 As noted, the formation of a community is part of a post-Fordist fragmentation of the 'social'. The social realm was developed as an absolute entity towards the end of the eighteenth century. See Foucault (1989, esp. 261) and Donzelot (1979, 1991) for more on this.

16 For example, CBA, Task Force Report (1989), Hughes (1988), Pirie (1987), Pitsula (1987) and Smith (1989).

17 Various commentators have pointed out, however, that there is reason to believe that informal justice actually 'widens the control network' because it deals with cases that the court system would have rejected, or dealt with informally anyway (e.g. Cohen 1985, Tomasic 1982, Abel 1982a, 1982b, Harrington 1985, Hofrichter 1987).

18 This point derives from insightful observations by Fitzpatrick (1988: 193), Santos (1982) and Baskin (1988), each of whom seems to underscore (in their various ways) the importance of these with respect to the relationship between community mediation and the law.

19 This point echoes Fitzpatrick's (1988) contention that informal justice comes between the 'synoptic', universalising, dimensions of law and its 'syncretic' application in local contexts. However, in British Columbia at least, to make this general statement would be to overstate the case because community mediation is rather more specifically implicated in the liberal problem of increasing 'access to justice' (Hughes 1988, Smith 1989).

20 Interestingly, Donzelot (1991) suggests that it was the looming absence of a gap between the welfare state and the social domain that produced a severe crisis in the former, for, without sufficient distance between these, the state was in danger of becoming synonymous with 'society'. As the welfare state increasingly managed society's destiny through direct administration, it could no longer claim to be a watchdog of 'society's interests' or a regulator of a 'free' social domain.

21 As Foucault puts it,

> Modern society . . . has been characterised on the one hand, by a legislation, a discourse, an organisation based on public right, whose articulation is the social body and the delegative status of each citizen; and on the other hand, by a closely linked grid of disciplinary coercions whose purpose is in fact to assure the cohesion of this same social body. (1980: 106)

22 I have borrowed the term 'synoptic' from Fitzpatrick (1988) and used it to denote those political practices that operate across local contexts and social fields. The term 'envelope' comes from Foucault's (1978: 100) attempt to forge an intrinsic link between local tactics and wider strategies.

23 I attended one meeting of a regional network and was intrigued to observe the 'quiet presence' of a member of the Attorney General's office. The representative listened earnestly, and seemed genuinely interested in nurturing mediation, but offered little by way of overt support (financially or conversationally). His was, I suspect, a tacit – but detached – approval of the process.

24 For instance, when considering divorce or separations, there are various laws governing what can come out of a mediation session (e.g. people may not agree to abide by norms that are illegal). Conversely, observations of a family lawyer who practises mediation reveal the degree to which the 'norms of the community' influence her ways of interpreting statutes. See also C. Smart (1989) for an in-depth analysis of this issue.

25 This concept is conceptually related to Miller and Rose's 'government at a distance' (1990: 9), and I borrow many of their insights – somewhat out of context – in what follows. As will become apparent, my concept also borrows from N. Rose (1990), which, in turn, refers extensively to Foucault (especially, 1979, 1981b, 1982, 1984).

26 This affirms the idea that, with the development of neo-conservatism, 'the law

operates more and more as a norm, and that the judicial institution is increasingly incorporated into a continuum of apparatuses ... whose functions are for the most part regulatory' (Foucault 1978: 144). Clearly, the community mediation movement should be seen as one of the apparatuses that regulates through the use of the norm. This normalisation provides far greater flexibility and discretion than a formal rule of law can provide.

27 Cohen suggests that this is a fundamentally irreconcilable paradox in that one cannot affirm the value of statist criminal law and decentralisation within a single framework. That is, he suggests, '[t]o be realistic about law and order must mean to be unrealistic (that is, imaginative) about the possibilities of order without law. To take decentralisation seriously means that you must be an abolitionist' (1988: 228). Although not all will agree with the anarchistic overtones of this thesis, it does allude to the realisation that an 'alternative' cannot 'complement' formal justice in the way that some adherents propose (e.g. Danzig 1973).

28 For more on the difficulties of postmodern politics of law, see Hunt (1990a, b), Carty (1990) and Fitzpatrick (1988), and, for an overview of legal pluralism, see Merry (1988).

29 In this respect, it may be instructive for community mediation advocates to learn from labour mediation, and even environmental mediation, where groups – rather than individuals – are brought as parties to a dispute.

30 Interview 17/09/1991. Indeed, early on in my research I came to understand that, in this domain, reputation was an important means of securing an established position in the network. I also observed the difficulties that confronted a new member in one of the regional networks, and the defensive postures that were adopted by those who felt threatened by her presence. The point here is that networks, and one's position within these, are crucial for being a successful member of the mediation community. Harrington (1985) came to a similar conclusion in her study.

31 In observing a series of family mediation sessions, I perceived various ways in which normal roles were ascribed to people on the basis of their gender, 'cultural background', etc. For example, one could see the effect of patriarchally ascribed roles in the mediation session itself in various ways, not least with respect to the heterosexist assumptions of the mediators (e.g. the 'husband' was asked if he was 'seeing' anybody else, ' ... another woman, perhaps?'). Also, this was rather graphically reflected in the fact that the chief mediator (who was a women) addressed most of her questions to the husband – especially those pertaining to household finances. However, on matters pertaining to custody, she directed her questions to mainly to the wife. In addition, the mediator kept referring to the women's 'cultural background' (e.g. 'is it the same in your culture?'), even though it became clear that raising this issue made the women feel somewhat uncomfortable. Thus it becomes clear just how far wider 'community' norms do pervade the mediation session.

32 As noted in chapter 1, some research has been conducted on the gendered nature of mediation. For instance, see Whittington and Ruddy's (n.d.) bibliography on the subject, and, inter alia Rifkin (1984), Lerman (1984), Scambler (1988) and Harrington and Rifkin (1989).

33 It is interesting to note, perhaps vindicating this assessment, that at least one advocate (Mica 1992) has expressed serious doubts about individualising disputes without addressing the 'social' background from which such conflict emerges.

BIBLIOGRAPHY

Abel, Richard L. 1973. 'A Comparative Theory of Dispute Institutions'. *Law and Society Review* 6(2): 217–347.

—— 1981. 'Conservative Conflict and the Reproduction of Capitalism: The Role of Informal Justice'. *International Journal of the Sociology of Law* 92: 245–267.

—— 1982a. 'Introduction'. In *The Politics of Informal Justice: The American Experience*, edited by Richard Abel, vol. 1. New York: Academic Press.

—— 1982b. 'The Contradictions of Informal Justice'. In *The Politics of Informal Justice: The American Experience*, edited by Richard Abel, vol. 1. New York: Academic Press.

—— 1983. 'Mediation in Pre-capitalist Societies'. *The Windsor Yearbook of Access to Justice* 3: 175–185.

Adamson, Walter L. 1980. *Hegemony and Revolution: A Study of Antonio Gramsci's Political and Cultural Theory*. Berkeley: University of California Press.

Adler, Peter, Karen Lovaas and Neal Milner. 1988. 'The Ideologies of Mediation: The Movement's Own Story'. *Law & Policy* 10(4): 317–339.

Agger, Ben. 1991. 'Critical Theory, Poststructuralism, Postmodernism: Their Sociological Relevance'. *Annual Review of Sociology* 17: 105–131.

Aglietta, Michel. 1979. *A Theory of Capitalist Regulation: The U.S. Experience*. London: New Left Books.

Alberta Law Reform Institute. 1990. *Dispute Resolution: A Directory of Methods, Projects and Resources*. Alberta: ALRI Research Paper No. 19.

Alexander, Jeffrey C. 1980. *Theoretical Logic in Sociology*, vol. 1. Berkeley: University of California Press.

Alfini, James. 1986. 'Alternate Dispute Resolution and the Courts: An Introduction'. *Judicature* 69(5): 252–253.

Alper, Benedict S. and Lawrence T. Nichols. 1981. *Beyond the Courtroom: Programmes in Community Justice and Conflict Resolution*. Massachusetts: Lexington Books.

Altieri, Charles. 1989. 'Judgment and Justice under Postmodern Conditions; or, How Lyotard Helps Us Read Rawls as a Postmodern Thinker'. In *Redrawing the Lines: Analytic Philosophy, Deconstruction, and Literary Theory*, edited by Reed Dasenbrock. Minneapolis: University of Minnesota Press.

American Bar Association. 1990. *Dispute Resolution Program Directory*. Washington, DC: American Bar Association.

Anderson, Perry. 1976/7. 'The Antinomies of Antonio Gramsci'. *New Left Review* 100: 5–78.

Angus, Ian. 1990. 'Habermas Confronts the Deconstructionist Challenge: On *The*

BIBLIOGRAPHY

Philosophical Discourse of Modernity'. Canadian Journal of Political and Social Theory 14(1–3): 21–33.

Armstrong, Timothy J. 1992. *Michel Foucault Philosopher.* New York: Harvester Press.

Aronowitz, Stanley. 1987/88. 'Postmodernism and Politics'. *Social Text* 18: 99–115.

Arthurs, H. W. 1980. 'Alternatives to the Formal Justice System: Reminiscing About the Future'. In *Cost of Justice*, Canadian Institute for the Administration of Justice. Toronto: Carswell Company.

Arts, Wil and Romke van der Veen. 1994. 'Sociological Approaches to Distributive and Procedural Justice'. In *Justice: Interdisciplinary Perspectives*, edited by Klaus R. Scherer. Cambridge: Cambridge University Press.

Auerbach, Jerold S. 1983. *Justice without Law.* Oxford: Oxford University Press.

—— 1985. 'Rethinking Alternatives to the Courts'. *Legal Studies Forum* IX(1): 89–100.

Balkin, J. M. 1987. 'Deconstructive Practice and Legal Theory'. *The Yale Law Journal* 96: 742–786.

—— 1994. 'Being Just with Deconstruction'. *Social and Legal Studies* 3(3): 393–404.

Barron, Anne. 1990. 'Legal Discourse and the Colonisation of Self in the Modern State'. In *Post-Modern Law*, edited by Anthony Carty, Edinburgh: Edinburgh University Press.

Baskin, Deborah R. 1988. 'Community Mediation and the Public/ Private Problem'. *Social Justice* 15(1): 98–115.

—— 1989. 'What is All the Fighting About? Privatism and Neighbor Disputes'. *Social Justice* 16(2): 165–187.

Bastein, R. 1981. *Federalism and Decentralization: Where Do We Stand?* Ottawa: Ministry of Supply and Services.

Baudrillard, Jean. 1983. *In the Shadow of Silent Majorities . . . or The End of the Social and Other Essays.* New York: Semiotext(e).

—— 1987. 'Modernity'. *Canadian Journal of Political and Social Theory* XI(3): 63–73.

—— 1988. *Selected Writings*, edited by Mark Poster, Standford, Calif.: Stanford University Press.

Bauman, Zygmunt. 1991. *Modernity and Ambivalence.* Cambridge: Polity Press.

—— 1992. *Intimations of Postmodernity.* London: Routledge.

—— 1994. 'Morality without Ethics'. *Theory, Culture and Society* 11: 1–34.

Baumgartner, M. P. 1984. 'Social Control from Below'. In *Toward a General Theory of Social Control*, edited by Donald Black. New York: Academic Press.

Beck, Ulrich, Anthony Giddens and Scott Lash. 1994. *Reflexive Modernization: Politics, Tradition and Aesthetics in the Modern Social Order.* Cambridge: Polity Press.

Becker, Calvin. 1975. 'Conflict and the Uses of Adjudication'. In *Studies on Diversion*, edited by the Law Reform Commission of Canada. Ottawa: Queen's Printer.

Beer, Jennifer E. 1986. *Peacemaking in Your Neighborhood: Reflections on an Experiment in Community Mediation.* Philadelphia: New Society Publishers.

Bell, David. 1994. 'Justice and the Law'. In *Justice: Interdisciplinary Perspectives*, edited by Klaus R. Scherer. Cambridge: Cambridge University Press.

Bell, Vikki. 1993. 'Governing Childhood: Neo-liberalism and the Law' *Economy and Society* 22(3): 390–405.

Benhabib, Seyla. 1989. 'On Contemporary Feminist Theory'. *Dissent* 36 (Summer): 366–370.

Benjamin, Andrew, ed. 1992. *Judging Lyotard.* London: Routledge.

BIBLIOGRAPHY

Bennett, William R. 1978. *Towards an Economic Strategy for Canada: The British Columbia Position*. Victoria: Province of British Columbia.

Benoit, John H., W. Stephen MacDonald, E. Grant MacDonald and S. Bennet. 1984. *Assessing the Impact of Mediation*. Ottawa: Ministry of the Solicitor General.

Berman, Marshall. 1988. *All That Is Solid Melts into Air: The Experience of Modernity*. New York: Penguin Books.

Bernauer, James W. 1990. *Michel Foucault's Force of Flight*. London: Humanities Press.

Bernstein, Richard J., ed. 1985. *Habermas and Modernity*. Cambridge, Mass.: MIT Press.

Bierne, Piers and Richard Quinney, eds. 1982. *Marxism and the Law*. New York: John Wiley.

Black, Donald, ed. 1984. *Toward a General Theory of Social Control*. vol. 1. New York: Academic Press.

Blair, Robert A. 1988. 'Impetus for the Movement towards Non-court Mechanisms for Dispute Resolution'. Presented at the Canadian Bar Association's (Ontario) Conference on Alternative Dispute Resolution (October 3, 1988). Ontario: CBAO.

Blake, Donald E. 1984. 'The Electoral Significance of Public Sector Bashing'. *BC Studies* 62: 29–43.

Blake, Donald E., Richard Johnston and David Elkins. 1981. 'Sources of Change in the B.C. Party System'. *BC Studies* 50:3–28.

Blum, Alan and Peter McHugh. 1984. *Self-Reflection in the Arts and Sciences*. New Jersey: Humanities Press.

Bobbio, Norberto. 1989. *Dictatorship and Democracy*. Minneapolis: University of Minnesota Press.

Bock, K. 1979. 'Theories of Progress Development and Evolution'. In *A History of Sociological Analysis*, edited by Tom Bottomore and Robert Nisbet. London: Heinemann.

Bocock, Robert. 1986. *Hegemony*. New York: Tavistock.

Boggs, Carl. 1976. *Gramsci's Marxism*. London: Pluto Press.

—— 1984. *The Two Revolutions: Antonio Gramsci and the Dilemmas of Western Marxism*. Boston: South End Press.

Bohannan, Paul. 1957. *Justice and Judgment amongst the Tiv*. Oxford: Oxford University Press.

——, ed. 1967. *Law and Warfare*. New York: National History Press.

Bonner, Frances and Paul du Guy. 1992. 'Representing the Enterprising Self: *Thirtysomething* and the Contemporary Consumer Culture'. *Theory, Culture and Society* 9(2): 67–92.

Bossy, John, ed. 1983. *Disputes and Settlements: Law and Human Relations in the West*. Cambridge: Cambridge University Press.

Bothwell, Robert, Ian Drummond and John English. 1981. *Canada Since 1945: Power, Politics and Provincialism*. Toronto: University of Toronto Press.

Bottomley, Anne and Jeremy Roche. 1988. 'Conflict and Consensus: A Critique of the Language of Informal Justice'. In *Informal Justice?* edited by Roger Matthews. London: Sage.

Bowler, K. Christie. 1993/4. 'Victim Offender Mediation/Reconciliation Programs Research'. *The Mediator* 39: 3.

Brinton, Crane. 1963. *The Shaping of Modern Thought*. New Jersey: Prentice Hall.

British Columbia Government Employees Union. 1985. *A Broken Promise: The Effects of Restraint on Delivery of Social Services in British Columbia*. In 'Report by the BCGEU', September.

BIBLIOGRAPHY

British Columbia, Attorney General. 1979. *Justice Councils*. Victoria: Queen's Printer.

Bromley, Simon. 1991. 'The Politics of Postmodernism'. *Capital and Class* 45: 129–150.

Brown, Mykie. 1991. 'Small Claims Settlement Conferences Welcome – But No Substitute for Community Mediation'. *The Mediator* 31 Winter 1–2.

Buchanan, Allen E. 1982. *Marx and Justice: The Radical Critique of Liberalism*. New Jersey: Rowman & Allanheld.

Buckle, Leonard G. and Suzanne R. Thomas-Buckle. 1982. 'Doing Unto Others: Dispute and Dispute Processing in an Urban American Neighborhood'. In *Neighborhood Justice: Assessment of an Emerging Idea*, edited by Roman Tomasic and Malcolm Feeley. New York: Longman.

Burchell, Graham. 1991. 'Peculiar Interests: Civil Society and Governing "the System of Natural Liberty" '. Pp. 119–150 in *The Foucault Effect: Studies in Governmentality*, edited by Graham Burchell, Colin Gordon and Peter Miller. Chicago: Chicago University Press.

—— 1993. 'Liberal Government and Techniques of Self'. *Economy and Society* 22(3): 267–282.

Burchell, Graham, Colin Gordon, and Peter Miller, eds. 1991. *The Foucault Effect: Studies in Governmentality*. Chicago: Chicago University Press.

Burdine, Marje. 1990. *Mediation Skills Manual: 'How to Mediate a Dispute'*. Justice Institute of B.C. Vancouver: The Centre for Conflict Resolution Training.

—— 1991. 'Certifying Mediators No Easy Task'. *Interaction* 2(3): 7.

Burnham, Peter. 1991. 'Neo-Gramscian Hegemony and the International Order'. *Capital and Class* 45: 73–94.

Bush, Robert A. Baruch and Joseph P. Folger. 1994. *The Promise of Mediation: Responding to Conflict through Empowerment and Recognition*. San Francisco: Jossey-Bass.

Butcher, John. 1985. 'Restraint Economics and the Social Safety Net in British Columbia: The Political Economy of the Post-Welfare State in British Columbia's "New Reality" '. Unpublished manuscript, Department of Geography, University of British Columbia.

Butler, Nancy. 1990. 'Gender Trouble, Feminist Theory and Psychoanalytic Discourse'. In *Feminism/Postmodernism*, edited by Linda J. Nicholson. New York: Routledge.

Cadava, Eduardo, Peter Connor and Jean-Luc Nancy. 1991. *Who Comes after the Subject?* New York: Routledge.

Cain, Maureen. 1988. 'Beyond Informal Justice'. In *Informal Justice?* edited by Roger Matthews. London: Sage.

Cain, Maureen and Christine Harrington, eds. 1994. *Lawyers in a Postmodern World: Translation and Transgression*. Buckingham: Open University Press.

Cain, Maureen and Alan Hunt, eds. 1979. *Marx and Engels on Law*. London: Academic Press.

Cain, Maureen and Kalman Kulscar, eds. 1983. *Disputes and the Law*. Budapest: Akademiai Kiado.

Calavita, Kitty and Seron Carroll. 1992. 'Postmodernism and Protest: Recovering the Sociological Imagination'. *Law and Society Review*. 26(4): 765–772.

Callahan, Marilyn. 1984. 'The Human Costs of Restraint'. *The New Reality: The Politics of Restraint in British Columbia*, edited by Warren Magnusson *et al*. Vancouver: New Star Books.

Callahan, Marilyn and Chris McNiven. 1988. 'British Columbia'. In *Privatization and Provincial Social Services in Canada: Policy, Administration and Service*

179

Delivery, edited by Jacqueline S. Ismael and Yves Vaillancourt. Edmonton: University of Alberta Press.

Campbell, Tom. 1988. *Justice*. Basingstoke: Macmillan Educational.

Canada. 1979. *The Task Force on Canadian Unity: A Future Together*. Quebec: Minister of Supply and Services.

—— 1985. *A Profile of Divorce Mediation and Reconciliation Services in Canada*. Ottawa: Department of Justice.

—— 1986. 'Divorce Law for Counsellors'. Ottawa: Department of Justice.

Canadian Bar Association. 1988. *Alternate Dispute Resolution: What's All the Fuss and Where Is It Going?* edited by Robert A. Blair. CBA, Continuing Legal Education manuscript.

Canadian Bar Association (Task Force Report). 1989. *Alternate Dispute Resolution: A Canadian Perspective*. Ottawa: Canadian Bar Association.

Canadian Bar Foundation. 1984. *The Windsor-Essex Mediation Centre: History and Pilot Project Evaluation*. Ontario: Canadian Bar Foundation.

Canadian Criminology and Corrections Association. 1976. *Crime: A Community Responsibility*. Ottawa: CCCA.

Capital Region (Justice Council). 1977. 'Symposium of Justice Councils: Bringing Justice Back into the Community'. Unpublished report.

Cappelletti, Mauro and Bryant Garth. 1981. 'Access to Justice and the Welfare State: An Introduction'. In *Access to Justice and the Welfare State*, edited by Mauro Cappelletti. Alphen aan den Rijn: Sijthoff.

Carnoy, Martin. 1984. *The State and Political Theory*. New Jersey: Princeton University Press.

Carroll, David. 1984. 'Rephrasing the Political with Kant and Lyotard'. *Diacritics*, Fall: 75–88.

Carroll, William, K. 1984. 'The Solidarity Coalition'. In *The New Reality: The Politics of Restraint in British Columbia*, edited by Warren Magnusson *et al.* Vancouver: New Star Books.

Carroll, William K. and R. S. Ratner. 1989. 'Social Democracy, Neo-conservatism and Hegemonic Crisis in British Columbia'. *Critical Sociology* 16(1): 29–53.

Carty, Anthony, ed. 1990. *Post-Modern Law*. Edinburgh: University of Edinburgh Press.

Castel, Robert. 1991. 'From Dangerousness to Risk'. Pp. 281–298 in *The Foucault Effect: Studies in Governmentality*, edited by Graham Burchell, Colin Gordon and Peter Miller. Chicago: Chicago University Press.

Caygill, Howard. 1988. 'Post-Modernism and Judgement'. *Economy and Society* 17(1): 1–20.

Chalke, Douglas, R. 1984. *Family Mediation Newsletter* 3: 7.

—— 1988. 'Mediation of Family Disputes: B.C. Practice in 1988'. *The Advocate* 46: 579–591.

—— 1991. 'Vancouver Centre for Commercial Disputes'. *The Mediator* 31: 3.

Chomsky, Noam and Foucault, Michel. 1974. 'Human Nature: Justice versus Power'. In *Reflexive Water: The Basic Concerns of Mankind*, edited by Fons Elders. London: Souvenir Press.

Clague, Michael, Robert Dill, Roop Seebaran and Brian Wharf. 1984. *Reforming Human Services: The Experience of the Community Resource Boards in B.C.* Vancouver: University of British Columbia Press.

Cohen, Stanley. 1984. 'The Deeper Structures of Law; or Beware the Rulers Bearing Justice'. *Contemporary Crisis* 8: 83–93.

—— 1985. *Visions of Social Control: Crime, Punishment and Classification*. Cambridge: Polity Press.

BIBLIOGRAPHY

—— 1988. *Against Criminology*. Oxford: Transaction Books.

—— 1989. 'The Critical Discourse on "Social Control": Notes on the Concept as a Hammer'. *International Journal of the Sociology of Law* 17: 347–357.

Coles, Romand. 1991. 'Foucault's Dialogical Artistic Ethos'. *Theory, Culture and Society* 8(2): 99–120.

Comaroff, John L. and Simon A. Roberts. 1977. 'The Invocation of Norms in Dispute Settlement: The Tswana Case'. In *Social Anthropology and the Law*, edited by Ian Hamnet. London: Academic Press.

—— 1981. *Rules and Processes: The Cultural Logic of Dispute in an African Context*. Chicago: University of Chicago Press.

Conner, Ross F. and Ray Surette. 1977. *The Citizen Dispute Settlement Program*. Washington, DC: American Bar Association.

Connor, Des. 1988. 'Your Marketing Plan'. *The Mediator* 16 (Spring): 1.

Cook, Royer F., Janice A. Roehl and David I. Sheppard. 1980. *Neighborhood Justice Centers Field Test: Final Evaluation Report*. Washington, DC: US Department of Justice.

Corlett, J. Angelo, ed. 1991. *Equality and Liberty: Analyzing Rawls and Nozick*. London: Macmillan.

Cornell, Drucilla. 1992. *The Philosophy of the Limit*. London: Routledge.

Cossom, John and David Turner. 1985. 'The Rise and Fall of Justice Councils in British Columbia'. Unpublished manuscript.

Cotterrell, Roger. 1984. *The Sociology of Law*. London: Butterworths

Critchley, Simon. 1992. *The Ethics of Deconstruction: Derrida and Levinas*. Oxford: Blackwell.

Cullen, Bernard. 1994. 'Philosophical Theories of Justice'. In *Justice: Interdisciplinary Perspectives*. Cambridge: Cambridge University Press.

Danzig, Richard. 1973. 'Towards the Creation of a Complementary, Decentralized System of Criminal Justice'. *Stanford Law Review* 26: 1–54.

Davidson, Arnold I. 1986. 'Archaeology, Genealogy, Ethics'. Pp. 221–234 in *Foucault: A Critical Reader*, edited by David Couzens Hoy. Oxford: Basil Blackwell.

Davis, Albie. 1986. 'Community Mediation in Massachusetts: Lessons from a Decade of Development'. *Juridicature* 69(5): 307–309.

Davis, Albie M. and Richard A. Salem. 1984. 'Dealing with Power Imbalances in the Mediation of Interpersonal Disputes'. Pp. 17–26 in *Mediation Quarterly No. 6: Procedures for Guiding the Divorce Process*, edited by John Allen Lemmon. San Francisco: Jossey-Bass.

Dean, Mitchell. 1991. *The Constitution of Poverty: Towards a Genealogy of Liberal Governance*. New York: Routledge.

—— 1992. 'A Genealogy of the Government of Poverty'. *Economy and Society* 21(3): 215–251.

—— 1994. *Critical and Effective Histories: Foucault's Methods and Historical Sociology*. London: Routledge.

Defert, Daniel. 1991. '"Popular Life" and Insurance Technology'. Pp. 211–234 in *The Foucault Effect: Studies in Governmentality*, edited by Graham Burchell, Colin Gordon and Peter Miller. Chicago: Chicago University Press.

Delgado, Richard. 1988. 'ADR and the Dispossessed: Recent Books about the Deformalization Movement'. *Law and Social Inquiry* 13(1): 145–154.

Derrida, Jacques. 1976. *Of Grammatology*. Baltimore, Md.: Johns Hopkins University Press.

—— 1992. 'Force of Law: The "Mystical Foundation of Authority"'. In *Deconstruction and the Possibility of Justice*, edited by Drucilla Cornell, Michel Rosenfeld and David Carlson. London: Routledge.

BIBLIOGRAPHY

Dews, Peter. 1984. 'Power and Subjectivity in Foucault'. *New Left Review* 144: 72–95.

—— 1987. *Logics of Disintegration: Post-Structuralist Thought and the Claims of Critical Theory.* London: Verso.

Diamond, Irene and Lee Quinby, eds. 1988. *Feminism and Foucault: Reflections on Resistance.* Boston: Northeastern University.

Di Stefano, Christine. 1990. 'Dilemmas of Difference: Feminism, Modernity and Postmodernism'. In *Feminism/Postmodernism*, edited by Linda J. Nicholson. New York: Routledge.

Dolan, Norman. 1989. *The Victoria Dispute Resolution Centre: An Evaluation of the Mediation Project.* Victoria, BC: Ministry of the Attorney General.

Donzelot, Jacques. 1979. *The Policing of Families.* New York: Pantheon Books.

—— 1991. 'The Mobilization of Society'. Pp. 169–180 in *The Foucault Effect: Studies in Governmentality*, edited by Graham Burchell, Colin Gordon and Peter Miller. Chicago: Chicago University Press.

Douzinas, Costas, Peter Goodrich and Yifat Hachamovitch. 1994. *Politics, Postmodernity and Critical Legal Studies.* London: Routledge.

Douzinas, Costas and Ronnie Warrington. 1991. ' "A Well-founded Fear of Justice": Law and Ethics in Postmodernity'. *Law and Critique* II(2): 113–147.

—— 1994. 'The Face of Justice: A Jurisprudence of Alterity'. *Social and Legal Studies* 3(3): 405–426.

Dreyfus, Hubert L. and Paul Rabinow. 1982. *Michel Foucault: Beyond Structuralism and Hermeneutics.* Chicago: Chicago University Press.

Durkheim, Emile. 1982. *The Rules of Sociological Method.* Basingstoke: Macmillan.

Dussault, Donna. 1993. 'Community Mediation Programs: Where Do They Fit?' *The Mediator.* 36: 6.

Edge, Hoyt L. 1994. *A Constructive Postmodern Perspective on Self and Community: From Atomism to Holism.* Lewiston: E. Mellen Press.

Edwards, Connie. 1988. 'Victoria School District to Initiate Mediation Project'. *The Mediator* 17 (Summer): 1.

—— 1990. 'Growing Interest in School Conflict Management'. *The Mediator* 25 (Summer): 1.

Elliff, John T. 1971. *Crime, Dissent and the Attorney General: The Justice Department in the 1960's.* Beverly Hills: Sage.

Emond, Paul. 1988. 'Alternative Dispute Resolution: A Conceptual Overview'. Presented at the Canadian Bar Association's (Ontario) Conference on Alternative Dispute Resolution (October 3, 1988). Ontario: CBAO.

Epstein, Barbara. 1990. 'Rethinking Social Movement Theory'. *Socialist Review* 20(1): 35–64.

Estey, Willard. 1981. 'Who Needs Courts?' In *The Windsor Yearbook of Access to Justice*, edited by William E. Conklin. Ontario: University of Windsor Press.

Etheridge, Caroline F. 1988. 'Review of Richard Hofrichter, *Neighborhood Justice in Capitalist Society*'. *Socialism and Democracy* 2: 232–236.

Ewald, François. 1991. 'Insurance and Risk'. Pp. 197–210 in *The Foucault Effect: Studies in Governmentality*, edited by Graham Burchell, Colin Gordon and Peter Miller. Chicago: Chicago University Press.

Featherstone, Mike. 1988. 'In Pursuit of the Postmodern'. *Theory, Culture and Society* 5(3–5): 195–216.

—— 1991. *Consumer Culture and Postmodernism.* London: Sage.

Felsinger, Leon. 1984. 'The Logic of Mediation'. In *Toward a General Theory of Social Control*, edited by Donald Black, vol. 2. New York: Academic Press.

Femia, Joseph V. 1981. *Gramsci's Political Thought: Hegemony, Consciousness and the Revolutionary Process*. Oxford: Clarendon Press.

Feyerabend, Paul. 1975. *Against Method*. London: Verso.

Fine, Bob. 1979. 'Struggles against Discipline: The Theory and Politics of Michel Foucault'. *Capital and Class* 10: 75–96.

Finkelstein, Linda J. 1986. 'The D.C. Multi-door Courthouse'. *Juridicature* 69(5): 305–306.

Fisher, Eric A. 1975. 'Community Courts: An Alternative to Conventional Adjudication.' *American University Law Review* 24: 1253–1291.

Fisher, Roger and William Ury. 1983. *Getting to Yes: Negotiating Agreement without Giving in*. New York: Penguin Books.

Fisk, Milton. 1989. *The State and Justice: An Essay in Political Theory*. Cambridge: Cambridge University Press.

Fitzpatrick, Peter. 1980. *Law and State in Papua New Guinea*. New York: Academic Press.

—— 1983. 'Law, Plurality and Underdevelopment'. In *Legality, Ideology and the State*, edited by David Sugarman. London: Academic Press.

—— 1988. 'The Rise and Rise of Informalism'. In *Informal Justice?*, edited by Roger Matthews. London: Sage.

—— 1992a. 'The Impossibility of Popular Justice'. *Social and Legal Studies* 1(2): 199–216.

—— 1992b. *The Mythology of Modern Law*. London: Routledge.

—— 1993. 'Relational Power and the Limits of Law'. In *Law and Power: Critical and Socio-Legal Essays*, edited by Kaarlo Tuori, Zenon Bankowski and Jyrki Uusitalo. Liverpool: Deborah Charles Publications.

Fitzpatrick, Peter and Alan Hunt, eds. 1987. *Critical Legal Studies*. Oxford: Basil Blackwell.

Floyd, Richard Heath. 1991. 'Mediation as a Form of Social Exchange'. Unpublished MA thesis, Department of Anthropology and Sociology, University of British Columbia.

Flynn, Thomas, R. 1989. 'Foucault and the Politics of Postmodernity'. *Nous* 23: 187–198.

Folberg, Jay and Alison Taylor. 1984. *Mediation: A Comprehensive Guide to Resolving Conflicts without Litigation*. San Francisco: Jossey-Bass.

Ford Foundation. 1978. *Mediating Social Conflict*. New York: Ford Foundation.

Foucault, Michel. 1973. *The Order of Things: An Archaeology of the Human Sciences*. New York: Vintage Books.

—— 1977a. *Language, Counter-Memory, Practice: Selected Essays and Interviews*. edited by Donald F. Bouchard. New York: Cornell University Press.

—— 1977b. *Discipline and Punish: The Birth of the Prison*. New York: Vintage.

—— 1978. *The History of Sexuality: An Introduction*, vol. 1. New York: Pantheon Books.

—— 1979. 'Governmentality'. *Ideology and Consciousness* 6: 5–21.

—— 1980. *Power/Knowledge: Selected Interviews and Other Writings 1972–1977*. Brighton: Harvester Press.

—— 1981a. 'Foucault at the College de France I: A Course Summary'. *Philosophy and Social Criticism* 8(2): 235–242.

—— 1981b. 'Foucault at the College de France II: A Course Summary'. *Philosophy and Social Criticism*, 8(3): 351–359.

—— 1981c. 'Sexuality and Solitude'. *London Review of Books*, 21 May–2 June: 3–6.

—— 1981d. 'Omnes et Singulatim'. In *The Tanner Lectures on Human Values (Vol. 2)*, edited by S. McMurrin. Cambridge: Cambridge University Press.

——. 1982. 'The Subject and Power'. In *Michel Foucault: Beyond Structuralism and Hermeneutics*, edited by Hubert L. Dreyfus and Paul Rabinow. Chicago: Chicago University Press.

—— 1984. *The Foucault Reader*, edited by Paul Rabinow. New York: Pantheon Books.

—— 1985. *The History of Sexuality II: The Use of Pleasure*. New York: Pantheon Books.

—— 1986. *The History of Sexuality III: Care of the Self*. New York: Vintage Books.

—— 1988a. *Politics, Philosophy, Culture*. New York: Routledge.

—— 1988b. *Technologies of the Self*. Amherst: University of Massachusetts Press.

—— 1988c. 'The Ethic of Care for the Self as a Practice of Freedom'. Pp. 1–20 in *The Final Foucault*, edited by James Bernauer and David Rasmussen. London: MIT Press.

—— 1989. *Foucault Live (Interviews 1966–1984)*. New York: Semiotext(e).

—— 1991. *Remarks on Marx: Conversations with Duccio Trombadori*. New York: Semiotext(e).

Frank, Jerome. 1970. *Courts on Trial: Myth and Reality in American Justice*. New York: Atheneum.

Fraser, Nancy and Linda J. Nicholson. 1990. 'Social Criticism without Philosophy'. In *Feminism/Postmodernism*, edited by Linda J. Nicholson. New York: Routledge.

Fuhr, Jeffrey. 1987. 'What's Wrong with Mediation?' *The Mediator* 12 (Spring): 4.

Fuller, Lon. 1971. 'Mediation – Its Forms and Functions'. *Southern California Law Review* 44: 305–339.

Galanter, Marc. 1981. 'Justice in Many Rooms'. In *Access to Justice and the Welfare State*, edited by Mauro Cappelletti. Alphen aan den Rijn: Sijthoff.

Gallagher, William T. 1988. 'The Transformation of Justice: Hofrichter's Neighborhood Justice and Harrington's Shadow Justice'. *Law and Social Inquiry* 13(1): 133–143.

Garth, Bryant. 1982. 'The Movement towards Procedural Informalism in North America and Western Europe: A Critical Survey'. In *The Politics of Informal Justice: The American Experience*, edited by Richard Abel, vol. 2. New York: Academic Press.

Gibbins, Roger. 1982. *Regionalism: Territorial Politics in Canada and the U.S.* Toronto: Butterworths.

Giddens, Anthony. 1990. *The Consequences of Modernity*. Cambridge: Polity Press.

—— 1991. *Modernity and Self-Identity: Self and Society in the Late Modern Age*. California: Stanford University Press.

Giroux, Henry A. 1991. *Postmodernism, Feminism and Cultural Politics: Redrawing Educational Boundaries*. Albany: SUNY Press.

Gluckman, Max. 1965. *Politics, Law and Ritual in Tribal Society*. Oxford: Basil Blackwell.

Goldberg, Stephen B., Eric D. Green and Frank E. A. Sander. 1985. *Alternative Dispute Resolution*. Boston: Little, Brown.

Gordon, Colin. 1987. 'The Soul of the Citizen: Max Weber and Michel Foucault on Rationality and Government'. Pp. 293–316 in *Max Weber, Rationality and Modernity*, edited by Scott Lash and Sam Whimster. London: Allen & Unwin.

—— 1991. 'Governmental Rationality: An Introduction'. Pp. 1–52 in *The Foucault*

BIBLIOGRAPHY

Effect: Studies in Governmentality, edited by G. Burchell, C. Gordon and P. Miller. Chicago: Chicago University Press.

Gramsci, Antonio. 1978a. *Selections from Political Writings (1910–1920)*. London: Lawrence & Wishart.

—— 1978b. *Selections from Political Writings (1921–1926)*. London: Lawrence & Wishart.

—— 1980. *Selections from the Prison Notebooks*. New York: International Publishers.

—— 1985. *Selections from Cultural Writings*. London: Lawrence & Wishart.

Gregory, Jeanne. 1987. *Sex, Race and the Law: Legislating for Equality*. London: Sage.

Gulliver, P. H. 1977. 'On Mediators'. In *Social Anthropology and the Law*, edited by Ian Hamnet. London: Academic Press.

Gustafson, Dave. 1989. 'Victim Offender Mediation'. *Interaction*, September, 9–10.

Habermas, Jürgen. 1976. *Legitimation Crisis*. London: Heinemann.

—— 1984. *The Theory of Communicative Action (Vol. 1)*. Boston: Beacon Press.

—— 1986. 'Taking Aim at the Heart of the Present'. Pp. 103–108 in *Foucault: A Critical Reader*, edited by David Couzens Hoy. Oxford: Basil Blackwell.

—— 1987. *The Philosophical Discourse of Modernity*. Cambridge, Mass.: MIT Press.

Hacking, Ian. 1986. 'Self-improvement'. Pp. 235–240 in *Foucault: A Critical Reader*, edited by David Couzens Hoy. Oxford: Basil Blackwell.

—— 1991. 'How Should We Do the History of Statistics?' In *The Foucault Effect: Studies in Governmentality*, edited by Graham Burchell, Colin Gordon, and Peter Miller. Chicago: University of Chicago Press.

Hamilton, Roberta and Michele Barrett, eds. 1986. *The Politics of Diversity: Feminism, Marxism and Nationalism*. Montreal: Book Centre.

Hamnett, Ian, ed. 1977. *Social Anthropology and the Law*. London: Academic Press.

Hampson, Norman. 1990. *The Enlightenment*. London: Penguin Books.

Handler, Joel. 1992. 'Postmodernism, Protest and the New Social Movements'. *Law and Society Review* 26(4): 697–732.

Harrington, Christine B. 1982. 'Delegalizing Reform Movements: A Historical Analysis'. In *The Politics of Informal Justice: The American Experience*, edited by Richard Abel, vol. 1. New York: Academic Press.

—— 1984. 'The Politics of Participation and Nonparticipation in Dispute Processes'. *Law & Policy* 6(2): 203–229.

—— 1985. *Shadow Justice: The Ideology and Institutionalization of Alternatives to the Court*. Connecticut: Greenwood.

—— 1988. 'Regulatory Reform: Creating Gaps and Making Markets'. *Law and Policy* 10(4): 293–316.

—— 1992. 'Popular Justice, Populist Politics: Law in Community Organising'. *Social and Legal Studies*. 1(2): 177–198.

—— 1993. 'Community Organising through Conflict Resolution'. In *The Possibility of Popular Justice: A Case Study of Community Mediation in the United States*, edited by Sally Engle Merry and Neal Milner. Ann Arbor: University of Michigan Press.

Harrington, Christine B. and Sally Merry. 1988. 'Ideological Production: The Making of Community Mediation.' *Law and Society Review* 22(4): 709–735.

Harrington, Christine B. and Janet Rifkin. 1989. 'The Gender Organization of Mediation: Implications for the Feminization of Legal Practice.' *Institute for Legal Studies* 4(2).

185

BIBLIOGRAPHY

Hartsock, Nancy. 1990. 'Foucault on Power: A Theory for Women? In *Feminism/ Postmodernism*, edited by Linda J. Nicholson. New York: Routledge.

Harvey, David. 1991. 'Flexibility: Threat or Opportunity?' *Socialist Review* 21(1): 65–78.

Hastings, Ross and Ronald P. Saunders. 1987. 'Social Control, State Autonomy and Legal Reform: The Law Reform Commission of Canada'. In *State Control: Criminal Justice Politics in Canada*, edited by R. S. Ratner and John L. McMullan. Vancouver: University of British Columbia Press.

Havelock, Eric A. 1978. *The Greek Concept of Justice From Its Shadow in Homer to Its Substance in Plato*. Cambridge, Mass.: Harvard University Press.

Hebdidge, D. 1988. *Hiding in the Light: On Images and Things*. London: Routledge.

—— 1989.'New Times: After the Masses'. *Marxism Today*, January.

Heidegger, Paul. 1962. *Being and Time*. Translated by John Macquarrie and Edward Robinson. Oxford: Basil Blackwell.

Heilbroner, Robert. 1987. 'A Vision of Socialism'. *Dissent* 36: 562–565.

Hekman, Susan. 1991. 'Reconstructing the Subject: Feminism, Modernism and Postmodernism'. *Hypatia* 6(2): 44–63.

Held, David. 1987. *Models of Democracy*. Stanford, Calif.: Stanford University Press.

Heller, Agnes. 1987. *Beyond Justice*. Oxford: Basil Backwell.

Henry, Stuart. 1983. *Private Justice: Towards Integrated Theorising in the Sociology of Law*. London: Routledge & Kegan Paul.

Hepworth, Mike and Bryan S. Turner. 1982. *Confession: Studies in Deviance and Religion*. London: Routledge and Kegan Paul.

Hiley, David. 1984. 'Foucault and the Analysis of Power'. *Praxis International* 4(2): 192–207.

—— 1985. 'Foucault and the Question of Enlightenment'. *Philosophy and Social Criticism* 1: 63–83.

Hipkin, Brian. 1985. 'Looking for Justice: The Search for Socialist Legality and Popular Justice'. *International Journal of the Sociology of Law* 13: 117–132.

Hirsch, Joachim. 1981. 'The New Leviathan and the Struggle for Democratic Rights'. *Telos* 48: 79.

—— 1983. 'The Fordist Security State and New Social Movements'. *Kapitalistate* 10(11): 75.

—— 1988. 'The Crisis of Fordism, Transformations of the "Keynesian" Security State and New Social Movements'. *Research in Social Movements, Conflicts and Change* 10: 43–55.

Hirst, Paul and Phil Jones. 1987. 'The Critical Resources of Established Jurisprudence'. In *Critical Legal Studies*, edited by Peter Fitzpatrick and Alan Hunt. Oxford: Basil Blackwell.

Hirst, Paul and Jonathan Zeitlin. 1991. 'Flexible Specialization versus Post-Fordism: Theory, Evidence and Policy Implications.' *Economy and Society* 20(1): 1-56.

Hobbes, Thomas. 1968. *Leviathan*, edited by C. B Macpherson. Harmondsworth: Penguin.

Hofrichter, Richard. 1982. 'Neighborhood Justice and the Social Control Problems of American Capitalism: A Perspective'. In *The Politics of Informal Justice: The American Experience*, edited by Richard Abel, vol. 1. New York: Academic Press.

—— 1987. *Neighborhood Justice in Capitalist Society: The Expansion of the Informal State*. New York: Greenwood.

Hogarth, John. 1974. 'Alternatives to the Adversary System'. In *Studies on Sentencing*, edited by the Law Reform Commission of Canada. Ottawa: Queen's Printer.

Horrocks, Russell L. 1982. 'Alternatives to Courts in Canada'. *Alberta Law Journal* 20: 326–334.

Howlett, Michael and Keith Brownsey. 1988. 'The Old Reality and the New Reality: Party Politics and Public Policy in British Columbia 1941–1987'. *Studies in Political Economy* 25: 141–176.

Hoy, David Cousins, ed. 1986. *Foucault: A Critical Reader*. Oxford: Basil Blackwell.

——1988. 'Foucault: Modern or Postmodern?' In *After Foucault: Humanistic Knowledge, Postmodern Challenges*, edited by Jonathan Arac. New Jersey: Rutgers University Press.

Huber, Marg. 1990. 'Update on Community Mediation in B.C.' *The Mediator* 24 (Spring): 5.

—— 1991a. 'Native Mediation Model for Urban Communities'. *Interaction*, Spring: 1–4.

—— 1991b. 'Medicine Wheel Featured in Native Mediation Model'. *The Mediator* 28 (Spring): 1.

Hughes, E. N., chairperson. 1988. *Access to Justice: Report of the Justice Reform Committee of British Columbia*. Victoria BC: Ministry of the Attorney General.

Hunt, Alan. 1978. *The Sociological Movement in Law*. Philadelphia: Temple University Press.

—— ed. 1980. *Marxism and Democracy*. London: Lawrence & Wishart.

—— 1987. 'The Critique of Law: What Is Critical about Critical Legal Theory?' In *Critical Legal Studies*, edited by Peter Fitzpatrick and Alan Hunt. Oxford: Basil Blackwell.

—— 1990a. 'The Big Fear: Law Confronts Postmodernism'. *McGill Law Journal* 35(3): 507–540.

—— 1990b. 'Postmodernism and Critical Criminology'. *Critical Criminologist* 2(1): 5–6, 17–18.

—— 1993. *Explorations in Law and Society: Toward a Constitutive Theory of Law*. New York: Routledge.

Hunt, Alan and Gary Wickham. 1994. *Foucault and Law*. London: Pluto Press.

Hutchinson, Allan C. 1992. 'Doing the Right Thing? Toward a Postmodern Politics'. *Law and Society Review* 26(4): 773–787.

Ietswaart, Heleen F. P. 1982. 'The Discourse of Summary Justice and the Discourse of Popular Justice: An Analysis of Rhetoric in Argentina'. In *The Politics of Informal Justice: The American Experience*, edited by Richard Abel, vol. 2, New York: Academic Press.

Ingram, David. 1987/8. 'Legitimacy and the Postmodern Condition: The Political Thought of Jean-Francois Lyotard'. *Praxis International* 7(3/4): 286–305.

Ismael, Jacqueline S. and Yves Vaillancourt, eds. 1988. *Privatization and Provincial Social Services in Canada: Policy, Administration and Service Delivery*. Edmonton: University of Alberta Press.

Jameson, Fredric. 1984. 'Postmodernism or the Cultural Logic of Capitalism'. *New Left Review* 146.

—— 1989. 'Marxism and Postmodernism'. *New Left Review* 176.

Janowitz, Morris. 1975. 'Sociological Theory and Social Control'. *American Journal of Sociology* 81(1): 82–108.

Jenkins, Fredell. 1980. *Social Order and the Limit of the Law: A Theoretical Essay*. New Jersey: Princeton University Press.

Jenson, Jane. 1990. 'Representations in Crisis: The Roots of Canada's Permeable Fordism'. *Canadian Journal of Political Science* XXIII(4): 653–684.

—— 1991. 'All the World's a Stage: Ideas, Spaces and Times in Canadian Political Economy'. *Studies in Political Economy* 36 (Autumn): 43–72.

Jessop, Bob. 1990. 'Regulation Theories in Retrospect and Prospect'. *Economy and Society* 19(2): 153–216.

Johnson, Earl. 1981. 'The Justice System of the Future: Four Scenarios for the Twenty First Century'. In *Access to Justice and the Welfare State*, edited by Mauro Cappelletti. Alphen aan den Rijn: Sijthoff.

Justice Council (Cranbrook). 1976. 'Justice Council's Conference: Community Involvement in Justice.' In *Report of Conference Held at Cranbrook, 27–29 November, 1976.*

Justice Council (Kamloops). 1978. 'Symposium: Community Justice Exchange.' In *Report, B.C. Association of Justice Councils.*

Justice Development Commission. 1974a. *The Justice Development Commission.* Vancouver: Attorney General, British Columbia.

—— 1974b. *The Work of the Justice Development Commission.* Vancouver: Attorney General, British Columbia.

Justice Development Commission (Courts Division). 1974. *Program Report for Period April 1 to November 30, 1974 and Proposal for Continuing Development and Future Programs.* Vancouver: Attorney General, British Columbia.

—— 1976. *Final Report: Small Claims Project.* Vancouver: Attorney General, British Columbia.

Kairys, David. 1982. *The Politics of Law: A Progressive Critique.* New York: Pantheon Books.

Kalpatoo, Tom. 1994. 'The Vancouver Inter-Cultural Dispute Resolution Project'. *The Mediator* 41: 2.

Kant, Immanuel. 1990. *Foundations of the Metaphysic of Morals and What is Enlightenment?* New York: Macmillan.

Kauffman, L. A. 1990. 'The Anti-Politics of Identity'. *Socialist Review* 20(1): 67–80.

Keane, John, ed. 1988a. *Civil Society and the State: New European Perspectives.* London: Verso.

—— 1988b. *Democracy and Civil Society.* London: Verso.

Keenan, Thomas. 1982 'Michael Foucault: Is it really Important to Think?' *Philosophy and Social Criticism* 9(1): 31–40.

Keene, Roger and David C. Humphreys. 1980. *Conversations with W.A.C. Bennett.* Toronto: Methuen.

Kennedy, Leslie. 1985. 'Resolving Community Disputes: Social Conflict and Social Control'. University of Alberta, Edmonton Area Series Report, No. 37.

Knowles, Molly. 1987. 'Family Mediation Canada'. *The Mediator* 13 (Summer): 1.

Kolb, Deborah M. 1983. *The Mediators.* Cambridge, Mass.: MIT Press.

Kolb, Deborah *et. al.* 1993. *When Talk Works: Profiles of Mediators.* San Francisco: Jossey-Bass.

Kressel, Kenneth and Dean G. Pruitt, eds. 1989. *Mediation Research: The Process and Effectiveness of Third-Party Intervention.* San Francisco: Jossey-Bass.

Kumar, Krishan. 1988. *The Rise of Modern Society.* Oxford: Basil Blackwell.

Laclau, Ernesto and Chantal Mouffe. 1982. 'Hegemony and the New Political Movements'. *Socialist Review* 12(6): 91–113.

—— 1985. *Hegemony and Socialist Strategy: Towards a Radical Democratic Politics.* London: Verso.

Lajeunesse, Theresa. 1976a. *Justice Councils: A Study.* Victoria BC: Department of the Attorney General.

—— 1976b. *Justice Councils: A Summary Report.* Victoria BC: Department of the Attorney General.

Landau, Barbara. 1988. 'Mediation: An Option for Divorcing Families'. *Advocates' Quarterly* 9: 1–21.

Landau, Barbara, Mario Bartoletti and Ruth Mesbur. 1987. *Family Mediation Handbook*. Toronto: Butterworth.

Lash, Scott. 1990. *Sociology of Postmodernism*. London: Routledge.

Law Reform Commission of Canada. 1975a. *Studies on Diversion*. Ottawa: Queen's Printer.

—— 1975b. *Diversion, Working Paper 7*. Ottawa: Queen's Printer.

Lederach, John P. and Ron Kraybill. 1993. 'The Paradox of Popular Justice: A Practioner's View'. In *The Possibility of Popular Justice: A Case Study of Community Mediation in the United States*, edited by Sally Engle Merry and Neal Milner. Ann Arbor: University of Michigan Press.

Leonard, Jerry D. 1990. 'Foucault, Genealogy, Law, Praxis'. *Legal Studies Forum* XIV(1): 3–25.

Lerman, Lisa. 1984. 'Mediation of Wife Abuse Cases: The Adverse Impact of Informal Dispute Resolution on Women'. *Harvard Women's Law Journal* 7: 57–113.

Levin, David. 1989. 'The Body Politic: The Embodiment of Praxis in Foucault and Habermas'. *Praxis International* 9(1/2): 112–132.

Levinas, Immanuel. 1989. *The Levinas Reader*, edited by Sean Hume. Oxford: Basil Blackwell.

Lipietz, Alain. 1984. 'The Globalization of the General Crisis of Fordism'. Kingston: Program of Studies in National and International Development, Queens University.

—— 1988. 'Reflections on a Tale: The Marxist Foundations of the Concepts of Regulation and Accumulation'. *Studies in Political Economy* 26: 7–36.

Lotz, Don. 1994. 'Multiculturalism – An Alternative View' *The Mediator* 41: 2.

Lover, John and Andrew Pirie. 1990. *Alternative Dispute Resolution for the Community: An Annotated Bibliography*. Victoria, BC: UVic Institute for Dispute Resolution.

Lowman, John, Robert J. Menzies and T. S. Palys, eds. 1987. *Transcarceration: Essays in the Sociology of Social Control*. Aldershot: Gower.

Lyotard, Jean-François. 1984. *The Postmodern Condition: A Report on Knowledge*. Minneapolis: University of Minnesota Press.

—— 1988. *The Different: Phrases in Dispute*. Manchester: Manchester University Press.

—— 1991. *The Inhuman: Reflections on Time*. Stanford: Stanford University Press.

—— 1992. 'Sensus Communis'. In *Judging Lyotard*, edited by Andrew Benjamin London: Routledge.

Lyotard, Jean-François and Jean-Loup Thebaud. 1985. *Just Gaming*. Minneapolis: University of Minnesota Press.

Macaulay, Stewart. 1984. *Private Government*. Madison: Disputes Processing Research Program, University of Wisconsin-Madison.

McBride, Stephen. 1992. *Not Working: State, Unemployment and Neo-Conservatism in Canada*. Toronto: University of Toronto Press.

McCann, Michael. 1992. 'Resistance, Reconstruction and Romance in Legal Scholarship.' *Law and Society Review* 26(4): 733–750.

MacDonald, Eleanor. 1991. 'Feminist, Marxist and Poststructural Subjects'. *Studies in Political Economy* 35: 43–72.

McGillis, Daniel. 1986. *Community Dispute Resolution Programs and Public Policy*. Washington, DC: US Department of Justice.

McGillis, Daniel and Joan Mullen. 1977. *Neighborhood Justice Centers: An Analysis of Potential Models*. Washington, DC: US Government Printing Office.

McGowan, John. 1991. *Postmodernism and Its Critics*. Ithaca: Cornell University Press.

MacIntyre, Alisdair. 1988. *Whose Justice? Which Rationality?* Indiana: University of Notre Dame Press.

Mackie, Karl J., ed. 1991. *A Handbook of Dispute Resolution: ADR in Action*. London: Routledge and Sweet & Maxwell.

McNay, Lois. 1992. *Foucault and Feminism: Power, Gender and Self*. Cambridge: Polity Press.

—— 1994. *Foucault: A Critical Introduction*. New York: Continuum.

Macpherson, C. B. 1987. *The Life and Times of Liberal Democracy*. Oxford: Oxford University Press.

Maffesoli, Michel. 1990. 'Post-Modern Sociality'. *Telos* 35: 89–92.

Magnusson, Warren, William K. Carroll, Charles Doyle, Monika Langer and R. B. J. Walker, eds. 1984. *The New Reality: The Politics of Restraint in British Columbia*. Vancouver: New Star Books.

Mahon, Rianne. 1991. 'From "Bringing" to "Putting": The State in Late Twentieth-century Social Theory'. *Canadian Journal of Sociology* 16(2): 119–144.

Maine, Henry S. 1965. *Ancient Law*. New York: J. M. Dent.

Malcolmson, John. 1984. 'The Hidden Agenda of "Restraint" '. In *The New Reality: The Politics of Restraint in British Columbia*, edited by Warren Magnusson *et al*. Vancouver: New Star Books.

Mandel, Michael. 1989. *The Charter of Rights and the Legalization of Politics in Canada*. Toronto: Wall & Thompson.

Manning, D. J. 1976. *Liberalism*. London: J. M. Dent Ltd.

Marchak, Patricia. 1984. 'The New Economic Reality: Substance and Rhetoric'. In *The New Reality: The Politics of Restraint in British Columbia*, edited by Warren Magnusson *et al*. Vancouver: New Star Books.

—— 1985. *The New Right and the New Economic Reality*. Kingston: Program of Studies in National and International Development, Queens University.

—— 1986. 'The Rise and Fall of the Peripheral State: The Case of British Columbia'. In *Regionalism in Canada*, edited by Robert J. Brym. Toronto: University of Toronto Press.

Marshall, Tony F. 1985. *Alternatives to Criminal Courts*. Aldershot: Gower.

—— 1988. 'Informal Justice: The British Experience'. In *Informal Justice?*, edited by Roger Matthews. London: Sage.

Marx, Karl. 1973. *Grundrisse*. Harmondsworth: Penguin.

Matthews, Roger. 1987. 'Taking Realist Criminology Seriously'. *Contemporary Crisis* 11: 371–401.

—— 1988. 'Introduction'. In *Informal Justice?*, edited by Roger Matthews. London: Sage.

—— ed. 1989. *Privatizing Criminal Justice*. London: Sage Publications.

May, Todd G. 1990. 'Kant the Liberal, Kant the Anarchist: Rawls and Lyotard on Kantian Justice'. *The Southern Journal of Philosophy* XXVIII(4): 525–538.

Mediation Development Association of British Columbia. 1989. *Brief on Standards and Ethics for Mediators*. Bound document.

—— 1990. 'B.C. Mediators to Examine Standards'. *The Mediator* 24 (Spring): 3–4.

Medycky, Christine. 1988. 'An Overview of Alternative Dispute Resolution Processes'. Presented at the Canadian Bar Association's (Ontario) Conference on Alternative Dispute Resolution (October 3, 1988). Ontario: CBAO.

Merry, Sally Engle. 1979. 'Going to Court: Strategies of Dispute Management in an American Urban Neighborhood'. *Law and Society Review* 13: 891.

—— 1982. 'The Social Organization of Mediation in Nonindustrial Societies: Implications for Informal Community Justice'. In *The Politics of Informal Justice: The American Experience*, edited by Richard Abel, vol. 2. New York: Academic Press.

—— 1984. 'Rethinking Gossip and Scandal'. In *Toward a General Theory of Social Control*, edited by Donald Black, vol. 2. New York: Academic Press.

—— 1988. 'Legal Pluralism'. *Law & Society Review* 22(5): 869–901.

—— 1992. 'Popular Justice and the Ideology of Social Transformation'. *Social and Legal Studies* 1(2): 161–176.

—— 1993. 'Sorting out Popular Justice'. In *The Possibility of Popular Justice: A Case Study of Community Mediation in the United States*, edited by Sally Engle Merry and Neal Milner. Ann Arbor: University of Michigan Press.

Merry, Sally Engle and Neal Milner eds. 1993. *The Possibility of Popular Justice: A Case Study of Community Mediation in the United States*. Ann Arbor: University of Michigan Press.

Merry, Sally Engle and Susan S. Silbey. 1984. 'What Do Plaintiffs Want? Reexamining the Concept of Dispute'. *The Justice System Journal* 9(2): 151–178.

Mica, Harry. 1992. 'Social Conflict, Local Justice: Organizational Responses to the Astructural Bias'. *Interaction (supplement)*, Spring.

Miller, David. 1974. 'The Ideological Backgrounds to Conceptions of Social Justice'. *Political Studies* 22(4): 387–399.

Miller, Peter and Nikolas Rose. 1988. 'The Tavistock Programme: The Government of Subjectivity and Social Life'. *Sociology* 22(3): 171–192.

—— 1990. 'Governing Economic Life'. *Economy and Society* 19(1): 1–30.

Miller, Toby. 1993. *The Well-Tempered Self: Citizenship, Culture and the Modern Subject*. Baltimore Md.: Johns Hopkins University Press.

Mills, C. Wright. 1959. *The Sociological Imagination*. New York: Oxford University Press.

Minson, Jeffrey. 1985. *Genealogies of Morals: Nietzsche, Foucault, Donzelot and the Eccentricity of Ethics*. London: Macmillan.

Moffat, Gary. 1982. *A History of the Peace Movement in Canada (Bibliography)*. Ottawa: Grape Vine Press.

Mohr, Richard D. 1988. *Gays/Justice: A Study of Ethics, Society and Law*. New York: Columbia University Press.

Moir, Donald S. 1987. 'Unity of Mediators Needed in Canada'. *The Mediator* 13 (Summer).

Moller Okin, Susan. 1989. *Justice, Gender and the Family*. New York: Basic Books.

Moore, Christopher. 1986. *The Mediation Process: Practical Strategies for Resolving Conflict*. San Francisco: Jossey-Bass.

Moore, Sally Falk. 1977. 'Individual Interests and Organizational Structures: Dispute Settlements as Events of Articulation'. In *Social Anthropology and the Law*, edited by Ian Hamnet. London: Academic Press.

—— 1978. *Law as Process: An Anthropological Approach*. London: Routledge & Kegan Paul.

Morrison, Kathleen M. 1984. *Small Claims Dispute Resolution Project*. Victoria, BC: Queen's Printer.

Morsley, J. Terrence, Norman J. Ruff, Neil A. Swainson, R. Jeremy Wilson and Walter D. Young. 1983. *The Reins of Power: Governing British Columbia*. Vancouver: Douglas & McIntyre.

BIBLIOGRAPHY

Mouffe, Chantal, ed. 1979. *Gramsci and Marxist Theory.* London: Routledge & Kegan Paul.
Mouzellis, Nicos. 1988. 'Marxism or Post-Marxism?' *New Left Review* 167: 107–123.
Murphy, Peter. 1991. 'Postmodern Perspectives and Justice'. *Thesis Eleven.* 30: 117–131.
Nader, Laura. 1979. 'Disputing without the Force of Law'. *The Yale Law Journal* 88(5): 998–1022.
—— 1984. 'From Disputing to Complaining'. In *Toward a General Theory of Social Control,* edited by Donald Black, vol. 2. New York: Academic Press.
—— 1988. 'The ADR Explosion – The Implications of Rhetoric in Legal Reform'. *The Windsor Yearbook of Access to Justice* 8: 269–291.
—— 1993. 'When Is Popular Justice Popular?' In *The Possibility of Popular Justice: A Case Study of Community Mediation in the United States,* edited by Sally Engle Merry and Neal Milner. Ann Arbor: University of Michigan Press.
Nader, Laura and Linda Singer. 1976. 'Dispute Resolution and the Future: What Are the Choices?' *California State Bar Journal* 51: 281.
Nader, Laura and Harry F. Todd. 1978. 'Introduction: The Disputing Process.' In *The Disputing Process in Ten Societies,* edited by Laura Nader and Harry Todd. New York: Columbia University.
Network, The. 1991a. *Directory of Canadian Dispute Resolution Programs.* Kitchener: The Network for Community Justice and Conflict Resolution.
—— 1991b. *Learning for Life: Conflict Resolution.* Kitchener: The Network for Community Justice and Conflict Resolution.
—— 1993/94. *Membership Handbook.* Kitchener: The Network for Community Justice and Conflict Resolution.
Ng, Roxana, Gillian Walker and Jacob Muller, eds. 1990. *Community Organizing and the Canadian State.* Toronto: Garamond Press.
Nicholson, Linda J. 1990. *Feminism/Postmodernism.* New York: Routledge.
Nietzsche, Friedrich. 1967. *The Will to Power.* New York: Vintage Books.
Northey, Wayne. 1990. 'Restorative Justice: Victim-Offender Meetings'. *Accord* 9(2): 5–6.
Nowell-Smith, Geoffrey. 1975. 'The Question of Hegemony'. *Radical Philosophy* 5: 23–25.
O'Connor, James. 1973. *The Fiscal Crisis of the State.* New York: St. Martin's Press.
Offe, Claus. 1984. *Contradictions of the Welfare State.* London: Hutchinson.
—— 1985. 'New Social Movements: Challenging the Boundaries of Institutional Politics'. *Social Research* 52: 817.
O'Hagan, Timothy. 1988. 'Four Images of Community'. *Praxis International* 8(2): 183–192.
O'Neill, John. 1995. *The Poverty of Postmodernism.* London: Routledge.
Palmer, Bryan D. 1987. *Solidarity: The Rise and Fall of an Opposition in British Columbia.* Vancouver: New Star Books.
Pascal, Blaise. 1962. *Pascal's Pensées* (trans. Martin Turnell). London: Harvill Press.
Pasquino, Pasquale. 1979. 'Theatrum Politicum. The Genealogy of Capital – Police and the State of Prosperity'. *Ideology and Consciousness* 4: 41–54.
Pateman, Carol. 1988. *The Sexual Contract.* Cambridge: Polity Press.
Patterson, Dennis, ed. 1994. *Postmodernism and the Law.* Sydney: Dartmouth.
Pavlich, George C. 1990. 'Contesting Social Limits: Diagnosis, Evaluation and Prescription'. *Journal of Human Justice* 2(1): 117–124.
—— 1992a. 'Mediating Community Disputes: The Regulatory Logic of Govern-

ment through Pastoral Power'. Unpublished PhD thesis, University of British Columbia.

—— 1992b. 'People's Courts, Postmodern Difference, and Socialist Justice in South Africa'. *Social Justice* 19(3): 29–45.

—— 1995. 'Contemplating a Postmodern Sociology: Genealogy, Limits Critique'. *The Sociological Review* 43(3): 548–567.

—— Forthcoming 'A Genealogy of Community Mediation in British Columbia: Economic, Political and Legal Lines of Descent'. *BC Studies.*

Peachey, Dean E. 1989a. 'The Kitchener Experiment'. In *Mediation and Criminal Justice: Victims, Offenders and Community*, edited by Martin Wright and Burt Galaway. London: Sage.

—— 1989b. 'What People Want from Mediation'. In *Mediation Research: The Process and Effectiveness of Third-Party Intervention*, edited by Kenneth Kressel and Dean G. Pruitt. San Francisco: Jossey-Bass

Peachey, Dean E., Cathy Skeen and Anne-Marie Tymec. 1988. *Directory of Canadian Dispute Resolution Programs.* Kitchener: The Network for Community Justice and Conflict Resolution.

Peachey, Dean E., Brian Snyder and Alan Teichroeb. 1983. *Mediation Primer: A Training Guide for Mediators in the Criminal Justice System.* Waterloo: Community Justice Initiatives of the Waterloo Region.

Peachey, Dean E. and Anne-Marie Tymec. 1989. *Membership Handbook.* The Network, Interaction for Conflict Resolution.

Perry, Linda, Theresa Lajeunesse and Anna Woods. 1987. *Mediation Services: An Evaluation.* Manitoba: Ministry of the Attorney General.

Perry, Nick. 1995. 'Travelling Theory/Nomadic Theorizing'. *Organization* 2(1): 35–54.

Pfohl, Stephen J. 1985. *Images of Deviance and Social Control: A Sociological History.* New York: McGraw Hill.

—— 1990. 'Terror of the Simulacra: Struggles for Justice and the Postmodern'. In *New Directions in the Study of Justice, Law and Social Control.* Prepared by School of Justice Studies, Arizona State University. New York: Plenum Press.

Pinkelle, Carl F. and William C. Louthan. 1985. *Discretion, Justice and Democracy: A Public Policy Perspective.* Ames: Iowa State University Press.

Pipkin, Ronald M. and J. Rifkin. 1984. 'The Social Organization in Alternative Dispute Resolution: Implications for the Professionalization of Mediation'. *The Justice System Journal* 9(2): 204–227.

Pirie, Andrew J. 1987. *Dispute Resolution in Canada: Present State, Future Direction.* Victoria, BC: The Law Reform Commission of Canada.

Pirie, Andrew J. and Dinah Stanley. 1992. *Dispute Resolution and You: What You Need to Know.* Victoria, BC: UVic Institute for Dispute Resolution.

Pitsula, Pat. 1987. *Report on Alternative Dispute Resolution Projects.* Burnaby: Simon Fraser University.

Plato. 1973. *The Republic.* Oxford: Oxford University Press.

Plotke, David. 1990. 'What's So New about Social Movements?' *Socialist Review* 20(1): 81–102.

Poster, Mark. 1984. *Foucault, Marxism and History: Mode of Production versus Mode of Information.* Cambridge: Polity Press.

Poulantzas, Nicos. 1978. *State, Power, Socialism.* London: New Left Books.

Pound, Roscoe. 1922. *An Introduction to the Philosphy of Law.* New Haven, Conn.: Yale University Press.

Pruitt, Dean G. and Peter J. Carnvale. 1993. *Negotiation in Social Conflict.* Buckingham: Open University Press.

Rajchman, John. 1985. *Michel Foucault: The Freedom of Philosophy*. New York: Columbia University Press.

—— 1986. 'Ethics after Foucault'. *Social Text* 13/14: 165–183.

—— 1991. *Truth and Eros: Foucault, Lacan and the Question of Ethics*. New York: Routledge.

Ratner, R. S. and John L. McMullan. 1987. *State Control: Criminal Justice Politics in Canada*. Vancouver: University of British Columbia Press.

Ratner, R.S. and George Pavlich, 1993. 'Critical Criminology in Canada: Transformations in the Post-modernist Phase'. *Socialist Studies Bulletin* 32: 27–36.

Rawls, John. 1973. *A Theory of Justice*. Oxford: Oxford University Press.

—— 1988. 'Priority of Right and Ideas of the Good'. *Philosophy and Public Affairs*, 17(4): 251–276.

Ray, Larry. 1989. 'Emerging Options in Dispute Resolution'. *ABA Journal* June: 66–68.

—— 1990. *American Bar Association Dispute Resolution Directory*. Washington DC: ABA.

Reiman. Jeffrey. 1990. *Justice and Modern Moral Philosophy*. New Haven, Conn.: Yale University Press.

Resnick, Philip. 1984. 'The Ideology of Neo-Conservatism'. In *The New Reality: The Politics of Restraint in British Columbia*, edited by Warren Magnusson *et al*. Vancouver: New Star Books.

—— 1985. 'B.C. Capitalism and the Empire of the Pacific'. *BC Studies* 67: 29–46.

—— 1987. 'Neo-Conservatism on the Periphery: The Lessons from B.C.' *BC Studies* 75: 3–23.

Richardson, C. James. 1988. *Court-Based Mediation in Four Canadian Cities: An Overview of Research Results*. Ottawa: Deptartment of Justice, Canada.

Rifkin, Janet. 1982. 'Mediating Disputes: An American Paradox'. *ALSA Forum* VI(3): 263–277.

—— 1984. 'Mediation from a Feminist Perspective: Promise and Problems'. *Law and Inequality: Journal of Theory and Practice* 2: 21–31.

Roberts, Simon. 1979. *Order and Dispute: An Introduction to Legal Anthropology*. Oxford: Martin Robinson.

Roehl, Janice A. and Royer F. Cook. 1985. 'Issues in Mediation: Rhetoric and Reality Revisited'. *Journal of Social Issues* 41(2): 161–178.

Rose, Gillian. 1994. 'Athens and Jerusalem: A Tale of Three Cities'. *Social and Legal Studies* 3(3): 323–332.

Rose, Nikolas. 1990. *Governing the Soul: The Shaping of the Private Self*. London: Routledge.

—— 1992. 'Governing the Enterprising Self'. In *The Values of the Enterprise Culture: The Moral Debate*, edited by P. Heelas and P. Morris. London: Routledge.

Rose, Nikolas and Peter Miller. 1992. 'Politcal Power beyond the State: Problematics of Government.' *British Journal of Sociology* 43(2): 173–205.

Rothenberg, Randall. 1984. *The Neo-Liberals: Creating the New American Politics*. New York: Simon & Schuster.

Rousseau, Jean-Jacques. 1974. *The Essential Rousseau*, edited by Lowell Bair. New York: Merridian Books.

Russel, Peter H. 1987. *The Judiciary in Canada: The Third Branch of Government*. Toronto: McGraw-Hill Ryerson.

Rustin, Michael. 1989. 'The Politics of Post-Fordism: Or, the Trouble with "New Times" '. *New Left Review* 175: 54–77.

Salem, Richard A. 1985. 'The Alternative Dispute Resolution Movement: An Overview'. *The Arbitration Journal* 40(3): 3–11.

Sander, Frank E. A. 1976. 'Varieties of Dispute Processing'. *Federal Rules Decisions* 70: 79.

—— 1977. *ABA Report on the National Conference on Minor Disputes Resolution.* Washington, DC: American Bar Association.

—— 1980. 'Community Justice'. *Harvard Law School Bulletin* 31(2): 18–19.

—— 1990. 'ADR Explosion, Perfection and Institutionalization'. *ABA/Dispute Resolution* 26: 1.

Santos, Boaventura De Sousa. 1982. 'Law and Community: The Changing Nature of State Power in Late Capitalism'. In *The Politics of Informal Justice: The American Experience*, edited by Richard Abel, vol. 1. New York: Academic Press.

—— 1985. 'On Modes of Production of Law and Social Power'. *International Journal of the Sociology of Law* 13: 299–336.

Sarat, Austin. 1983. 'Informalism, Delegalization, and the Future of the American Legal Profession'. *Stanford Law Review* 35: 1217–1235.

Sauvé, Robert *et al.* 1977. *Community Involvement in Criminal Justice: Report of the Task Force on the Role of the Private Sector in Criminal Justice.* vol. 1. Ottawa: Ministry of Supply and Services.

Sawicki, Jana. 1991. *Disciplining Foucault: Feminism, Power and the Body.* New York: Routledge.

Scambler, Catherine. 1988. 'What is Power?' *The Mediator* 18 (Autumn): 1.

—— 1989. 'Family Mediation: The Feminist Critique of Mediation'. *Interaction* 1(1): 7.

Schapera, I. 1955. *A Handbook of Tswana Law and Custom.* London: Oxford University Press.

Scott, Alan. 1990. *Ideology and the New Social Movements.* Boston: Unwin Hyman.

Scott, Ian. 1988. 'The Government Perspective'. Presented at the Canadian Bar Association's (Ontario) Conference on Alternative Dispute Resolution (October 3, 1988). Ontario: CBAO.

Scull, Andrew. 1982. 'Community Corrections: Panacea, Progress, or Pretense?' In *The Politics of Informal Justice: The American Experience*, edited by Richard Abel, vol. 1. New York: Academic Press.

—— 1984. *Decarceration: Community Treatment and the Deviant – A Radical View*, 2nd edn. New Jersey: Rutgers University Press.

Selva, Lance H. and Robert M. Bohm. 1987. 'A Critical Examination of the Informalism Experiment in the Administration of Justice'. *Crime and Social Justice* 29: 43–57.

Shailor, Jonathan G. 1994. *Empowerment in Dispute Mediation: A Critical Analysis of Communication.* London: Praeger.

Shapiro, Martin. 1981. *Courts: A Comparative and Political Analysis.* Chicago: University of Chicago Press.

Shonholtz, Raymond. 1978. 'Community Board Program'. Mimeograph.

—— 1984. 'Neighbourhood Justice Systems: Work, Structure and Guiding Principles'. *Mediation Quarterly* 5: 3–30.

—— 1987. 'The Citizens' Role in Justice: Building a Primary Justice and Prevention System at the Neighborhood Level'. *Annals of the American Academy of Political and Social Science* 494: 42–53.

—— 1988/89. 'Community as Peacemaker: Making Neighborhood Justice Work'. *Current Municipal Problems* 15: 291–330.

BIBLIOGRAPHY

—— 1993. 'Justice from Another Perspective: The Ideology and Developmental History of the Community Boards Program'. In *The Possibility of Popular Justice: A Case Study of Community Mediation in the United States*, edited by Sally Engle Merry and Neal Milner. Ann Arbor: University of Michigan Press.

Showstack Sassoon, Anne. 1982. *Approaches to Gramsci*. London: Lawrence & Wishart.

Silbey, Susan S. and Sally Engle Merry. 1986. 'Mediator Settlement Strategies'. *Law and Policy* 8(1): 7–32.

Silbey, Susan S. and Austin Sarat. 1989. 'Dispute Processing in Law and Legal Scholarship: From Institutional Critique to the Reconstruction of the Juridical Subject'. *Denver University Law Review* 66(3): 437–498.

Simon, Jonathan. 1987. 'The Emergence of a Risk Society: Insurance, Law and the State'. *Socialist Review*, 95: 61–89.

—— 1988. 'The Ideological Effects of Actuarial Practices'. *Law and Society Review* 22(5): 772–800.

Singer, Linda. 1985. 'Nonjudicial Dispute Resolution Mechanisms: The Effects on Justice for the Poor'. In *Dispute Resolution*, edited by Stephen B. Goldberg, Eric D. Green and Frank Sander. Boston: Little, Brown.

Sloan, Gordon B. 1989. *Continuing Legal Education Society of British Columbia Curriculum for Dispute Resolution: Designer's Report*. Vancouver: Continuing Legal Education Society.

—— 1992. 'Power: Its Uses and Abuse in Mediation'. *Interaction* 4(1): 1.

Smart, Barry. 1985. *Michel Foucault*. Chichester, Sussex: Ellis Horwood.

—— 1991. 'Theory and Analysis after Foucault'. *Theory, Culture and Society* 8(2): 145–155.

—— 1992. *Modern Conditions, Postmodern Controversies*. London: Routledge.

—— 1993. *Postmodernity*. London: Routledge.

—— 1995. 'The Subject of Responsibility'. *Philosophy and Social Criticism* 21(4): 93–109.

Smart, Carol. 1989. *Feminism and the Power of Law*. London: Routledge.

—— 1990. 'Feminist Approaches to Criminology or Postmodern Woman Meets Atavistic Man'. Pp. 70–84 in *Feminist Perspectives in Criminology*, edited by Loraine Gelsthorpe and Allison Morris. Philadelphia: Open University Press.

Smith, Brian. 1989. *Access to Justice*. Victoria, BC: Ministry of the Attorney General.

Solicitor General, Canada. 1977. *Diversion: A Canadian Concept and Practice*. In *A Report of the First National Conference on Diversion, October 23–26, Quebec City*. Ottawa: Ministry of Supply and Services.

—— 1981. *Highlights of the Federal Initiatives in Criminal Justice: 1966–1980*. Ottawa: Ministry of Supply and Services.

Soper, Kate. 1986. *Humanism and Anti-Humanism*. London: Hutchinson.

—— 1990. 'Feminism, Humanism and Postmodernism'. *Radical Philosophy* 55: 11–17.

—— 1991. 'Postmodernism, Subjectivity and the Question of Value'. *New Left Review* 186: 120–128.

Spitzer, Steven. 1979. 'The Rationalization of Crime Control in Capitalist Society'. *Contemporary Crisis* 3: 187–206.

—— 1982. 'The Dialectics of Formal and Informal Control'. In *The Politics of Informal Justice: The American Experience*, edited by Richard Abel, vol. 1. New York: Academic Press.

Starr, June and Anne Collier. 1989. *History and Power in the Study of Law: New Directions in Legal Anthropology*. Ithaca, NY: Cornell University Press.

Stead, Denis George. 1986. 'The Effectiveness of Criminal Mediation: An Alternative to Court Proceedings in a Canadian City'. PhD dissertation, University of Denver.

Steinmetz, Heinz. 1984. 'The Development of "Discipline" According to Michel Foucault: Discourse Analysis vs. Social History'. *Crime and Social Justice* 20: 83–98.

Stenson, Kevin. 1992. 'Community Policing as a Governmental Technology'. *Economy and Society.* 22(3): 373–387.

Stephanson, Anders. 1987. 'Regarding Postmodernism – A Conversation with Fredric Jameson'. *Social Text* 17 (Fall): 29–54.

Stevens, Sam. 1991. 'An Aboriginal View of the Canadian Justice System'. *Accord* 10(1): 1–5.

Sugarman, David, ed. 1983. *Legality, Ideology and the State.* London: Academic Press.

Sumner, Colin. 1990. 'Foucault, Gender and the Censure of Deviance'. Pp. 26–40 in *Feminist Perspectives in Criminology,* edited by Loraine Gelsthorpe and Allison Morris. Philadelphia: Open University Press.

Tannis, Ernest G. 1989. *Alternative Dispute Resolution That Works.* Ontario: Captus Press.

Taylor, Charles. 1986. 'Foucault on Freedom and Truth'. Pp. 69–102 in *Foucault: A Critical Reader,* edited by David Couzens Hoy. Oxford: Basil Blackwell.

Taylor, Ian, Paul Walton and Jock Young. 1973. *The New Criminology: For a Social Theory of Deviance.* London: Routledge & Kegan Paul.

Theophanous, Andrew C. 1993. *Understanding Social Justice: An Australian Perspective.* Victoria: Elikia Books.

Thompson, Bonita J. 1991. 'Building an Arbitration and Mediation Centre from International Foundations to Domestic Rooftops: A Case Study of the BCICAC'. In *A Handbook of Dispute Resolution: ADR in Action,* edited by Karl Mackie. London: Routledge.

Thompson, Janna. 1992. *Justice and World Order: A Philosophical Inquiry.* London: Routledge.

Tomasic, Roman. 1982. 'Formalized "informal" Justice – A Critical Perspective on Mediation Centres'. In *Proceedings of the Institute of Criminology: Community Justice Centres,* edited by Lawrence Street, Sydney: University of Sydney Press.

Tomasic, Roman and Malcolm Feeley, eds. 1982. *Neighborhood Justice: Assessment of an Emerging Idea.* New York: Longman.

Touraine, Alain. 1989. 'Is Sociology Still the Study of Society?' *Thesis Eleven* 23: 5–63.

Tucker, Kenneth. 1991. 'How New Are the New Social Movements?' *Theory, Culture and Society* 8(2): 75–98.

Turner, Bryan S., ed. 1990. *Theories of Modernity and Postmodernity.* London: Sage.

—— 1994. *Orientalism, Postmodernism and Globalism.* London: Routledge.

Turner, David and Keith Jobson. 1990. *The Decision to Mediate, Not Litigate.* Victoria, BC: University of Victoria Institute for Dispute Resolution.

Turner, John. 1971. 'Law for the Seventies: A Manifesto for Law Reform'. *McGill Law Journal* 17(1): 1–10.

Umbreit, Mark. 1994. *Victim Meets Offender: The Impact of Restorative Justice and Mediation.* New York: Criminal Justice Press.

Unger, Roberto. 1983. 'The Critical Legal Studies Movement'. *Harvard Law Review* 96: 620–625.

Urry, John. 1981. *The Anatomy of Capitalist Societies: The Economy, Civil Society and the State*. London: Macmillan.

Vattimo, Guivani. 1992. *The Transparent Society*. Baltimore, Md.: Johns Hopkins University Press.

Wahrhaftig, Paul. 1981. 'Dispute Resolution Retrospective'. *Crime and Delinquency* 27(1): 99–105.

—— 1982. 'An Overview of Community-oriented Citizen Dispute Resolution Programs in the United States'. In *The Politics of Informal Justice: The American Experience*, edited by Richard Abel, vol. 1. New York: Academic Press.

—— 1984. 'Nonprofessional Conflict Resolution'. *Villanova Law Review* 29(6): 1463–1476.

Walker, Samuel. 1980. *Popular Justice: A History of American Criminal Justice*. Oxford: Oxford University Press.

Wall, Victor D. and Marcia L. Dewhurst. 1991. 'Mediator Gender: Communication Differences in Resolved and Unresolved Mediations'. *Mediation Quarterly* 9(1): 63–85.

Walzer, Michael. 1983. *Spheres of Justice: A Defense of Pluralism and Equality*. New York: Basic Books.

—— 1986. 'The Politics of Michel Foucault'. Pp. 51–68 in *Foucault: A Critical Reader*, edited by David Couzens Hoy. Oxford: Basil Blackwell.

—— 1987. *Interpretation and Social Criticism*. Cambridge, Mass.: Harvard University Press.

Wapner, Paul. 1989. 'What's Left?: Marx, Foucault and Contemporary Problems of Social Change'. *Praxis International* 9(1–2): 88–111.

Warren, Carol. 1981. 'New Forms of Social Control: The Myth of Deinstitutionalization'. *American Behavioral Scientist* 26(6): 724–740.

Weber, Max. 1976. *The Protestant Ethic and the Spirit of Capitalism*. London: Allen & Unwin.

—— 1978. *Economy and Society*, 2 vols. Berkeley: University of California Press.

—— 1980. *Basic Concepts in Sociology*. Secaucus, NJ: The Citadel Press.

Weinstein, Michael A. 1991. 'The Dark Night of the Liberal Spirit and the Dawn of the Savage'. In *Ideology and Power in the Age of Lenin in Ruins*, edited by Arthur and Marilouise Kroker. New York: St. Martins Press.

Wellbank, J. H., Denis Snook and David T. Mason. 1982. *John Rawls and his Critics: An Annotated Bibliography*. New York: Garland.

Wellmer, Albrecht. 1985. 'Reason, Utopia and the *Dialectic of Enlightenment*'. In *Habermas and Modernity*, edited by Richard Bernstein. Massachusetts: The MIT Press.

White, Deborah. 1988. 'Mediation and Women's Rights: Can They Work Together?' *The Mediator* 17 (Summer): 1–2.

White, Stephen K. 1987/8. 'Justice and the Postmodern Problematic'. *Praxis International* 7(3/4): 306–319.

Whittington, Barbara. 1987. 'Sexual Harassment Mediation'. *The Mediator* 12 (Spring): 1.

Whittington, Barbara and Karen Burgess Ruddy. N.d. 'Mediation, Power and Gender: An Annotated Bibliography'. University of Victoria Institute for Dispute Resolution.

Wickham, Gary. 1989. 'Cautious Postmodernism and Legal Truths'. *Law in Context* 7(2): 39–53.

—— 1990. 'The Political Possibilities of Postmodernism'. *Economy and Society* 19(1): 121–149.

—— N.d. 'Justice, Democracy and the Demise of Politics'. School of Social Studies, Murdoch University.

Wittgenstein, Ludwig. 1983. *Philosophical Investigations*. Oxford: Basil Blackwell.

Wood, Alan W. 1972. 'The Marxian Critique of Justice'. *Philosophy and Public Affairs* 1: 244–282 .

Worth, Dave. 1986. 'VORP: A Look at the Past and Future'. *Community Justice Report* supplement (September).

—— 1989. 'Mediation and Values'. *Accord* 8(3): 11–12.

Wright, Martin and Burt Galway, eds. 1989. *Mediation and Criminal Justice: Victims, Offenders and Community.* London: Sage.

Yeatman, Anna. 1990. 'A Feminist Theory of Social Differentiation'. In *Feminism/Postmodernism*, edited by Linda J. Nicholson. New York: Routledge.

Yin, Robert K. 1989. *Case Study Research: Design and Methods.* London: Sage.

Yngvesson, Barbara 1993. 'Local People, Local Problems and Neighborhood Justice'. In *The Possibility of Popular Justice: A Case Study of Community Mediation in the United States*, edited by Sally Engle Merry and Neal Milner. Ann Arbor: University of Michigan Press.

Yngvesson, Barbara and Lynn Mather. 1983. 'Courts, Moots and the Disputing Process'. In *Empirical Theories about Courts*, edited by Keith O. Boyum and Lynn Mather. New York: Longman.

Young, Iris Marion. 1990. *Justice and the Politics of Difference.* New Jersey: Princeton University Press.

—— 1992. 'Recent Theories of Justice'. *Social Theory and Practice.* 18(1): 63–79.

Young, Jock. 1987. 'The Task Facing a Realist Criminology'. *Contemporary Crisis* 11: 337–356.

Zehr, Howard. 1986. 'Retributive Justice, Restorative Justice'. *Peace Section Newsletter* 16(1): 9–11.

—— 1994. *Changing Lenses: A New Focus for Crime and Justice.* Scottsdale: Herald Press.

Zuber, T. G. 1987. *Report of the Ontario Courts of Inquiry.* Ontario: Ministry of the Attorney General.

INDEX

Abel, R.L. 68–69, 71
alternative dispute resolution (ADR) 3, 40, 44, 152–53; alternative politics of 1, 4, 148–155; *see also* community mediation
American Sociological Association 14

Baskin, D.R. 74–76, 80
Bauman, Z. 11, 22, 87
British Columbia: and ADR 4–5, 43–51, 132–133, 135; calculations of community justice in 51–55, 99–101; Community Resource Boards 52; and divorce mediation 45–46; Justice Councils of 53, 115; Justice Development Commission of 52–53; mediation services 44–51, 111–131; neo-liberalism in 13, 137–138; privatisation and deregulation within 13; rise of community mediation in 1–3, 43–46, 145
Burdine, M. 47–51

calculated social fields 151–152
Cameralism 108
Canada: absence of community justice critics in 3
Canadian Bar Association 45, 58, 63
class-based conflict 69
community: community mediation advocates' visions of 58–59, 113–116; conflict in 59, 115, 151–152; ideals of 153; and the individual self 113; integrating with individuals and selves 129–131; and neo-liberalism 13–14; strength and peace 57–59, 124; visions of 113–116

Community Justice Initiatives Network 44, 46
community mediation 2, 3, 8–9, 10; advocates in British Columbia 42–43; assessment of value of 61, 150–151; and the capitalist state 67, 72, 76–78; and confession 86, 118, 123–129; critiques of 3–4, 66–81; and dearth of clients 53; definition of 4–5; and individual empowerment 55–57; expanding/intensifying state control 4, 66–68, 71, 73, 75, 78–79; funding of 45, 61, 141, 150; governmental rationality of 4, 106, 130; governmentalising the state 91–92, 132–158; individual, disputing selves 96–97, 116–129; neo-Marxist analysis of 67, 71, 76; neo-Weberian analyses of 67–71, 76; and pastoral power 86, 106–113; physical setting for 122; political contests in 69–70; as a postmodern idiom 40, 64–65; and power relays 152–153; and state power 91, 99, 100, 147–148, 150; structural logic of 71–74; system-based form of 149; and techniques of self 96–97, 98, 118; and voluntarism 116; and volunteers 54, 111
confession 123–129
conflict resolution 9
consensus-based politics 70–71, 72, 155
courts 5, 134–135; and adjudication 51, 139; and advocates of community mediation 3, 138; in British Columbia 51–52; problems associated with 52
criticism 5–8
customary law 40

200

deconstruction 6–7, 34, 37, 100
Derrida, J. 36–39
discipline 86–87, 97; techniques of
  118–123
discourse 9–10; advocates' discourse on
  community mediation 51–60, 100;
  aporias in critics' discourse 78–81;
  critics' discourse on community
  mediation 66–77; distinction between
  'elements' and 'moments' 10; and
  'floating signifiers' 10
'disenchantment of the world' 20
Dispute Resolution Act (US) 70

Enlightenment 21, 31
enterprise culture 12, 97
examination, the 121–123

Fisk, M. 30
Fitzpatrick, P. 42, 79, 83–88, 147–149
Foucault, M. 9, 88–98; art of
  government 108; and bio-power 88,
  90, 109; carceral archipelago 90;
  criticisms of 101–105; discipline 88,
  89–90, 93, 118–121 (see also
  discipline); ethical work 123–124,
  127–129; ethics 154; on freedom 103;
  governmentality 4, 88, 90, 92–94;
  individuals and selves 96–98; law and
  sovereign power 89–92; live
  individuals 95; omnes et singulatim
  95, 129; pastoral power 4, 94–95,
  107–108; population 90–91, 109–110;
  power-knowledge 7–8, 86, 95–96;
  and power outside the state 91–92;
  and power relations 146; techniques
  of self 4, 93–94
Fraser Institute (BC) 13

genealogy 7
Good, the 17–18
Gramsci, A. 73, 74

Harrington, C. 68, 69–70, 80–81
hegemony 16, 72
Hofrichter, R. 71–74
Homer's formulation of justice 18
human nature 21

individual disputing selves 116–129
informal alternatives 69

jurisprudence 8, 16, 18, 28
justice 2–3, 5–6, 17–18; community 5,
  43, 55, 145, 156 (see also community
  mediation); and decline of modern
  auspices 16–17; Derrida on 1, 36–39;
  as fairness 25; fragmented 2, 4, 16, 29,
  32, 41; informal 1, 42, 70–71, 83–85
  (see also community mediation); and
  modern auspices 16, 25, 28–29, 32;
  modern theories of 19–29, 35–36;
  mystical promise of 36; popular 42,
  70, 83 (see also justice, informal);
  postmodern conditions of 2, 4,
  29–32, 36–39; as process 28;
  professional 5, 42, 104, 145, 150; and
  professionalism 133, 150; radical 30;
  restorative see restorative justice;
  social 26; spheres of 29–30; and state
  control 67–69; and universal
  principle 16, 32
Justice Councils (BC) 53
Justice Development Commission (BC)
  43, 51, 52–53
'justice without law' 156

Kant, I. 21; universal moral foundations
  22–25

law: and community mediation 133,
  136–140, 150; 'dark side' of 85, 90,
  137; formal equality of 1; and order
  8, 133, 136, 141; rule of 28; and
  state 76
Law Reform Commission of Canada
  (LRC) 51–52
legal anthropology 43
lex eterna 1
lex temporalis 1
liberal legality 84
liberal political rationalities 87
liberty and security 149–151
litigation 1, 3
Lyotard, J.F. 71; the differend 39–40;
  'incredulity towards metanarratives'
  33; knowledge legitimacy crises
  33–34, 143; pagan 39

MacIntyre, A. 29–30
Marx, K. 67
Matthews, R. 79, 80
mediation 9; and justice 39, 45
mediators: in British Columbia 53–54,

111–112, 151; guiding the process
126–127; neutrality of 61–64, 127;
normalising gaze of 121–123;
training of 44–45; volunteers 54, 111
Merry, S. 10, 43, 69–70
Milner, N. 10, 43
minor dispute resolution 9
modern society 19–20; calculations of
justice in 19–29; epistemological
ethos of 101–102

Nader, L. 67
neighbourhood dispute resolution 9
neo-Fordist modes of regulation 74–76
neo-Fordist state 74
neo-liberalism 110–111, 137–138; and
British Columbia 13; and regulation
12–14
New Democratic party (BC) 52, 137
new informalism 4, 82–88
normalising judgement 119–121

panopticon 119
pastoral power 107–111
patria potestas 133
Pavlich, G. 13, 35, 44, 46, 53, 111, 112,
149
Plato's formulation of justice 17–18
polis 133
politics of difference 31, 103–104
population as object of government
109–110
postmodern conditions 4, 10–12, 87–88,
98, 101, 111; counter-modern
politics under 103; political theatre of
106
power see Foucault, M.

rationalism see reason
Ratner, R.S. 153
Rawls, J. 25–26, 27
reason 23, 27, 28, 34–35
'reason of state' 108
regulatory practices 14

Reiman, J. 25, 26–27
remote control 5, 142–145
resistance 146–149
restorative justice 59–61
Rose, N. 80, 142, 144

San Francisco Community Boards
Project 43
Santos, B. 76–78, 80
science of police 108
secular rationalism 21
settlement 59–61
Shonholtz, R. 41, 57, 59, 112
Smart, B. 11, 20, 21, 33, 87, 89, 101
Social Credit Party (BC) 13, 137
social domain 13–14, 58, 97–98, 110; as
a 'community of communities' 14,
110
social movements 74, 104, 153
social reproduction 71
Socrates' formulation of justice 17–18
sovereign-law model 133–135, 136–137,
150
spectacles of power 89, 135
state control 66–79
Stoicism, sixteenth century 108
subjective aspiration 142, 153–155
Surrey/White Rock Mediation Services
Society 55, 56, 57, 61
surveillance 119, 154

Tomasic, R. 68

Vattimo, G. 33, 35

Walzer, M. 7, 29–30, 101
Weber, M. 20, 21, 47, 70
welfare state 12, 13, 110; Keynesian 75,
116
Westcoast Mediation Services Society
54, 56, 57, 61
Wittgenstein, L. 9

Young, I. 30–31, 103, 152, 153